Divided Mastery

DIVIDED MASTERY

Slave Hiring in the American South

JONATHAN D. MARTIN

HARVARD UNIVERSITY PRESS
Cambridge, Massachusetts
London, England
2004

Library of Congress Cataloging-in-Publication Data

Martin, Jonathan D.
Divided mastery : slave hiring in the American South /
Jonathan D. Martin.
p.   cm.
Includes bibliographical references (p.) and index.
ISBN 0-674-01149-X
1. Slavery—Southern States—History.
2. Slaves—Employment—Southern States—History.
I. Title.

E443.M38 2003
306.3'62'0975—dc22   2003057118

Designed by Gwen Nefsky Frankfeldt

For my parents

Contents

Divided Mastery

Introduction: Slaves with Two Masters

New Year's Day was always called Hiring Day by the slaves . . .
Slaves went to a place called the hiring grounds to hire their labors
out for the next year. That's where that sayin' comes from that
what you do on New Year's Day you'll be doin' all the rest of the
year.

Former slave Sister Harrison, interviewed in 1937

"THE thing *is* an evil, existing among us." These insistent words appeared in the December 1852 issue of the *Southern Planter,* in an article penned by the journal's editor, Frank Ruffin. The sinister "thing" to which Ruffin referred was the practice of renting out slaves. Slave hiring was not a new phenomenon in the 1850s, so the journal's subscribers were well acquainted with the source of Ruffin's consternation, even if they did not share his alarm. Throughout the colonial and antebellum periods, Southern slaves were routinely bought and sold, but they were even more frequently rented out—usually by the year, but also by the month, week, or day. Hired slaves, ubiquitous in the South, did all kinds of labor. They worked as field hands and domestic laborers; they built turnpikes, canals, and railroads; they staffed coal pits, tobacco factories, and ironworks; they were sailors, blacksmiths, carpenters, cobblers, porters, hucksters, laundresses, and wetnurses. They were skilled and unskilled, male and female, old and young. Some were "self-hired" slaves, sent out to live on their own and find their own work, who turned over wages to their owners. The rental market in slaves added needed flexibility to the slave labor system and incorporated new, if temporary, members into the master classes. But the shared mastery on which slave hiring depended was also a source of social conflict. All hired slaves were somewhat anomalous, for each was a slave with two masters: owner and hirer. The social fallout from this anomaly prompted Frank Ruffin to denounce slave hiring in the pages of the *Southern Planter.*

As Sister Harrison pointed out to her interviewer decades later, many hiring transactions began, by custom, on New Year's Day. Across the South, that day was "hiring day" on countless town squares, courthouse steps, and rural roads. Other transactions were carried out privately between friends, family members, and business associates, commonly through an exchange of letters. For all slaves in the South, there was a significant likelihood that they would be hired out at least once in their lifetimes. In fact, a slave was more likely to be rented out to another person than sold to a new master. That prospect was an unavoidable aspect of slave life. At the same time, the vast numbers of hired slaves staffing the farms, factories, and big houses of the South put slave hiring at the center of the region's society and economy. But the significance of the practice, to slaves themselves and to the South as a whole, was attributable to more than its mere prevalence. While playing a fundamental role in such signal transitions as the market revolution and westward expansion, slave hiring shaped the everyday lives of black and white Southerners. It influenced the economic strategies of slave owners, the family lives of slaves, the tenor of master-slave relationships, and the relations between slaveholders and nonslaveholders. The pages that follow tell what life was like for hired slaves in the Old South, and what life was like in the Old South as a whole, given the existence of hired slaves.[1]

The story reads like a paradox. At first glance, slave hiring would seem to have bolstered the system of slavery, and in many ways it did. The practice was, in no small measure, a godsend for slaveholders. It was largely responsible for keeping slavery viable in the Chesapeake region during the unsteady years surrounding the American Revolution, when tobacco was becoming increasingly unprofitable to cultivate and when egalitarian rhetoric urging planters to manumit their slaves was on the rise. Slave hiring also facilitated westward migration by making it easier for small and large slaveholders to pursue the tantalizing vistas opened up by surging world demand for cotton. Moreover, hiring ushered many more white Southerners into the slaveholding ranks than would have been possible if the costly slave pens had been the only place to acquire slave labor.

But that is only half the story. The everyday unfolding of hiring transactions actually did as much to strain the social relations of the slave South as to strengthen them. Whether sealed by an auctioneer's cry on hiring day or with a handshake between neighbors, hiring transactions were intrinsically and idiosyncratically triangular. Where there had been two people, now there were three, and the dynamics immediately changed. Asked to resolve a dispute over the rate of hire for Moses in 1822, for example, Virginian Joseph Hobson asserted that the price would be "a matter of little import," so long as there existed "a mutual agreement between master, slave, and hirer," and so long as "each person" was "accommodated."[2] Such three-way relationships altered everything. The conventional polarity of master-slave relationships was reconfigured once a slave could have two masters.

Unlike in slave sales, where total rights to property and mastery were transferred between white Southerners, in hiring arrangements those rights were divided into separate spheres with awkward temporal boundaries. With contracts signed and cash tendered, hirers considered themselves temporarily entitled to the full prerogatives of mastery, including the power to force slaves to work and to punish them for substandard displays of submissiveness. Owners, by contrast, continued to defend their long-term property rights in the same slaves—including rights to future labor, future hiring earnings, and future sales—and did so by circumscribing as strictly as possible the mastery they transferred to hirers. Owners and hirers jockeyed to assert their rights of mastery and property over the same slaves because those rights were the wellspring of prosperity and prominence in the Old South. The jockeying did not go unnoticed, for between the two principals were the hired slaves themselves, who understood best that a slave with two masters was a contradiction neither law nor custom could readily accommodate. Such knowledge opened up for them frequent opportunities to shape their work and family lives, to bring white people into conflict with each other, and to destabilize the system that trapped them.

Indeed, it was the subversive potential of slaves with two masters that inspired Frank Ruffin's 1852 diatribe in the pages of the *Southern Planter.* His editorial offered a contemporary account of the paradox of slave hiring. On the one hand, Ruffin noted, the fact that slaves could be rented (and not merely sold) allowed "a certain profit to accrue" to both owners and hirers. Owners earned money on slaves they could not use, and hirers acquired needed labor that they could not afford to purchase in the slave pens. But on the other hand, Ruffin insisted, slave hiring was "felt everywhere to be a serious evil." He discerned in particular two deplorable consequences of the practice. First, the triangularity of hiring arrangements, by allowing one master to be played off the other, gave slaves a leverage over their enslavers that they ordinarily would not have had. Second, the inevitable conflicts between owners and hirers—especially over how slaves should be treated—resulted in a discord that was perilous to any slave society, especially one that required racial solidarity among free persons. Slave hiring was thus "an injury to all parties," Ruffin declared, "the hirer, the hiree, the negro himself, and society at large."

To Ruffin's mind, first among the injuries inflicted by slave hiring was the change it effected in hired slaves. Too many owners, Ruffin maintained, were allowing their slaves to participate in decisions about where they would be hired out. He thought the underlying reason for such behavior was clear. Owners were increasingly viewing their slaves as units of investment return, and that vantage point sometimes obscured the absolute necessity of unabated and complete domination over slaves. Owners wanted quick profits, and these were more easily secured when slaves were amenable to hiring transactions. Disgruntled and resentful slaves were more likely to antagonize hirers, to malinger, and to run away. Owners therefore selected hirers on the grounds that "the negro will bring his value from somebody and give no *trouble* in getting it." But this was a "weakness," Ruffin opined, and through it owners had exposed themselves—and hirers as well—to circumstances in which slaves could exert substantial influence over the way hiring transactions unfolded. To make the point, Ruffin observed that owners were often "compelled to persuade, exhort, and even pay their own negroes to go where they had been hired." At other times, slaves left hirers in the middle of their terms and "refused to return in defiance of command and entreaty." In the event, hirers and owners alike were left to wallow in their "share of inconvenience, chagrin, and humiliation." Ruffin thus lamented what seemed to him the obvious consequences of slave hiring: slaves with two masters were able to control their own destinies and, in the process, sow discord in white social relations.

Such a situation was less than ideal in a slaveholding world predicated on subordination of an entire race. Indeed, Ruffin went so far as to assert that hired slaves not only destabilized the social relations of slave society but nearly turned them on their head. In perverse overstatement, Ruffin claimed that both owners and hirers were "made to feel—only in reverse—'the horrors of slavery.'" He insisted that one need only be present on hiring day to witness this state of affairs: "All this is owing to the simple fact that the old rule is reversed, and the *man* enquires, aye, enquires with insolence, into the character of the *master*. 'Are you for hire?' said the late Judge Scott to a likely black. 'I am, sir, what is your name?' 'John Scott,' said the Judge. 'Very well,' rejoined the black, 'I'll enquire into your character, sir, and if I like it, I'll come and live with you.' The Judge never made another effort to hire." Ruffin knew that all those who had ever "met the scowl of the hireling" would grasp his point: the triangular nature of hiring arrangements changed the dynamics of master-slave relationships enough to give slaves an influence over the course of their lives. By dividing mastery, Ruffin suggested, slave hiring had attenuated the absolute domination on which slavery must rest. Of course, hiring did not make slaves any less enslaved, as Ruffin implied, but their occasional hiring-day "scowls" suggest that hired slaves did in fact cultivate a self-reliance and defiant resourcefulness that helped, in some ways, to forestall dependence on paternalist white masters.

The injuries inflicted by slave hiring, Ruffin insisted, did not end with changes in slaves' character, for the dynamics of the practice also poisoned white social relations generally. In their efforts to defend their (often diametrically opposed) interests, owners and hirers blindly allowed slaves' resistance to foster strife in their own relations. Ruffin maintained that owners and hirers were prevented from seeing the havoc wreaked by slave hiring in Southern society because they were mesmerized by their competing self-interests. "Each distrusts another's inflexibility, each fears the influence of competition from his fellow, and so all follow a road which will do more to render the slave worthless than all the efforts" of abolitionists, Ruffin admonished. Hirers had reason to be especially resentful, he added. Because a hirer "must have the labor," Ruffin observed, he was "compelled to succumb" to the restrictions placed on him by an owner—"or lose his money" when the owner repossessed the slave for some treatment later deemed improper. Especially restrictive was the diminished punitive power to which hirers could lay claim. A hirer was forced "to electioneer with negroes whom he wishes to hire," and that relaxation of discipline resulted in "the consequent detriment of his affairs." In such circumstances, a hirer could no longer stand as absolute master before either the slaves he rented or those he already owned. In short, as Ruffin saw it, to divide mastery was a virtual impossibility, for it gave slaves undue influence and produced, among whites, inordinate rancor.[3]

Despite Frank Ruffin's insistent remonstrance and despite the disquieting tensions arising from the practice, slave hiring was a vigorous and conspicuous presence in Southern life, and its proponents sanctioned it, along with slave selling, as a natural concomitant of bound servitude. Edward B. Bryan, South Carolina's vociferous advocate for reopening the African slave trade in the 1850s, began his proslavery tract *The Rightful Remedy* (1850) with a biblical justification of three institutions that he thought defined the South: slavery, the slave trade, and slave hiring. According to Bryan, slave hiring was "recorded in the history of the most remote ages," ranking next in antiquity only to the slave trade. He claimed that the first instance of slave hiring could be found in the biblical account of the building of Solomon's temple. For that monumental effort, Bryan noted, King Solomon hired a contingent of skilled bondsmen from Hiram, king of Tyre, in exchange for wheat and oil. Thus emerged the ostensible prototype for the thousands of hiring transactions carried out every year by white Southerners—transactions sanctioned, so Bryan believed, by no less an authority than the Bible itself. Indeed, Bryan thought that by attaching to slave hiring this pedigree of nearly three millennia he could meet abolitionist arguments from a position of historical strength. He asserted boldly that "the custom of *hiring slaves prevailed two thousand, eight hundred and sixty-four years ago.*"[4]

Antislavery loyalists would have impugned on principle the tendentious claims Edward Bryan conjured from his biblical exegesis. Fanny Kemble, for one, blasted slave hiring as "a new form of iniquity." To her, it was not a labor arrangement with firm historical moorings, but just one more hateful invention of Southern slaveholders, a novelty that could have only the most insidious consequences.[5] But both Kemble and Bryan, in their different ways, obscured the actual historical context in which slave hiring emerged. White Southerners who rented out their slaves had precedents to follow that were considerably more recent than the construction of Solomon's temple yet considerably better established than Fanny Kemble would have allowed. The practice had recognizable roots in English and then Anglo-American labor traditions reaching back to the sixteenth century. The customs and practices that surrounded slave hiring—from the typical yearlong terms and periodic "hiring days" to the rules regarding the maintenance and treatment of hired slaves—grew out of Anglo-American standards governing the employment of apprentices, servants, and indentured laborers. In sixteenth- and seventeenth-century England, for example, farmers commonly hired extra laborers by the year, and laws required employers in other trades to hire workers for the term of a year as well. Those who wished to take on additional labor went to "hiring fairs," where they would negotiate the details of food, clothing, shelter, and wages for the year with potential workers. Servants could choose not to renew contracts at year's end if they wished, and in some limited circumstances they could abrogate contracts before their terms had expired.[6]

In the seventeenth century, these traditions accompanied English planters and their indentured servants when they crossed the Atlantic to the colonies of the New World. Indentured servitude itself derived from sixteenth-century precedents; in return for passage to the American colonies, indentured servants bound themselves for seven-year terms, rather than the customary year. As a result of these special arrangements, an essential difference separated indentured servants from the farm laborers of earlier periods. Because they had received payment at the outset in the form of ocean passage, indentured servants could not dissolve their contracts. They became, to all intents and purposes, the property of those who had paid their passage to the colonies: planters and colonial authorities made little distinction between possessing the labor and possessing the laborer.

The consequences of this proprietary stake the planters had in their laborers were difficult to reverse. Once laborers in the American colonies came to be regarded as possessions, few checks were placed on their employers. Given the abiding respect for private property rights during that era, property owners could rarely be restricted in the use of they made of that property. As a result, the right of planters and other employers to sell or hire out their bonded laborers was recognized from the time the first indentured servants arrived in the New World. As early as the 1620s, Edmund S. Morgan notes, Virginia servants were "traded about as commodities." In 1643, in deciding to sell all his indentured servants, Lord Baltimore reasoned that to hire servants from other Maryland planters—at 1500 pounds of tobacco per year—would be less expensive than to maintain a full complement of servants to work his farm. For Lord Baltimore and for the men who sent him their servants in exchange for tobacco, hiring bonded labor was from the start an effort to increase profits. Profit tempted later slaveholders as well, but the absolute right over personal property would, in many ways, torment them.[7]

Slave hiring's deep roots in Anglo-American labor practices guaranteed that as the practice emerged in the South it would take firm hold. Though it is impossible to calculate exactly how many slaves were hired out in any given year, historians agree that the numbers were sizable. The difficulties in estimating arise both from the sources that are available and from the nature of hiring transactions themselves. The manuscript slave schedules of the 1860 census included places for census marshals to record whether slaves were owned or hired, but the numbers in these tabulations are of limited reliability. Some census marshals ignored altogether the distinction between whether slaves were owned or hired, and others made only haphazard observations. As a result, many regions display suspiciously low levels of hired slaves. Marshals ignored the distinction in such large urban centers as Charleston, Savannah, Mobile, New Orleans, Natchez, and Montgomery—all hotbeds of slave hiring.[8] Even if they were reliable, the census numbers would apply only to 1860, for they cannot be extrapolated backward and no baseline exists in previous censuses to show relative rates of change. For the years before 1860, the best sources for counting the numbers of hired slaves are the contracts, estate probate records, and other documents in which transactions were recorded. Finding and counting all such sources would be a virtually impossible task in itself. It would also doom researchers to underestimate from the start because so many hiring transactions were carried out privately. Ultimately, however, exact numbers matter less in determining the significance of slave hiring than does the scale of the practice. The same is true of slave sales: imprecise estimations of the numbers of slaves auctioned each year cannot dislodge the slave market from its centrality to Southern history.

The scale of slave hiring was nothing short of monumental. More hiring transactions occurred every year than sales; more slaves faced the prospect of working for a temporary master than of being transferred to a new owner. Historian Barbara Jeanne Fields found that in nineteenth-century Maryland hiring was "much more common than sale." Likewise, Frederic Bancroft speculated that in some Virginia towns hire transactions on one day could outnumber all the sales carried out in those locations for a year. Eugene D. Genovese estimates that between 5 and 10 percent of all slaves in the South were hired out every year. Robert Fogel and Stanley Engerman contend that the figure was more likely 15 percent or higher, and that in some regions nearly a third of all slaves in the local population could be hired out at any given time.[9] To make these percentages intelligible, it is useful to take slave sales as a rough benchmark. Historians have estimated that, on average, the chance that a slave would be sold in any given year in the antebellum period would have been roughly between 2 and 3.5 percent. Even these numbers, though they might seem low at first glance, would have made it unlikely that a slave could live to age thirty-five without being sold at least once. The likelihood of being hired out, by contrast, was three to five times greater, and perhaps more. Sarah S. Hughes found that in Elizabeth City County, Virginia, between 1782 and 1810, few slaves living in the county escaped being rented out; most slaves were likely to be hired out several times, and few children left adolescence without spending at least one year working in households of people other than their owners. Brenda E. Stevenson found that in Loudoun County, Virginia, in 1860, no fewer than 34 percent of adult slaves—or 20 percent of the county's slave population—were hired out for the year. The threat of hire loomed extremely large in the lives of the enslaved.[10]

Though hiring was at the center of life in the slave South, it has been relegated to the periphery of scholarly attention. The commanding presence that hiring held in the South is by no means reflected in histories of the region. Almost invariably, historians of slavery devote a few paragraphs to the prevalence of the practice in the region they are studying, but they do not attempt to make sense of it or to sort out its implications for slaves, for whites, or for the system as a whole. This neglect is no doubt due in part to scholarly suspicion that slave hiring was merely one of the "business" aspects of slavery, an insipid subject that reflects only on the viability and profitability of the system. In addition to historians' tendency to shy away from an apparently economic study of slavery, there may be a historical explanation for this scholarly neglect as well. From the days of slavery itself, slave hiring was overshadowed by the slave trade. Abolitionists trumpeted the exploitation and brutality of the slave market, rendering it paradigmatic of the wrenching pain inflicted by the system of slavery. Slave hiring never acquired the same aura of gravity and consequence, even though many slaves were torn from friends and family through hiring, as well. For whatever reason, then, slave hiring has attracted scarce attention as a topic in itself, and it is impossible, therefore, to trace out any broad historiographic shifts in its interpretation.[11]

Historians who have attempted to attach some significance to slave hiring routinely conclude that the importance of the practice lies in the flexibility it infused into the slave labor system. White Southerners could rent slaves when they needed them, for as long as they could afford them, and at prices well below the cost of purchase. Perhaps it should not be surprising, then, that the first two sentences of the entry for "Hiring Out" in the *Dictionary of Afro-American Slavery* use the words "elasticity," "adaptability," and "flexibility."[12] This lexicon of maneuverability is unquestionably central to any understanding of slave hiring. But that lexicon does not tell the whole story, and is by no means the *end* of the story. As a conclusion, highlighting "adaptability" is something like arguing that the slave trade's ultimate significance resided in "how people got slaves."

Beginning rather than ending with the issue of flexibility leaves a simple question unanswered: "So what?" What difference, if any, did this "flexibility" make? The word should, of course, be understood always to be braced by quotation marks (even when it is not in the following pages), for it hardly takes into account the experiences of those actually hired out. The flexibility that white Southerners sought would have been labeled dispersal or separation (or something much more pejorative) by slaves. More than simply myopic in its one-sidedness, however, the notion of flexibility actually explains very little in itself. The importance of flexibility lies in the way it changed the lives and relationships of black and white Southerners. In the chapters that follow, I take the story of slave hiring beyond the basic economics of supply and demand and delve into the exuberant prospects of westward-moving cotton farmers; into the fragile but resilient family lives of the enslaved; into the courtrooms where acrimonious conflicts over rights to mastery and personal property played themselves out; into the everyday situations where hired slaves were able to play their two masters off each other; and into the Southern cities where white workers angrily resented being forced to compete with hired slaves for jobs.

A significant weakness in the existing scholarship on slave hiring is that it omits the perspectives of slaves themselves. Historians who have looked at slave hiring have rarely, if ever, turned to slaves' own narratives to learn about the practice, and that failure has necessarily limited the arguments they could make. I began this project convinced that hiring needed to be understood from slaves' viewpoints. I was equally convinced, as I set out, that I would find only a trickle of sources produced by hired slaves themselves. Somewhat daunting, for example, was the observation that the book most historians regard as the magisterial account of slave life in the antebellum South—Eugene D. Genovese's *Roll, Jordan, Roll*—devotes only two of its nearly seven hundred pages to slave hiring. To my surprise, however, I quickly had to find ways to incorporate a veritable flood of remarkably rich sources produced by slaves. To begin with, numerous slave narratives discuss the practice at length. Many authors—Henry Clay Bruce and William Wells Brown are just two examples—spent their lives as slaves rented out to a succession of different masters. In addition, still filed inconspicuously in Southern manuscript collections are such archival gems as letters from self-hired slaves to their owners. And former slaves interviewed by the American Freedman's Inquiry Commission in 1863 and by the Works Progress Administration in the 1930s recounted experiences that they or their friends and families had while hired out. The testimony taken down in the 1930s, for all its potential pitfalls, is especially invaluable in understanding the experiences that slave children had while hired out.[13] All of these slave sources are indispensable in disclosing the motivations of owners and hirers, as well, another outcome on which I had not counted when I started, but one I find both ironic and felicitous. It is important to note that in these sources, and especially in those generated by whites, slaves are often referred to by only their first names; for this reason, in the chapters that follow I am able to refer to slaves by their surnames only when that name is part of the historical record.

In addition to centering the story of slave hiring on the perspectives of slaves, I have broadened it to the entire South. Anyone who has studied American slavery knows that the institution differed greatly from region to region in the South. The rice districts of coastal South Carolina, the black belt of Mississippi, the yeoman communities in the Georgia mountains— each evolved work and living patterns that made slavery in that region different. Slavery's diversity and particularity make local studies invaluable to the study of the institution, and these studies sometimes allow for more detailed investigations. But while microhistories can delve more deeply into the everyday life of a particular region (often one county in a state), they can also obscure the larger picture with their accumulation of local evidence. I have chosen to focus on the South as a whole—which I define as the slave states that existed in 1860, not simply those which eventually joined the Confederacy—because slave hiring offers some new and important insights into the big picture of Southern history. An understanding of

how slave hiring influenced the politics, the economy, and the social relations of the slave South challenges some of the long-held assumptions of
historiography on slavery and the South. My intent here is less to give an
accounting of hiring's distinct character in different regions of the South
than to elaborate the factors that were largely present whenever and wherever hiring transactions were carried out, and then to use those commonal-
ities to shed light on the history of the slave South as a whole. Slave hiring
was a major factor in everyday life in the South under slavery, and for that
reason alone the practice deserves continued attention from scholars. The
case presented here is a beginning, and it will no doubt be challenged and
refined by further inquiry into the local dynamics of slave rental markets.

This is a social history of slave hiring that is at the same time a social history of the slave South. Politics thus figures centrally in the account. The
story of slave hiring is in part about consensus. It is, at one level, an account of poor white Southerners given an enticing taste of slave mastery
through hiring. In no small part, hiring allowed whites from different
classes to "share" slaves among themselves in a way that reassured them of
their power and superiority. I am convinced, however, that the story of hiring is, at bottom, one about conflict. First of all, the history of slavery is
fundamentally about the day-to-day combat between owners and their unwilling slaves, and a study of hiring helps to illuminate the economic and
ideological terrain on which those daily battles were carried out. Second,
the history of slave hiring highlights the power that slaves and slavery had
to sow serious discord in the social relations of Southern whites. An understanding of the dynamics of slave hiring will thus clarify the ongoing
negotiations that characterized the social relationships between masters
and slaves and between slaveholders and nonslaveholders. I analyze the
broader historical significance and implications of those negotiated relationships by exploring how they affected power relations in Southern society and, in particular, whether they served to weaken or strengthen the system of slavery. To answer such questions, as historian James Oakes writes,
"the historian must necessarily step beyond the confines of the social relationship itself, to examine in some systematic way the political, economic,
or intellectual context within which slavery operated." I therefore begin
with the premise that the social relations engineered by slave hiring—those
between owners and hirers, between slaves and hirers, and between slaves
and owners—can be understood only within the larger political context in
which they unfolded: liberal capitalism. As Oakes himself has argued,
"Southern slave society emerged within rather than apart from the liberal
capitalist world, and that made a crucial difference." Slave hiring reveals
just how crucial that difference could be.[14]

That slave hiring should be viewed in relation to the larger political atmosphere surrounding American slavery was understood by contemporaries as well. In the issue of the *Southern Planter* following Frank Ruffin's exposition on slave hiring a subscriber responded with a letter-to-the-editor. While concurring with Ruffin's conclusions, the letter's author asserted that "a more careful consideration of the subject will lead you to the conclusion that the root of the evil is more deeply involved in the laws of political economy than one would suppose."[15] The author blamed the "evils" that accompanied slave hiring on the rising demand for labor in the slave South (he may in fact have been making an oblique argument for reopening the African slave trade). The rising demand for labor to which the author alluded was tied in turn to the rising demand for cotton and other staples produced by the South in the 1850s. The "laws of political economy" to which the subscriber referred were the laws of the market, the forces that kept white Southerners scrambling to find ever more efficient ways to meet the demands of those who consumed their products the world over. Slave hiring was a crucial aspect of that effort to rationalize production for the market.

Implicit in the letter to the editor was the idea that the "laws of political economy" had placed Southern slaveholders in something of a bind. In a world where laborers were owned by masters, the value liberal capitalism placed on labor efficiency worked at cross-purposes with its exaltation of absolute property rights. To defend slavery in a capitalist world, slaveholders had long armored their slave ownership and their slave mastery with the liberal protection of absolute right to property. Slaves and the right of mastery were both considered personal property in the South, and they were tenaciously guarded by their possessors. That conception of slavery, however, made sharing mastery, if not entirely impossible, at least an inevitably acrimonious affair. Under slave-hiring arrangements, both owners and hirers felt entitled to property rights in mastery over the same slaves, the former to long-term and the latter to short-term rights. Thus, even as responsiveness to the needs of the market required flexibility, which the rental market in slaves supplied, capitalist devotion to absolute property and a Southern fixation on mastery as a cornerstone of personal identity combined to undermine the shared mastery on which that rental market was based. The history of slave hiring highlights the crucial difference that capitalism made in the development, and the everyday experience, of Southern slavery.

Using slave rentals to rationalize production for the market inevitably affected the way that slaveholders viewed their slaves. This is one answer to the simple question posed earlier—"So what?"—concerning the consequences of the flexibility that hiring afforded. In particular, I argue that hiring markets induced slave owners to see their slaves less as a "force" that could be thinned or expanded only through sale and more as individual units of investment return. The simple fact that hiring allowed slave owners to imagine more uses for their slaves—more ways to earn a profit off their capital value—helped to alter how they viewed those slaves. With hiring as a possibility, owners could individualize their plans for each slave's productivity. Some could be sent to the fields, but only as many as were needed; others could be used to staff kitchens, stables, and houses; and when all necessary work had been assigned, the remaining slaves could be hired out to the highest bidders. They could, of course, also be sold, but slaves who were currently superfluous might be needed in the future, and if they were children, they might be more valuable at auction at some later date. Hiring opened up options to slave owners, and the way they conceived of their slaves in light of those options is one of the major themes of the chapters that follow. Hiring was largely, although not solely, responsible for placing property, profit, and production at the heart of the relations between masters and slaves. When owners had recourse to rental markets, no slave had to be a complete loss; even young children, for whom there was often little work, could be hired out to poorer neighbors for their "victuals and clothes." Slaves, in turn, we will see, shaped their enslavement by using their status as property to their own advantage.

The manner in which slave hiring induced slave owners to conceive of their slaves also profoundly influenced social relations among white Southerners. As already noted, slaveholders turned to liberal capitalism to safeguard their personal property rights when they felt their mastery threatened by neighbors, by upcountry yeomen, or, especially, by Northern abolitionists. But this position, while it helped to make slave mastery inviolable in the face of antislavery onslaughts, also made mastery in many ways indivisible, and this fact had repercussions for the practice of slave hiring. How could two Southerners—one with sturdy long-term property rights at stake, the other with equally viable short-term rights—peaceably share mastery over a single slave? Whenever they tried to do so—and the promise of profits kept them at it year after year—the situation was potentially volatile. It was especially volatile because issues of gender and race were always intertwined with the commodification of black slaves. Property in slaves was a touchstone of both patriarchy and whiteness in the South, and as such it was fundamental to constructions of self-worth and personal identity. At the same time that white Southerners were trying to make money with slaves, they were also trying to "make"—that is, sustain—patriarchy, honor, race, and proslavery solidarity. These simultaneous efforts, however, could conflict when slaves had two masters. The white Southerners involved in hiring transactions felt that their honor, status, wealth, and independence hung in the balance. In this state of precariousness, hired slaves were well placed to tip the scales.

Chapter 1 maps the geographic spread of slave hiring, charting the practice's place in the development of Southern slavery, and suggests the ways that it changed how slaves and their owners viewed each other. The history of hiring begins in the colonial Carolinas, continues in the Revolutionary-era Chesapeake region, and culminates in the cotton-booming Southwest. At every step, white Southerners turned to slave hiring, and the flexibility it promised, to increase either their production for the market or their returns on slave capital. A widow in colonial Charleston, a Virginia farmer switching from tobacco to wheat cultivation in the late eighteenth century, a nineteenth-century migrant clearing land in Alabama for a new cotton plantation—all are examples of white Southerners who hired or hired out slaves in order to maximize their profits on slave capital. The "flexibility" of slave hiring was inseparable from, and needs to be understood in the context of, the slave South's experience of the market revolution and the westward migration it spurred. It also needs to factor into our understanding of how owners viewed their slaves and how slaves viewed their owners.

Chapter 1 thus traces change in slave hiring over time, from the colonial to the antebellum period. The remaining chapters are more thematic. They delve into the persistent triangularity of hiring arrangements and take a close look at its influence on the social and political economies of the slave South. Chapters 2 through 4 should be read as a piece, for they explore slave hiring from the perspectives of the three principal participants. I begin with slaves, for whom family life was always foremost: Chapter 2 documents the concerns they had when hired out. The mobility that hiring caused in slaves' lives could be at once an impediment and a resource in the effort to keep families together. Chapter 3 considers the perspective of owners, by tracing their motives for hiring out their slaves and the lengths to which they went to safeguard their slave capital from the feared predation of hirers. Chapter 4 examines the unending efforts of hirers to secure for themselves the mastery they felt they had rightfully purchased. They faced continual checks on that mastery from owners, from Southern judges and, most significantly, from the slaves they rented. These three chapters, when read together, delineate the intrinsic triangularity of hiring, showing the divergent aims, desires, and convictions that crisscrossed every transaction. The brute reality of power in the slave South meant that slaves were hamstrung from the beginning in their efforts to shape situations to their advantage, but they were not always the weakest leg of the triangle.

Slave resistance was a major factor in the everyday functioning of hiring, as it was with slavery as a whole, and it is a major theme in every chapter, but Chapter 5 takes a close look at a form of resistance unique to hired slaves: running away from a hirer to an owner to protest abuse. Such situations reveal just how considerably the three-way relationship altered the customary dynamics of master-slave interactions. Slaves who ran away to protest abuse could often bring their two masters into conflict while distracting attention from their own acts of resistance. I take these instances of flight as an opportunity to explore the ways that slave resistance, even if not collective or aimed at overthrowing the system, could have a powerful effect on master-slave relationships, on the law of slavery, and on social relations among white people. Individual acts of resistance could have systemic resonance by creating serious dissension among white Southerners over how the system of slavery should operate.

Chapter 6 addresses the practice of self-hire. Owners sometimes hired their slaves out to themselves, sending them out to find their own work with strict orders to turn over specific sums of money every month. Historians have been drawn to these seemingly aberrant arrangements between masters and slaves more than to any other aspect of hiring, and they frequently conclude that self-hired slaves enjoyed a "privilege" that made them "quasi-free." Each of the following chapters accentuates the ways in which being subject to the claims of two masters gave slaves more leverage in shaping their lives than they might ordinarily have enjoyed, but it is important to stress that hired slaves, including those who hired their own time, were always slaves. They were perpetually subject to all the physical and emotional torture that slavery inflicted. This final chapter uses the words of self-hired slaves themselves to deflate the assertions of many contemporary white Southerners and not a few modern scholars that these slaves lived in "quasi freedom." In addition, the protests of white workers against the practice of self-hire demonstrate further instances in which hiring put slavery at the contentious heart of white social relations.

The arguments that follow tease out slave hiring's paradoxical place in the colonial and antebellum South. While the practice enhanced production and speculation with slave capital, while it brought more white Southerners into the master classes every year, and while it facilitated the spread of slavery over time and across space, it also played out in ways that ultimately kept the slave system from consolidating its hold. Hired slaves understood the contradictions of divided mastery, and they aggravated them whenever possible in their daily encounters with owners and hirers. By using that leverage both to shape their work and family lives and to bring white people into conflict over slavery, hired slaves disturbed the social and power relations of Southern society enough to weaken the system that trapped them. For these reasons, Frank Ruffin might label slave hiring an evil, yet Thomas Jefferson would wax enthusiastic over the "hopeful prospect" it offered. Investigating why both men were accurate in their descriptions—coming to terms with slave hiring's central paradox—can help illuminate the fundamental nature of American slavery.

Slave Hiring in the Evolution of Slavery

The torment of mind I will endure till the moment shall arrive
when I shall not owe a shilling on earth is such really to render life
of little value. I cannot decide to sell my lands . . . Nor would I
willingly sell the slaves as long as there remains any prospect of
paying my debts with their labour . . . In a question between hiring
and selling them (one of which is necessary) the hiring will be temporary only . . . Hiring presents a hopeful prospect.

Thomas Jefferson, 1787

*W*HEREVER slavery exists, it rests on a unique dualism: slaves are both labor and capital, both people and property. Over time, slave-holders in the American South and elsewhere understood and exploited that dualism in different ways. The manner in which they did so always shaped the social and cultural evolution of their societies. For a long time after slaves arrived in the seventeenth-century American South, for example, they were workers first and foremost. The early South was a "society with slaves," a society in which slavery was just one labor system among many. The Chesapeake tobacco planters who first bought African slaves were investing not so much in capital as in a labor force that, by virtue of being permanently unfree, carried with it fewer of the troubles associated with indentured servitude. Especially appealing to these planters was the certainty that African slaves, unlike indentured servants bound to work finite terms, would never one day acquire land of their own and become competing tobacco growers.

In time, however, the South became a "slave society," as unfree black labor predominated, as slaveholders consolidated their power at the top of the social order, and as a slaveholding culture emerged that was predicated on patriarchy, on white supremacy, and on the pursuit of wealth through slave markets at home and commodity markets abroad.[1] In the process, the manner in which white Southerners conceived of slaves and slavery changed. By 1818, Louisianan James Steer could write that "for a young man just commencing life, the best stock in which he can invest Capital, is, I think, negro Stock . . . ; negroes will yield a much larger income than any bank dividend."[2] By the time that Southern slavery reached its peak in the eighteenth and nineteenth centuries, most white Southerners imagined slavery in the way that James Steer did, reckoning the profits to accrue as much through speculation as through production. Slavery was no longer one labor system among many. Instead, Southern slaveholders exploited both sides of slavery's intrinsic dualism. They expected, as before, to see proceeds from the fruits of slave *labor*—among them, tobacco, cotton, wheat, sugar, and indigo—but they also expected returns on slave *capital*. Sale and hire markets operated in tandem to provide these investment returns, but hiring was unique in that it allowed for capital returns on slaves without the necessity of relinquishing title to them. How slaveholders arrived at a conception of slaves and slavery that rested as much on speculation as on production—how they increasingly saw themselves as managers of capital as well as managers of workers—is the story of hiring's influence on the evolution of Southern slavery.

Suffusing slave hiring, as it did the South as a whole, was a culture that relied on the adaptability of slave rentals and that facilitated the conception of slaves as both capital and labor: a market culture. It is hard to overstate the significance of expanding markets, both local and international, in the development of Southern slavery. Production for the market drove change in the slave South. Market expansion spurred westward migration, separated black families, and bred the tormented ambivalence of master-slave relationships. It was the hidden hand behind a slaveholder's every move, from making quotidian calculations in a farm journal to brutally whipping a recalcitrant slave. From the Revolution onward, farms and plantations became increasingly more efficient, many closely approximating "factories in the fields." Merchants of a thriving domestic slave trade, in supplying these enterprises, picked up where the trade in African slaves had left off in 1808. Southern urban and industrial economies, though not so developed as their counterparts in the North, emerged as slave-based complements to agriculture. Because of these changes, slavery was in a state of perpetual transformation: from the colonial period to the Civil War, slaveholders sought to capitalize on changing markets by shifting from one staple crop to another, by heading west to "new" land, and by refining methods of control over their slaves. Southerners, slave and free, were squarely in the midst of the nation's market revolution as well as the national political culture—liberal capitalism—that sustained that revolution. Liberalism's appealing doctrines of equal opportunity, individual enterprise, and material acquisition supported slaveholders' overriding aim of efficient production for the market.[3]

Slave hiring reinforced this market culture in two ways. First, slave hiring provided some flexibility in a labor system based on lifetime service and thus helped white Southerners to compensate for some of the natural drawbacks of a slave system. One of those drawbacks, succinctly captured by Eugene D. Genovese, is that "slavery requires all hands to be occupied at all times." In a labor system based on compulsion rather than wages, idle workers are at once dangerous and uneconomical. Hiring markets, however, offered a way to make the slave labor supply more elastic, by mediating between slaveholders who needed extra labor and those who had more slaves than they could use profitably. By allowing slaveholders to shed or, alternatively, to acquire extra labor as required, hiring counteracted one of slavery's inherent disadvantages and mitigated the sclerotic tendencies of the slave system by injecting some measure of the adaptability that characterizes wage labor systems. That flexibility—which for slaves translated to "movement" or "separation"—helped eighteenth-century white Charlestonians accommodate slave labor to the protean demands of an urban economy, aided Chesapeake farmers in their transition from tobacco to wheat cultivation in the Revolutionary period, and assisted enterprising nineteenth-century migrants in creating a cotton "kingdom" in the Southwest. Hiring bolstered the institution of slavery by at least somewhat democratizing access to slave labor, by streamlining production for the market, and by facilitating white Southerners' attempts to re-create their distinctive culture and political economy over time and across geographic space.[4]

The second way that slave hiring fortified the market's place in Southern slaveholding culture was by disposing owners to view their slaves primarily as pieces of property from which they could turn a profit. If slavery at times bred master-slave relations that were paternalistic, based on a sense of reciprocal obligations between master and dependent, slave hiring countered that trend by exposing the extent to which relations between owners and their slaves were mediated by the market, rather than by organic or mutual duties and responsibilities. Slave hiring thus worked against the tendency of slaveholders to think of the slaves they owned, in familial terms, as their "people." Indeed, as hiring figured into their economic strategies more centrally, owners increasingly imagined their slaves less as the aggregate of a plantation "force," and more as individual units of financial return. With hiring as an option, slaveholders could envisage their slaves as producers of lucrative staple crops or as producers of cash—as labor or as capital—according to their specific needs. Slave hiring thus played a large role, along with the vibrant domestic slave trade, in creating a conception of slavery in which slaves were not only the producers of cash crops but also a cash crop in themselves. But again, hiring was unlike sale because it entailed only temporary transfer of slave property. By making slave capital more fungible than even sale markets could do, hiring was an unparalleled impetus to owners to view their slaves as investments rather than dependents, as parts of an investment "portfolio" rather than members of a plantation "family." Little room was left for a conception of slaves as dependents in a paternalist system once Southern slaveholders began to look to hiring markets for returns on young, old, and superfluous slaves.

The words of Thomas Jefferson quoted at the outset of this chapter offer a convenient insight into the thoughts of one Chesapeake planter who was delighted by hiring's possibilities. In 1787, strangled by debt and unable to increase production on his own farms, Jefferson deemed slave rental, which had become a regular practice in his region only since the Revolution, "a hopeful prospect." The man who had prided himself on being a benevolent patriarch was inspired by the prospect of hiring out to think of his slaves as investments from which a variety of financial returns could be imagined. His straitened circumstances dictated that Jefferson had to pursue speculation rather than production with his slaves, and he chose hiring over sale because it would be "temporary only." Slave owners across the South exploited hiring as Jefferson did, paring down their workforces when and as they saw fit, disburdening themselves of any slave, of no matter what age or condition, at the slightest hint of outside demand for that slave's labor.[5]

This chapter offers a bird's-eye view of the emergence of slave hiring in the South. Hiring became a recognizable presence in different regions at different times, and that staggered development is largely explained by variations in slaveholding culture over time and from place to place in the South. But there was one important constant wherever slave hiring flourished: the practice emerged as white Southerners responded to new demands made by the world markets to which they catered. Specifically, as regional economies diversified, hiring became a crucial complement to slave ownership. This account of slave hiring's emergence follows a temporal and geographic arc, beginning in the colonial Carolinas, proceeding through the Revolutionary and early-national Chesapeake, and culminating on the cotton frontier of the Southwest in the antebellum period. But the structural changes that slave hiring wrought are only part of the story here. No mere economic adjunct to the system of slavery, slave hiring figured prominently in the culture and political economy of the South, not least of all by shaping the way white Southerners conceived of slaves and slavery.

The Southeast

At the turn of the eighteenth century, Charleston was an entrepôt for the moribund trade in Indian slaves and deerskins as well as the more auspicious trade in African slaves, rice, indigo, and naval stores. As a trade center that required the services of merchants, factors, lawyers, builders, and various other tradesmen and professionals, Charleston's economy was diversified enough to spur demand for temporary slave labor. Carpenters needed wood cut for their daily jobs; fishermen needed their catches hawked at market; lawyers and other professionals needed their offices dusted and countless other odd jobs performed; merchants needed their wares stacked, unstacked, and delivered. In response, owners of slaves in and around the city increasingly began to allow their slaves to seek out such short-term work on their own. As early as 1712, slave hiring was prevalent enough in Charleston to be the focus of legislative action. "Several owners of slaves," an act promulgated by the legislature in that year noted, "suffer their said slaves to do what and go whither they will and work where they please, upon condition that their said slaves do bring their aforesaid masters so much money as between the said master and slave is agreed upon." These slaves, the legislature claimed, had been found "looking for opportunities to steal, in order to raise money to pay their masters, as well as to maintain themselves, and other slaves their companions, in drunkenness and other evil courses." The important issue raised by this legislation is that, from its very inception in the American colonies, slave hiring was met with reservations. This reaction held true especially for the practice of self-hire, which not only left slaves less supervised but also put them into competition with white laborers.[6]

By 1720 Charleston was a statistical hair's breadth from having a black majority. Of 2805 residents, 1390 were slaves. The city's population doubled over the next two decades, as the city went through a period of rapid growth, and soon black slaves were not only Charleston's predominant workers but also its most numerous residents. Situated at the confluence of the region's major inland waterways, the Cooper and Ashley rivers, Charleston had become the transportation and marketing center for the growing trade in rice and indigo. It was also the center of the African slave trade, the entry point for some 40 percent of all black arrivals to North American shores. This economic activity spawned various subsidiary industries, and slaves were prominent in every aspect of the burgeoning economy. Slave men and women dominated Charleston's public markets, where they butchered meat and hawked milk, fruit, vegetables, and oysters. At local fish markets, slaves worked as both fishermen and peddlers. Slave boatmen piloted merchants and factors to inland plantations, where they then loaded crops onto flatboats for transport to Charleston's wharves and warehouses. Scores more slaves worked in the shipyards that built and repaired the schooners that bobbed continually in the harbor.

Many worked as skilled craftsmen, both independently and as apprentices, plying their trade as carpenters, blacksmiths, gunsmiths, cabinetmakers, painters, plasterers, shoemakers, stonemasons, and tailors. Slave women filled the endless demand among the city's absentee rice planters for house servants, cooks, washerwomen, wet-nurses, and seamstresses. Some of these slaves were employed by their owners, but many were hired out temporarily—by the day, week, month, or year—to those who needed their labor.[7]

Advertisements about runaway slaves testify to the importance of slave hiring in Charleston from early in the colonial period. They highlight hiring as a primarily urban practice and suggest that Charleston slave owners were increasingly viewing their skilled slaves as remunerative investments on which they could expect cash returns. "This is to forewarn all Manner of Persons whatsoever," began a 1733 notice in the *South Carolina Gazette,* "not to employ two Negro Carpenters, . . . Mingo and Norwich, belonging to Lawrence Dennis of Charles town, without first agreeing with the said Dennis, or his Spouse for the same." "This is to give Notice to all Persons," began another notice in the same year, "that they do not hire or employ these following Negroes . . . Cuffee and Beavour, two Caulkers, and Anselm a Bricklayer, without first agreeing with . . . Nicholas Trott, or Sarah his Wife." Ever more frequently, Charleston slave owners like Lawrence Dennis and his wife or Nicholas and Sarah Trent hired out their skilled slaves to the city's builders, shipwrights, and other tradesmen. As long as they could keep the slaves from disappearing into the city's large black population and pocketing their wages, these owners found that their slaves could generate flush returns, a circumstance that prompted them to see their slaves as investments rather than dependents.[8]

Not everyone was so sure that hiring out was the best way to employ slaves. Many white Charlestonians denounced the sort of freelancing in which Mingo, Norwich, Cuffee, Beavour, and Anselm were engaged, pointing out the adverse effects it had on white workers and on the slaves themselves. By comparison with the Chesapeake, white craftsmen were relatively scarce in the Carolinas, and many critics, suggesting that white workers avoided the region because they would have to compete with slaves for jobs, blamed this situation on the practice of hiring out skilled slaves.[9] Johann Martin Bolzius, a German pastor who arrived in Georgia in the 1730s, worried that "since the Negroes learn all kinds of common and useful crafts, the poor [white] craftsmen cannot succeed."[10] Other critics agreed that allowing slaves to find their own jobs was ill advised, but they pointed also to undesirable changes they perceived in the hired slaves themselves. To many, these slaves, especially when they found their own work in the city, seemed too autonomous, too independent. No doubt for many white Charlestonians just the sight of a slave posing a question to a white person—"Do you need your fence repaired?"—which led inevitably to some sort of negotiation—"How much are you willing to pay?"—was an egregious violation of their preferred view of slaves as passively servile and unthinking. The irony of the fact that many of these slaves were featured in advertisements about runaways—evidence that the slaves did not feel autonomous *enough*—would have been lost on these white Charlestonians.

Enough slave artisans were out for hire in Charleston that slaves could camouflage themselves and escape the long arm of a master or mistress, at least for a time. Such situations were deeply distressing to slave owners who depended on the income of hired slaves for their livelihood, and they reveal some of the opportunities for resistance that slaves had while hired out. In 1740, Elizabeth Smith advertised in the *South Carolina Gazette* that her "Negro-Man named Lancaster, commonly known about the Town for a White washer, and Fisherman, has . . . defrauded me of his Wages." "I do therefore advertise all Persons not to employ the said Lancaster," Smith wrote, "without first agreeing with me, or his producing a proper Ticket, unless they are willing to pay the Fine prescribed by Law." Almost a year later, Smith advertised again, noting that her earlier ultimatum regarding Lancaster had been "but to little Purpose; since he constantly earns Money (which he loses either by Gaming or spends among the little Punch-Houses)." She once again enjoined all potential employers from hiring Lancaster without her permission: "otherwise they will assuredly be prosecuted according to Law." Elizabeth Smith was just one of many independent women, unmarried or widowed, who relied on slave hiring as a source of income. Lancaster provided Smith with an annuity through his forced labor, and when he "defrauded" her of that money, she no doubt tottered on the verge of destitution—hence her threats to prosecute complicit white hirers who turned a blind eye to Lancaster's moonlighting. Smith's frustration with Lancaster reveals two important results of the increase in slave hiring in the Carolinas. First, slaves could sometimes exploit the unique situation to malinger or make their own money, to choose their own work or avoid it altogether. Second, such resistance had serious potential to bring white people into conflict because it was not snugly contained within the relationship of a single slave and a single master.[11]

Though hiring caused its share of frustrations, hired slaves were, by the Revolutionary period, a fixture on the Charleston scene. When Henry Laurens' brother James departed for England in 1775, he left his slaves in

Henry's hands to be hired out as profitably as possible. By this time, finding high wages for both men and women was not a problem in Charleston. Auba, for example, was hired out with her child to Mr. Thomson, the schoolmaster, for £90 per year. Statira brought in £60 per year doing "easy service in the House"—"easy" from Laurens' perspective, that is—for the Reverend Mr. Tennant. Chloe worked for a washerwoman in the city, turning in "30/ per Week" to Laurens and using the rest to maintain herself and her child. George and Cato were hired out by the month, and Taaff was apprenticed to learn the tailoring trade. Laurens' success in renting out his brother's slaves ensured that James would see profits on his slave capital even while he was away in England. Had there been no rental market in slaves in Charleston, Auba, Statira, and the others no doubt would have been sold upon James Laurens' departure for England, his empty house no longer requiring the usual contingent of slaves. But slave hiring allowed Laurens to exploit his slaves as capital even though he no longer needed their labor. When he returned from England, Laurens would collect all the wages earned by his slaves, not having paid a cent for their maintenance while he was overseas.[12]

Such profits came at a price. By hiring out the slaves and often leaving it to them to turn over their wages, the Laurens brothers opened up new avenues of resistance for their slaves. Thus, Henry Laurens would report to his brother in 1777 that, on the one hand, "your Negroes are earning Money more upon the whole than you would expect," but that, on the other hand, "some Individuals of them are faulty." Indeed, Laurens quickly learned that hiring out slaves involved a trade-off: while a source of great profits, hired slaves could be especially irksome and difficult. Hired slaves found ways to shirk their work, as did all slaves, but when slaves were rented out, that behavior was tougher to police and also very likely to spark disagreements with hirers. Laurens found, to his own dismay, that the slaves in whom he "most confided" ultimately gave him "the most trouble." Ishmael and George, for example, "kept themselves aloof" whenever Laurens tried to find them, and whenever he made them account for their time and wages, they "pretended they were in search for Masters and employment." Laurens suspected that these two were "working jobbs about Town" but not turning in their money, so he threatened Ishmael until the slave "brought in 30/ [that he] said he had earned as a Porter." Laurens was also suspicious of Cato, whom he would "see about the Street very fat," guessing that the slave was "passing his day in Play." The women he had hired out to individual masters were equally troublesome. Three days' worth of Chloe's wages were deducted for sickness, though Laurens was skeptical of her "invalidity," and Betty showed up one day to

rehearse a list of grievances she had with her present master. Laurens' perpetual threat was to send these querulous and delinquent slaves "in the
country"—that is, out of Charleston and into agricultural labor. But because the slaves he hired out were more mobile and less easily monitored,
Laurens faced the risk that defiant slaves would remove themselves from
Charleston before he did it for them. Laurens was not surprised to hear,
during the war, that the irregular Ishmael was one of twenty-five slaves
fishing outside the Charleston harbor bar who were "taken by a British
cruiser and carried off." While Laurens probably suspected that the experience of hiring had wrought regrettable changes in his brother's slaves,
he was no doubt oblivious to the concurrent changes it wrought in him
as well. When opportunities for slave rental abounded, slaveholders like
Henry and James Laurens increasingly had to imagine themselves as managers of capital as well as managers of workers.[13]

In dictating the work that men and women did while hired out, gender
was of prime importance in shaping the early experiences of hired slaves,
including those rented out by Henry and James Laurens. Men dominated
the skilled trades that were in demand among hirers in Charleston. As a result, they were often able to move about the city at will, as Ishmael and
George were, looking for odd jobs in a variety of occupations. Men were
hired as boatmen, fishermen, wagoners, carpenters, and blacksmiths—all
of which jobs could, potentially, place slaves at some remove from white
scrutiny. Women, by contrast, did not have nearly the same opportunities
for moving about the city, for diversified work assignments, or for getting
out from under the eyes of white supervision. Women—like Auba, Statira,
Chloe, and Betty—were hired almost exclusively to perform domestic labor. Because Charleston's planter elite was remarkably itinerant, moving
back and forth between the city and their outlying plantations, the women
hired out to these grandees were especially susceptible to forced travel.
Tinah, hired out in Charleston in 1780 to a Mr. Sosportas "to suckle his
child," was compelled to follow the Sosportas family to Camden during
the year. "Not being able to procure another nurse," Tinah's owner wrote
regarding the hirer, "I have agreed to let him have her to continue to do
it while he remains at Camden." Camden was 125 miles northwest of
Charleston, so Tinah was separated from her own family for the sake of a
white one, a pattern that black women experienced throughout the history
of slavery.[14]

Before we leave the Southeast, it is important to cast a sideways glance
here at the budding colony of Georgia, whose founders could not ignore
the growing practice of slave hiring. Even though Georgia's proprietors envisioned their new colony as developing without slave labor, hired slaves

were present in the colony from the very beginning. In 1733, when James Oglethorpe and his partners began to raise the first buildings in the town of Savannah, they brought with them, as one of the men there recorded, "a sufficient number of negro sawyers, who were hired from Carolina." The use of hired slaves by men determined to create a free-labor colony presaged the dependence that future westward-moving migrants would have on slave hiring. It also signaled the futility of attempting to exclude slave labor from the new colony. Indeed, Georgia proprietors found that they could not counter the vehement arguments early settlers made in favor of slave labor, but in acceding to the inevitable, they took certain precautions. One of the strongest pertained to slave hiring.[15]

The colonial assembly of Georgia, studiously aware of the early complaints made by Charleston's white workers and other critics of slave hiring, passed several measures to ensure that Georgia's hired slaves would not compete with white tradesmen. In 1758, Georgia legislators passed an act "to encourage white Tradesmen to Settle in the several Towns within this Province of Georgia by preventing the employing negroes & other Slaves being handicraft Tradesmen in the said Towns." The act stipulated that white carpenters, joiners, bricklayers, plasterers, "or other Tradesmen" had to be given preference—three days' notice—for any jobs in the colony. The act did not, however, "debar any person from hireing or employing Negroes or other Slaves in the said Towns as Ship wrights Calkers, Sawyers, Coopers, porters, or ordinary labourers." Nearly twenty years later, though, legislators did regulate the hiring of slaves to work as laborers or porters in Savannah; owners there were required to purchase a badge, at ten shillings, for any slave they hired out. The badges were intended to contain the growing trend toward owners' allowing slaves to lease their own time.[16]

From the beginning of large-scale settlement in Georgia, legislators wanted to make sure that the colony's towns did not resemble Charleston, where slaves moved about at will, made their own contracts, and even rented houses. An act "for the Better Ordering and Governing" of Georgia slaves averred that the practice of self-hire "occasioned such Slaves to pilfer and Steal to raise money for their Owners as well as to Maintain themselves in Drunkeness and evil Courses." The act explicitly prohibited slaves from working "out of their respective houses or Familys without a Tickett" and from being "permitted to Rent or Hire any house Room Store or plantation on his own or her own Account."[17] But hiring was not simply an urban phenomenon in colonial Georgia. By the early 1760s, the colony's farmers were well versed in the practice, and for Georgia slaves the possibility of working for people other than their owners became increasingly likely.[18]

By the Revolutionary period, hiring had taken root across the Carolinas, most solidly in Charleston but in surrounding towns and districts as well. Wilmington, Savannah, Georgetown, Beaufort, and Camden were urban refuges for seaboard planters, and they also grew into transportation and commercial centers for the trade in rice and indigo.[19] Johann Schoepf, traveling through the region in 1783 and 1784, found that on the steps of the Wilmington courthouse, Carolinians could rent in one stop both a house and the slaves to outfit it. A keen observer of life in the Carolinas, Schoepf found slave hiring particularly noteworthy, especially as it seemed to be spurring some significant changes in the conception of slaveowning. Schoepf was intrigued to find that those who owned slaves were often not the ones who worked them, and he noticed that this situation was helping to make slaveholding as much about speculation as about production. In South Carolina, for example, Schoepf found that "many idlers place their capital in negroes and . . . are by them supported, living careless on the bitter sweat of the hired." Such a conception of slavery would have long-term consequences. The revenue stream that slave hiring guaranteed rendered obsolete any notion of slaves as aggregate members of a "force," much less members of a plantation "family." Slaves were elements of an investment portfolio, and slaveowners were increasingly aware of the yield on each person they owned. Indeed, Schoepf observed that the "average" return a South Carolina owner might expect to earn on the capital value of a hired slave was no less than "a yearly interest of 15–20 per centum."[20] By thus making cash yields as well as crop yields a measure of profits on individual slaves, slave hiring nudged white Southerners toward a conception of slavery centered as much on the slave market as on the plantation.

The Chesapeake

In contrast to its early, vital presence in the urban economies of the Carolina low country, slave hiring did not become an integral aspect of Chesapeake economies until the 1750s and 1760s. In fact, its indispensability to the region would not be truly cemented until the American Revolution. This is not to say, however, that renting slaves was unknown in the Chesapeake in the first half of the eighteenth century. In 1718, for example, John Brodnax petitioned the Virginia General Assembly, asking that slaves in the common jail be hired out—each with "a strong iron collar ab[ou]t his neck"—until their owners were found. It was not uncommon for widows and orphans to have the slaves who had been bequeathed to them rented out by the administrators of their estates. In 1737, Joseph Wright advertised in the *Virginia Gazette* for the return of "Two Negro Boys, belonging to the Orphans of Mr. James Benn," both of whom he had hired out to

Nathaniel Magruder. And evidence from wills and orphans' court records shows that some slaves were being hired out as early as the 1720s in the Manakin area of King William Parish, Virginia. But even though estates in probate occasionally leased out slaves, slave hiring did not have a pervasive presence in the economies of the Chesapeake before midcentury. In contrast to the colonial legislatures in the Carolinas and Georgia, which had regulated the practice from the first years of the eighteenth century, Virginia's General Assembly did not feel compelled to mention slave hiring in legislation until 1782. Revealing the limited extent of slave hiring in the eighteenth-century Chesapeake, Peter Fontaine, a Virginia resident often looking for extra labor, insisted that before the French and Indian War, Virginians "could not hire a servant or slave for love or money."[21]

Several factors explain why slave hiring arrived later in the Chesapeake, and tobacco lies behind each one. The Chesapeake—stretching from the eponymous bay in the east to the Blue Ridge Mountains in the west and dipping down into the Cape Fear region of North Carolina—was dominated by tobacco throughout the colonial period. The crop shaped the Chesapeake economy, its slaveholding culture, even its landscape. Tobacco planters, for instance, were notably uninterested in developing regional trade centers, so towns in the Chesapeake were smaller, less developed, and generally poorer than their Carolina counterparts. Whereas all roads in the Carolinas led to Charleston, in the Chesapeake they led to London and Glasgow. The largest towns of the Chesapeake—Baltimore, Norfolk, and Richmond—were, until the Revolution, veritable hamlets, located on the periphery of the region both geographically and economically. As late as 1770 the ports of Baltimore and Norfolk were half the size of Charleston, and the capital cities of Williamsburg and Annapolis were nothing more than transient government towns until after the Revolution. Because clusters of urban tradesmen and professionals in need of short-term labor did not emerge in the region, the demand for a mobile labor force of skilled slaves was less intense. The urban services that hired slaves provided in Charleston—from blacksmithing to coopering and carpentry—were supplied throughout the Chesapeake on individual plantations.[22]

If the Chesapeake's small towns were not fertile ground for slave hiring, neither were more rural areas. That tobacco farmers did not turn to hiring with greater frequency early in the eighteenth century is in part explained by the weak urban roots of the practice, but slave hiring also fit poorly with the region's slaveholding culture. A hallmark of that culture was the idealization of the position of the "planter," or, to be more precise, the *self-sufficient* planter. In fact, one reason there was so little diversification in the paltry urban economies of the Chesapeake was that so many in the region considered tobacco planting—together with the exalted position of "planter"—to be the only worthwhile calling. Peter Fontaine noted in 1755 that Virginia had "no merchants, traders, or artificers of any sort," except those that "became planters in a short-time." Virginians' exalting of self-sufficiency was in part a response to their status as colonials. Those who became planters battled their sense of dependence on British officials and merchants by redoubling their efforts for individual autonomy at home. Autarchy thus became the plantation ideal. (Carolina planters, by contrast, relied less on the empire's factors and merchants, so self-sufficiency was a less prominent ideal in that region.) Chesapeake planters wanted their own tobacco houses, their own mills, their own blacksmiths, coopers, and carpenters. In such a slaveholding culture, the notion that one could or should borrow or rent workers from others would have been foreign. Hiring implied dependency on another person, a position most planters worked hard to avoid.[23]

Two major developments in Chesapeake society in the middle of the eighteenth century made the region's slaveholding culture more receptive to hiring. The first change was agricultural, and the second was demographic. During the latter half of the eighteenth century, many Chesapeake planters supplemented their production of tobacco with the cultivation of grains, especially wheat. World demand for American tobacco began to stagnate after 1750, and, in addition, the crop was seriously depleting from the soil the nutrients its cultivation required. In a stroke of luck for Chesapeake planters, however, food prices were beginning to rise at the same time. Wheat and other provisions were in demand in Europe, in the West Indies, and in the newly settled regions of the Virginia piedmont and the Carolina backcountry. Chesapeake planters transformed their agricultural practices to meet these new demands, and the result was an object lesson in how regions of the South were shaped socially, culturally, and economically by the staples they produced. Tobacco had always been a year-round, labor-intensive crop: it required constant supervision, and farmers needed legions of slaves to pick, press, roll, and process leaves. Most tobacco planters early in the eighteenth century found that they never had enough slaves to carry out all the work they needed done, and they added to their forces by purchasing Africans whenever possible. Wheat, by contrast, needed almost no attention from the time it was sown in September to the time it was reaped in late June and early July. Planters who shifted to grain production thus found that they needed far fewer workers than they had needed when growing only tobacco. George Washington, who was himself a paragon of efficient agricultural innovation, voiced what would have been a common lament when he stated that it was "demonstratively clear that . . . I have more working Negroes by a full moiety, than can be employed to any advantage in the farming system."[24]

The transition to mixed farming, with its more seasonal labor demands, ushered in a social economy predicated on self-sufficiency of the community, rather than the plantation. The demands of the wheat harvest made plantation autarchy less practicable, and thus less appealing. Wheat required a large contingent of laborers only during the harvest, when farmers needed to act fast: ripened wheat had to be reaped quickly before it shed its grain. But it made little sense for wheat planters to maintain all those slaves throughout the other fifty weeks of the year. As a consequence, hiring slave labor during the labor-intensive harvest became common, and central to the emerging community-based social economy. In July 1777, for example, Landon Carter hired three of his neighbor's slaves "to cut my Fork wheat down at 5/ the day." When wheat farmers hired extra labor in midsummer, they usually hired men rather than women, evidence that gender shaped the early work experiences of hired slaves in the Chesapeake, as it had for slaves in the Carolinas. Though work at harvest was difficult, it also entailed certain perquisites. To prevent losses due to overripe grain, farmers customarily offered slaves incentives to quicken their pace. Virginia farmer Richard Jones hired men to cut, pitch, cart, stack, and rake his wheat and barley, and each received one dollar and a pint of liquor daily. Thomas Jefferson routinely offered rations of meat and whiskey to his harvesting slaves, including those he hired, and he always hired male slaves. For Landon Carter, Richard Jones, and Thomas Jefferson, slave hiring was an expedient way to deal with the rapidly changing labor needs on their farms and plantations.[25]

Wheat farmers in the Chesapeake commonly hired out their slaves for the year but stipulated that the slaves should return for a week or two in midsummer so that they could assist in harvest. The strategy allowed slaveholders to exploit fully the characteristic duality of slavery: the fact that their slaves were both labor and capital. Thomas Massie, a planter in Nelson County, Virginia, hired out several of his slaves by the year in the 1790s, but he always reserved their labor for the weeks during which his wheat crop reached its peak ripeness. Massie hired Billy out to learn blacksmithing in 1791, but noted in his journal that "Billy came home the 25th June to harvest and continued until Thursday 5th July." And when Massie hired Nathan out to James Moore in 1799, Massie stipulated that he was "to have him in Harvest . . . but to return the time." In this way, slave hiring abetted the efforts of planters like Massie to take advantage of the double value their slaves possessed as labor and capital. Massie saw his slaves, by turns, as the workers who moved his cash crop from the ground to the market and as a cash crop in themselves. The transition to wheat farming, and the subsequent flourishing of slave hiring, brought Southern slave-holders another step toward a view of slavery based as much on specula-tion as on production.[26]

The shift to increased grain cultivation was just one factor behind the turn to slave hiring in the Revolutionary-era Chesapeake. This change in farming occurred alongside a major demographic event in the Chesapeake slave population. In a paradoxical turn of events, at the same time that many farmers found themselves in need of fewer slaves, the slave popula-tion as a whole was beginning to grow faster than it ever had before, pri-marily through natural increase. Planters had several responses to the ap-parent surplus of slave labor in the region. A few were sufficiently roused by the egalitarian ideology of the American Revolution, by evangelical re-vivals, and by the demands of their slaves to consider manumission. Many more planters, however, decided to sell their slaves to small farmers mov-ing into the piedmont regions of Virginia and North Carolina and, after 1790, to the cotton revolution states of the Southwest. Other planters es-chewed both manumission and sale in favor of hiring out their excess slaves locally. Thomas Jones, for example, a successful Maryland lawyer and planter, kept his slave force lean by hiring out women he did not need on the farm. In 1779, he sent Nan and her son Jack to his sister who lived in New Jersey, hired out Unity for the year, and bound out another young girl for thirteen years. Over the next thirty years Jones continued to hire out slaves, renting some of them out for ten years at a time, as a way to keep his slave force as small as possible.[27]

Those Chesapeake farmers who preferred hiring out their slaves to sell-ing them to migrating farmers largely had the American Revolution to thank for making slave rental a practical alternative. The Revolution wrought a number of dramatic economic changes in the Chesapeake. Most important, the Revolution prompted the American colonies to divest themselves of the economic straitjacket of British mercantilism.[28] Even be-fore the war, home manufacturing had increased as the colonies united in nonimportation agreements, and the wartime years made such industry an unavoidable necessity. Chesapeake manufacturers strove to meet the Continental Army's demands for cloth, munitions, and other supplies. New enterprises sprouted throughout the region, including ironworks, mines, shipyards, and ropewalks. Slave labor was a critical necessity for all these industrial enterprises, but few of them had the capital required to purchase the full quota of slaves they would require. Slave hiring became an indispensable resource for manufacturers in the growing and diversify-ing Chesapeake economy.

The budding industries of the wartime Chesapeake paid high prices for any slaves they could find to rent, a fortunate state of affairs for those struggling to maintain the slaves they owned. James Dick, whose Annapolis-based mercantile business was burdened by wartime disruptions in trade, was able to hire out his slaves as ropemakers in 1780. Ropewalks were just one of the enterprises spurred by the war effort. Ironworks quickly became the largest employers of hired slaves in the Chesapeake. David Ross, the owner of the Oxford Iron Works in Virginia's Bedford County, advertised in the *Virginia Gazette* in October 1777 that he would "hire . . . 50 or 60 Negro Men for one, two, or three Years." Promising a "healthy" work environment, "moderate" labor, and a "plentiful diet" for all hired slaves, Ross offered "an advanced Price for Carpenters and Wheelwrights." Joseph Habersham, a rice planter from Georgia, fled British-occupied Savannah with his hundred and fifty slaves and headed for Virginia. Once there, he found that slaves were easily hired out, and at increasing prices. Turnpike and canal construction, central to the creation of an American marketing system for burgeoning industries, increased soon after the war. Canal companies paid top prices for hired slaves when construction began in the 1780s: £20 plus food and lodging for common laborers, and even more for skilled slaves.[29]

The Revolution also urbanized the Chesapeake, thus opening up even more new markets for slave hiring. Towns in the region, following the pattern set much earlier in Charleston, became regional centers of trade and production. Grain mills, shipyards, warehouses, and tobacco factories were just some of the industries that gravitated toward developing towns, and each relied on hired slave labor. Norfolk, for example, became a center of shipbuilding, eventually making the Chesapeake second only to New England in that field. Baltimore emerged as a center of the grain and flour trade, and as a result witnessed a dramatic increase in slave hiring. Those wishing either to hire or to hire out slaves placed one out of every six advertisements concerning slaves in Baltimore newspapers between 1790 and 1820. As Chesapeake farmers grew more wheat for export, such services as milling and warehousing needed to be provided, as did such transportation services as shipping and cooperage. Boatmen, coopers, carpenters, and other slave artisans who had once practiced their crafts only on their home plantations were sent to the towns to meet the surging demand for their labor. As town populations grew, so too did the need for domestic labor, as numerous advertisements in regional newspapers attest. That it was becoming possible for slaveholders to gain returns even on small children by hiring them out is evident in an advertisement placed in the December 1777 issue of the *Virginia Gazette:* "Wanted to hire immediately, or at

Christmas, a negro or mulatto woman that understands something of cooking, can wash and iron; also a girl and Boy to wait in a house."[30]

A new professional class—hiring agents—emerged to serve the expanding market in hired slaves. These men devoted themselves to brokering deals between owners and hirers, both in cities and in the countryside. Agents charged owners a percentage of the hiring price, usually between 5 and 8 percent, a policy that made some owners leery, for they feared that agents might be disposed to overlook hirers' reputations for brutality if the price was right.[31] In this early period in slave hiring's development, the appearance of hiring agents was most significant for the way it facilitated the geographic spread of slave rental. Owners did not have to hire out slaves just in their own communities or to people with whom they were acquainted. With agents as their intermediaries, owners could send their slaves to distant farms, mines, and factories, sometimes across state lines. Migrants heading to the cotton "kingdom" of the Southwest in the coming decades would rely heavily on the services of hiring agents. The geographic diffusion of slave hiring, accelerated in no small measure by the emergence of professional agents, also precipitated the fragmentation of slave families and communities.

By the turn of the nineteenth century, the Chesapeake economy was vastly different from what it had been fifty years earlier. Freed from the constraints of British mercantilism, the region urbanized and diversified, developing coal mines, ironworks, shipyards, and other ventures. Planters and farmers also diversified their pursuits, cultivating wheat alongside tobacco in order to take advantage of shifting demand on world markets. In this economic transformation, hiring played a crucial role. Once the cultural barriers to slave hiring had been razed through agricultural, demographic, and economic changes, the practice thrived in both rural and urban areas of the Chesapeake, among householders, industrialists, and farmers of different sorts. By the 1790s, hire rates for slaves had become one among many economic indicators for local economies, something farmers followed as they followed prices for wheat, tobacco, and land.[32] Up until the Civil War, white Southerners would advise each other to settle in different regions in large part on the basis of the prices that slaves brought both for sale and for hire in local markets. With slave hiring and the domestic slave trade both in the ascendant, slaveholders judged communities in the South not just by the fecundity of the land but by the opportunities for speculation in slaves.

By the Revolutionary period, the traffic in hired slaves had become a substantial element in the daily economic strategies of Chesapeake farmers. Slaves could be viewed as individual assets that should provide a return, even when, as individuals, they were redundant or unsuited to work on large plantations. Once hiring became prevalent, no slaves were exempt, including the very young or the old. The age range of "workers" widened according to demand for their labor. If a small farmer wanted a six-year-old to assist his wife in the house, and was willing to pay for the child's food and clothing, most owners would jump at the chance. Indeed, tenants and small farmers were increasingly able to rent the young and old slaves from neighboring plantations at low prices. Perhaps there is no greater testimony to the early changes wrought by slave hiring than the fact that by 1810 three-fourths of the slaves working on small farms in Elizabeth City County, Virginia, were either children under the age of twelve or adults old enough for their owners to be exempt from taxation.[33] With such opportunities for remuneration, owners "cared for" slaves only when those slaves were too small, too frail, or too sick to work for the clothes on their backs. For slave owners throughout the Chesapeake, hiring was the key to transmuting young, old, or superfluous slaves into a source of lucre.

The Southwest

After the Revolution, American settlers scrambled westward over the Appalachians into the lands that Great Britain had ceded to the young United States under the Treaty of Paris. Kentucky and Tennessee were the first regions to be settled. Alabama, Mississippi, and other states to the south and west were not far behind. These lands were new to white Americans, and the first order of business was to wrest farmland from dense forest. Trees had to be felled and cleared; some of those trees had to be reduced to posts, rafters, shingles, and clapboards, which were in turn fashioned into houses for both slaves and masters. Food and staple crops also had to go into the ground as soon as possible.

In the expensive and labor-intensive process of relocation, settlers relied heavily on slave hiring, both as a source of labor and as a source of cash. When James Trezevant set up his Hopedale plantation in 1845 he hired extra slaves from his new neighbor for twelve dollars a month, putting the hired slaves "to riving clapboards, skinning poles, and cutting blocks," while he "went on clearing with my own hands." Henry Clay, born a slave in North Carolina, was carried off to Louisiana at age fourteen by his master, who "started to whittle a plantation right out of the woods." Clay spent many days cutting down trees to clear a settlement, before he was "hired off to work on one of the boats" steaming along the Mississippi River. By the time the land was cleared, Clay's owner probably needed cash more than he needed labor, and hiring out slaves was an easy way to raise that money. Leaving behind oversettled and overcultivated seaboard communities, slaveholding migrants like Henry Clay's owner were the most promising aspirants in the South's cult of prosperity. These enterprising slaveholders were heading west to make their fortunes and to re-create, on new lands, the slaveholding world of their parents. They followed the well-beaten Southern path to wealth and upward mobility: they acquired more land and more slaves farther west.[34] In the pursuit of that social, economic, and geographic mobility, slave hiring had a crucial place.

Kentucky's history demonstrates how considerably the earliest western settlers relied on slave hiring. Kentucky was well populated with slaves from the beginning of white settlement. In 1790 there were more than twelve thousand slaves in the state, and just ten years later there were over forty thousand. For settlers, the practical implication of this demographic fact was that slave labor would predominate in the region, and free laborers for hire would be scarce. When farmers needed extra labor, they had little choice but to hire slaves from others. Those who came to Kentucky with their own slaves thus found ample opportunities to rent them out. Robert Terry even wrote home to Virginia in 1808 to tell his family that he would "like extremely to have Coleman." Coleman was worth ten dollars per month in labor-hungry Kentucky, and he could bring even more "if he should be smart at overlooking." Such cash was handy for new arrivals, but migrants who hired out their slaves also created more work for themselves while setting up homes and farms in rough country. The "hurry of business," for example, kept Samuel Womack and his family very busy on their Kentucky farm. "As we hired out all 4 of the Black Boys last year," he explained to a friend, "we had to apply ourselves with all our might to keep up the farm." For whatever reason, Samuel Womack and his family opted to pursue speculation rather than production as they deployed their slave labor on the Kentucky frontier, and slave hiring made it possible for them to do so.[35]

When John Breckinridge decided to move from Virginia to Kentucky in the early 1790s, hiring out his slaves was a crucial part of the process. Breckinridge sent his slaves to Kentucky almost a full year before he himself moved with his family. Breckinridge placed his slaves under the direction of Kentuckians Samuel Meredith and William Russell, no doubt enticed by the former's claim that "Negroes hire very well in this Country." Upon taking control of Breckinridge's slaves, Meredith affirmed that he would give "every assistance in my power towards hiring them to advantage and to good masters," an outcome that Russell claimed would be easily achieved since there were many people already "anxious" to get the slaves. For potential migrants like Breckinridge, the ease with which slaves could be rented out on the frontier was a blessing. First, Breckinridge was able to wrap up his business in Virginia for a year before he left for his new land in Kentucky without losing money on idle slaves. Second, hiring continued to be an asset once he reached Kentucky in the spring of 1793. Finding that he had "no open ground to place my Negroes on," he "hired some of them out" while using "the Balance" to clear twenty-five acres of land. He planned to reconvene his entire slave force in the fall, to "attempt a large crop of corn, at least, next year." When moving westward, Breckinridge needed to exploit both the speculative and productive potential of his slave labor. He needed slaves to clear land and plant crops once he arrived, but he also needed them to produce cash to finance the move in the first place. As Breckinridge had been advised by Samuel Meredith and William Russell, agricultural production and slave speculation—especially through hiring—had to work in symbiosis on the risky and uncertain frontier.[36]

During the decades between 1790 and 1810, the pace of migration quickened among white slaveholders, and movement solidified as a central factor in the lives of both slave and free. These were pivotal decades in the history of slavery: the institution declined precipitously in the North; a sizable free black population emerged in the South; Chesapeake farmers groped their way through a transition from tobacco to wheat cultivation; Congress reserved the Northwest Territory for free labor; the African slave trade came to an end, but not before white Southerners went into a buying frenzy; major slave revolts unfolded in Haiti and in Virginia; and a cotton "kingdom," expanding westward, became part of the Southern imagination. Revolutionary improvements in the machinery of the British textile industry had driven up demand for cotton until it reached formerly unimaginable heights, and Eli Whitney's timely invention of the cotton gin allowed Southern planters to meet this demand as never before. The cotton revolution fueled westward migration, as farmers invested early profits in more slaves and more land farther west. Cotton country would spread, over several decades, until it stretched from Kentucky down to Florida, and from the seaboard westward to Texas. To abet expansion, the strong arm of the federal government muscled Native Americans off lands whenever white Americans deemed those lands optimal for growing cotton. The slaveholders who populated those lands led a double-barreled forced migration: while pushing whole tribes west of the Mississippi River, they also pulled with them many thousands of slaves. Some 75,000 Chesapeake slaves were transported to the Southwest by owners or through the domestic slave trade between 1790 and 1810; another 137,000 Chesapeake and Carolina slaves were moved to frontier regions over the next ten years.[37]

The ambitious white migrants, most of whom were in their twenties and thirties, who flooded into the promising lowlands—the fertile, dark-loamed "black belts"—of the Mississippi Valley relied heavily on slave hiring to reproduce in the Southwest the cultural and economic slaveholding worlds they had known in their youth. Moving to western lands was not a simple proposition for the majority of migrants. Above all, it was extremely expensive. Travel westward entailed transportation costs and lost income as well as other incidental expenditures, so those bent on reclaiming untried land were assured of months, even years, of privation. Most migrants were on the road for more than a month, and the average expenses for a white family and twenty slaves on such an expedition could exceed $1000.[38] In such circumstances, having capital tied up in slaves could represent an initial liability for many of those setting up homesteads in the west. And costs did not abate once migrants reached their destinations. A fact of life on the frontier, where farms were small and unproductive, was the high cost of provisions.[39] Feeding a full contingent of slaves, or even just three or four, could prove an impossible burden for many cash-strapped migrants.

One way to deal with this situation was to leave slaves in the more settled seaboard regions to be hired out by friends, family, or hiring agents. Gustavus Pope left Tennessee for Mississippi in the early 1830s and enlisted the support of his mother and brother in hiring out the slaves he had left behind. Thomas Williams asked his brother to take charge of hiring out his slaves in 1829 when he moved to Tennessee from Warren County, North Carolina. And Albert Charlton imposed on Thomas Fox to hire out his slaves in 1845 when he left for Kentucky. Once migrants had settled down, prepared their new homesteads, and cleared enough ground, they could send for their slaves, along with the money due for their hire.[40]

Another strategy was to bring slaves along to be hired out on arrival. When prospective migrants solicited advice from friends already in the West, the letters in reply almost invariably advocated just such a plan. Hire rates in the West were generally higher than those in the East, so migrants who transported their slaves overland stood to gain higher returns. In 1839, Philip Pitts, in writing to a friend who was thinking about relocating to the Cane Brake region of Alabama, warned him that all the fertile land would "in the course of time be owned by [a] few men of Capital." He added that the "best plan" would be to "come out with your negroes to my house." "I would say hire out your negroes here for 12 months," Pitts advised, noting that men hired for as much as $220 per year, women for about half that amount, and "boys and girls in prop[or]tion." The money that hired slaves brought in could be put toward the purchase of land—

land being quickly swallowed up, Pitts warned, by greedy speculators—
and thus begin to underwrite the heady dreams of fortune and success.[41]

The best plan, though, for those with the means to do so, was actually to
send slaves west first, even a year ahead, as John Breckinridge had done in
Kentucky in the 1790s. Not only could the money earned by a contingent
of slaves help pad the lean years a migrant faced upon arrival, but the time
spent in the West could serve as a training period for slaves unaccustomed
to growing cotton. When John Young Mason was casting about in the
1840s for land to set up a cotton plantation that his son could manage, an
adviser out west urged him to send his slaves ahead and "hire them out for
a few years." The adviser counseled this plan—"a better and safer way of
making money from them at once"—for two reasons. First, slaves on the
cotton frontier could "hire for more than they are worth," and, second, it
would give Mason's son and, more important, his slaves time to learn to
work a cotton plantation. Whether slaves were brought to the West or left
in the East, hiring was an important part of the initial financial planning
for a westward trek. On thousands of different settlements, migrants were
reproducing the slaveholding culture to which their parents had raised
them, and that process required, as John Young Mason's adviser understood, that migrants exploit their slaves as both capital and labor, for both
speculation and production.[42]

True to the cycle of settlement and prosperity on the frontier, new migrants were attracted to sparsely populated—and thus unclaimed—lands,
but their slaves were in greater demand in regions that had been settled
longer, where farmers were perhaps beginning to cobble together a workforce to get cotton crops in the ground. Migrants often had to travel some
distance to find regions where they could hire out the slaves they had
brought with them. In 1836, James Harrison moved to a county in Mississippi that had been so recently settled that people there "had not enough
land open for their own hands" to work. Harrison's father advised him
that he could "hire to the greatest advantage" in Perkins County, Alabama, a region so flush with cotton profits that one could easily unload
"inferior negroes for enormous prices." Hire rates thus ran in rough proportion to the amount of improved land available in a region. "There is no
demand for negroes here at present," P. Ricks wrote to Hilliard Fort in
1822, "as those who are not in debt are laying up money to buy land."
"But as soon as the land is sold or settled," Ricks predicted, "your country
will be full of the Alabamans after negroes."[43]

As evidence of this predictable cycle, Ricks cited the "great demand for
negroes" in the already settled area around Huntsville, Alabama: "Negroes hired out very well here this year, fellows $200, girls and boys 12

years old $75, women from $120 to $144." Excited declarations, such as this one, of surging slave values in frontier hiring markets are everywhere in migrants' letters to friends and relations; the writers marveled at the wonders of speculation in slaves. Ricks, for example, proffered his information as proof of "the present prospects of negro property," but only on the condition that Hilliard Fort keep it to himself, for Ricks hoped "to deal in that way when I come in." Like land and other commodities in high demand on the ambitious frontier, hired slaves were big business and thus the object of considerable calculation. Indeed, migrants sometimes suggested that friends at least send their slaves out west to take advantage of surging demand, even if they could not come themselves. In 1810 Charles Norton urged his cousin Betsey to send her slaves to Natchez—"There are great expectations and accounts of that Country, greater than you know of," he wrote—because there she could get at least fifteen dollars per month for her slave men and ten dollars for women. Informing his cousin of the elevated hire rates in New Orleans in 1816 ("a negro man hires for $15 per month, a woman $10 and $12"), John H. Norton declared without reservation that "a man with any property in this country must very light indeed if he does not increase it." The quick and considerable profits garnered through slave hiring conditioned slave owners to a view of slavery predicated not just on productive labor but also on the accumulation of capital.[44]

That hire rates became the object of speculation is not surprising, for the purpose of hiring out slaves was to accumulate wealth, in this case wealth that could be put toward making new lives in the kingdom of cotton. In April 1822, W. Felton traveled "six weeks on the road" with his family to Courtland, Alabama. Once there, Felton did what most migrants did: he secured a room and board for his wife and children, he made plans to set out to find unclaimed land, and he hired out the slaves he had brought with him. Even though people in the surrounding region "had picked their crops," Felton was able to rent his slaves out in two days, a strong indication of the demand for labor on the cotton frontier. In hiring out his slaves, Felton's aim was more than simply to avoid provisioning them or even than to recoup money lost in the overland move. He wanted to maximize the income he could earn off his slaves, thereby accruing money he could put toward his new enterprise in Alabama. When he hired out his slaves in April, he received between $10 and $12.50 per month for men, $8 for plough boys, and $5 for women with children. "The whole are earning me something like $150 per month," Felton bragged to a friend, but he committed to the prices only for four months because after that time, he noted, "cotton will be opened." At that time, he had been told by "people of veracity," he could surely get as much as two dollars per day for his slaves. Felton thus checked what would have been the natural inclination to rent out his slaves for the entire year, "knowing I could make a great deal more."[45]

Like Felton, many migrants to the west found that those who had established themselves on land and had begun cultivating cotton constituted an eager market for hired slaves. Three migrants who left for the Southwest in 1836 found equally propitious conditions for hiring out slaves in different regions of the South. John Tutt, who left Virginia for Missouri in that year, was able to hire out his three slaves immediately upon his arrival. When Eli Lide arrived in Alabama, he "put out a negro boy to learn the Blacks[mith] trade for whom I get $150 dollars a year hire." And John Preston found circumstances in Arkansas so favorable in 1836 that he could hire one of his slaves for twenty dollars per month and another for one dollar per day. This cash was important for short-term survival in a new region where steady sources of income could lie months in the future. The money could be used to purchase seeds, tools, or livestock; it could be put toward the construction of a frame house to replace uninviting log cabins; it could be used to vary monotonous diets of pork and corn; and it could purchase all sorts of amenities that reminded migrants of home, from glass windows to comfortable beds.[46]

For individual migrants, much thought had to be put into determining which slaves to hire out, into finding that tenuous equilibrium between one's own labor needs and the desire to maximize the returns earned on hired slaves—the equilibrium between speculation and production. When James Harrison moved to Mississippi in the 1830s, his father, Thomas Harrison, gave him some valuable advice about what to do with his slaves once he arrived. "Don't hire for the whole year," Thomas counseled his son, knowing that the younger Harrison would need his slaves "as early next fall as possible to open land." Hiring, the elder Harrison pointed out, was a temporary expedient, a way to make some money before he settled down to cultivating his own land. "Select a few of the best hands," the father advised, "and make the rest earn a support until next fall." Though the ideal would have been to keep all the strongest slaves and hire out the women and children, the more experienced Harrison knew that this was far from likely. "The greater number of the negroes must be put out," he explained, "because it would be out of the question to buy provisions for the women and children and no one would hire them without a sufficient proportion of working hands." The elder Harrison's advice captured a conception of slavery predicated on fully exploiting the duality of slave labor: slaves as at once productive workers and money-making capital. That conception of slavery ensured that mobility would be an ever more salient aspect of slave life with each passing year of the eighteenth and early nine-teenth centuries.[47]

Consider, for example, the experience of Henry Bruce, who endured all of the emotional and physical hardships that slaves faced through forced migration to the West. Bruce was taken by his owner to Missouri and Mis-sissippi, and in each location he was hired out immediately upon arrival. As his experience attests, slaves did not stop moving once they reached their masters' destinations. They were passed from stranger to stranger, sometimes more than one time in a year. When Bruce was just a boy, his owner, Mr. Perkinson, decided to "break up his Virginia home and take his slaves to Missouri." In 1844, slaves and master reached Keytesville, Mis-souri, where the majority of the slaves were "soon hired out to work in the tobacco factories." Bruce himself was hired out with his mother and some of his siblings to a brickmaker. Though he was only nine years old, Bruce had to feed livestock, cut firewood, and carry bricks. He probably dropped a fair share of bricks—not surprising given his age—for he remembered that when in the brickyard he "got whipped nearly every day." Bruce's ex-perience in the brickyard is a good example of how slave life for young children could change dramatically when their owners began to consider hiring out slaves. Children were never exempt; hiring allowed migrants like Perkinson to envisage a return on *all* their slaves, including the youn-gest ones.

Perhaps not enjoying the success for which he had hoped, Perkinson re-turned to Virginia in 1846, but he left his slaves in Missouri to be hired out by the year. He was no doubt persuaded in this plan by the fact that his sis-ter-in-law hired out her slaves in Missouri, receiving "more money yearly for them than when they worked upon the farm." But then in 1847 Perkin-son sent word that he wanted his slaves sent east. The slaves went, even though it was "contrary to [their] will." Bruce never explained precisely why the slaves did not want to return to Virginia, but a likely reason was that they had succeeded, despite being moved around to different hirers, in establishing new kin ties in Missouri and were reluctant to see them severed.

The slaves did return to Virginia, however, and—yet again—they fell victim to Perkinson's profit-seeking wanderlust. In October 1849, Perkin-son decided to move west again, this time to Mississippi. Like so many other itinerant slaveholders rushing headlong into ambitions of fortune, Perkinson knowingly and capriciously sundered loving bonds formed by his slaves when they got in his way. Bruce's sister Eliza, for example, had married someone while in Virginia, "and thus they were separated for-ever" when Perkinson continued his search for ever greater opportunities. Bruce and the other Perkinson slaves arrived in Holly Springs, Mississippi, just in time for the 1850 hiring day on January 1. But by March, Perkinson was "dissatisfied" again, and he decided to buy out the hiring contracts to which he had committed his slaves and move back to Missouri. With Missouri tobacco factories paying large sums to owners in order to guarantee a sufficient workforce, money was surely a motivating factor in this final move. Bruce remembered that, at the factories, his "master received from two hundred and fifty to three hundred dollars a year for each man or boy over seventeen years old." Henry Bruce, like so many other hired slaves, was a remunerative investment for his owner. He was a product in high demand in the labor-hungry western states. His experience, again like that of other hired slaves, is most notable for its inescapable movement. That transience was of course a threat to slave communities and families, but as the next chapter will explore, slaves responded to the threat of movement with strategies of their own for family survival, often by using to their own advantage the very mobility that plagued them.[48]

By the time that Henry Bruce's master was dragging his Virginia slaves westward in enterprising pursuit of profitable hire rates, slave hiring had dominated the everyday economic strategies of Chesapeake slaveholders for nearly a century. The practice had had an even longer history in the Carolina low country, and it was nearly indispensable to migrating slaveholders seeking gainful advantage in the nascent cotton country of the Southwest following the Revolution. The alacrity with which slaveholders latched onto the promise of improved labor efficiency through hiring— Thomas Jefferson's "hopeful prospect"—must be understood within its larger context. To say simply that slave hiring offered flexibility in the South's slave labor market is to miss its true significance. In fact, that slaveholders in the Chesapeake and the Southwest desired that flexibility in the first place is more telling than that they found their answer in the practice of hiring out slaves. It was no mistake that slave hiring emerged in those regions precisely as the market revolution was beginning to surge forward and as capitalism shaped the national political culture. Slave hiring emerged because it made possible the driving passion of the slave South: production for world markets. Slave hiring, indispensable to the westward migration of slavery (more production required more land), was the crutch on which migrants relied in their efforts to reproduce the South's distinctive culture and political economy in lands farther west. Perhaps most important, slave hiring combined with the domestic slave trade and with the reigning tenets of liberal capitalism to encourage Southern slaveholders to view both slaves and slavery from the vantage point of the market. When hiring was a possibility, owners calculated returns on individual slaves in terms of cash earned as well as cotton picked. Every slave, young or old, could produce a profit when placed temporarily in someone else's hands.

But slave hiring had an Achilles' heel. Ironically, the practice made the slave system more vulnerable—recall Frank Ruffin's denunciation in the pages of the *Southern Planter*—at the same time that it spurred production and facilitated the expansion of slave territory. This paradox grew out of the contradictions inherent in relying on slave labor in a capitalist world. Mastery was property in the slave South, just as a cart or a horse or a slave was property, and liberalism preached the absolute and inviolable nature of property rights. But when a slave was hired out, mastery was divided between two people, each of whom was certain of "owning" that slave. The implications of this situation are best explained by noting the crucial difference between renting a horse, another common practice in the slave South, and renting a slave, even though Southern jurists and other observers often tried to draw analogies between the two. The purpose of renting out a horse or livestock was often the same as renting out a slave—to reduce maintenance costs and raise a little cash into the bargain—but the owners of slaves, unlike the owners of horses or mules, did not own merely bodies. Slaveholders wished to own the total subordination of their slaves, and as liberal tenets became more entrenched in the South, it was this complete subordination of slave to master that the notion of absolute property made inviolable. The right to mastery raised problems during hiring transactions because both white people involved wanted to safeguard the mastery that each had, at different times, bought and paid for. Moreover, the interests of owners and hirers were fundamentally opposed: owners wished to protect the long-term worth of their investments; hirers, by contrast, wanted to ensure quick and profitable returns, which usually meant working hired slaves to unendurable limits.

Slave hiring made obvious economic sense, but its rewards came at a price. Dividing mastery was a source of financial adaptability and strength, but it was also a source of social and cultural strain, for it could engender dissension among whites over how the system of slavery should operate. This dissension manifested itself not just in disputes between disgruntled owners and hirers but also in the animosity that white tradesmen felt when forced to compete for jobs with slaves hired out by their owners. Slaves, who stood to lose the most in hiring transactions, viewed the practice through the prism of their family lives. Families were constantly under threat of dispersal by sale or hire, and slaves found that while hiring could be a curse to stable family lives, it could also, under the right circumstances, be a blessing.

A Blessing and a Curse

I am not very well at present on account of being separated from
my wife . . . My mind is so distracted on her acc[oun]t that I scarce
can tend to my work as I ought to have done. I hope you will take
it into consideration and send for her . . .

Edmund, a hired slave, to his owner, 1849

*I*N HIS proslavery tract *The Rightful Remedy* (1850), Edward B. Bryan
averred that one advantage of hiring temporary labor in a slave society
was that, unlike in a free-labor society, negotiations over work and wages
were carried out "regardless of the will of the individual hired." The slave
was "no party to the contract," Bryan explained, but rather "the matter
under contract, the material upon which others operate." In the manner of
those who know implicitly that they are bidding a weak hand, Bryan overstated his case. Only in the realm of the apologia could slaves be viewed as
pure commodities. In the realities of everyday life, slaves asserted themselves, guarded their interests, acted on their own, and ran away. Both
owners and hirers would have strongly, if regretfully, disagreed with Bryan
that slaves were "no party to" the transactions that kept them moving
from master to master in the slave South. Indeed, the triangularity of
hiring arrangements was forged through concerted attempts by slaves to
shape, as best they could, the particulars of those transactions, including
where the slaves would work, for whom, and who would come with them.
When hired slaves asserted themselves in this way, they inevitably aimed to
maintain the integrity of their family lives. While hired out, slaves did everything in their power to keep children, spouses, and other family members near at hand.[1]

Slaveholders had to be constantly aware of their slaves' views on being
hired out if they wanted transactions to be remunerative. They had to negotiate terms and conditions with hirers, but they also had to negotiate
with the slaves whose names would be on the contracts. Not surprisingly,
slaves reacted to the prospect of being hired out in the same way that people react to any significant life change: with a spectrum of emotions. Joy,

eagerness, fear, anxiety, indifference—all were possible feelings for slaves moving on to new masters. Some slaves eagerly embraced their hiring out as a way to escape an unbearable situation. Solomon Northup felt "gratification" on hearing that John M. Tibeats, a man he despised, had hired him out, "as any place was desirable that would relieve me of his hateful presence." Other slaves might have wished to live in particular regions or preferred to do certain kinds of work, and hiring could sometimes fulfill such small wishes. For various reasons, but usually to avoid separation from spouses or children, some slaves were so eager to be hired out that they actually initiated transactions themselves, asking whites they knew to hire them.[2]

If some slaves accepted their hiring with alacrity, just the prospect of it filled many others with anxiety and even dread. Frederick Douglass noted that slaves about to be sent off to new masters were afflicted by "deep consternation," caused in part by separations from kin but also by fear of the unknown, in this case the conduct of different masters. Hired slaves faced this uncertainty on a maddeningly regular basis, as they were forced almost yearly to break off ties with kin and worry about getting accustomed to the habits and whims of new masters. Harriet Jacobs watched these worries become obsession for some of her fellow slaves. She observed that for those facing the unknown of hiring day, New Year's Eve was a time to "wait anxiously for the dawning of the day." The anxiety was so strong that it could ruin the preceding Christmas holiday, the few days that most slaves looked forward to all year. "Were it not that hiring day is near at hand," Jacobs wrote, "and many families are fearfully looking forward to the probability of separation in a few days, Christmas might be a happy season for the poor slaves."[3] "On New Year's Day we were all scared," recalled an ex-slave from Virginia, because "we did not know who was to go or come."[4]

Going and coming were certainties in slave life. Slaves were moved by their owners from plantation to plantation or from farm to city; they were sold away; they were forced to migrate westward with owners; and, not least of all, they were hired out—both near and far, in groups or alone, with family members and without. Historians have recently begun to emphasize the centrality of movement to slave life, an effort that partly revises works published in the 1970s and early 1980s that left an impression of slave life as largely settled on big plantations. But this increased attention to movement has raised new questions, especially since historians continue to see relative stability as a hallmark of slave families. One question that arises is simple: if slaves were on the move so much, how were they able to maintain strong ties with friends and family? Looking at hiring from the perspectives of slaves themselves suggests one way to reconcile this apparent contradiction. The evidence from slave narratives, from the recollections of former slaves, and even from slaveholders' letters unmistakably demonstrates that family—and the attempt to keep as closely in contact with loved ones as possible—lay at the heart of slaves' efforts to shape the hiring transactions that kept them moving from place to place. In these efforts, slaves often used to advantage their value to their owners as investments, and in the process often brought owners and hirers into conflict.[5]

Herbert Gutman noted more than twenty years ago that "the relationship between hiring out and the slave family . . . needs careful study." That relationship was, in its own way, a paradox. On the one hand are the unsurprising stories of slave families brutally separated when husbands or wives or children were hired out. Former slave Rev. William Ruth, interviewed in Canada, remembered that he "often saw separations of families by sales and by hiring" in his native Kentucky. On the other hand are the adaptive strategies that slaves devised to combat such separations, strategies that were at the heart of slave resistance. There are remarkably numerous stories of slaves who actually used the mobility that hiring introduced in the service of family integrity. If hiring could tear families apart, it could also bring them together.[6]

In the process of discovering that they could use hiring as a means to keep loved ones close by, slaves learned to rely on themselves, not the capricious solicitude of masters, to maintain family integrity. What slaves did in the face of separation thus helps to shed light on the relationships that slaves formed, and re-formed, with their owners. Slaves at least implicitly understood that for their owners hiring was primarily a profit-making measure, and that knowledge often offered them a resource for keeping families together. When slaves attempted to control where and to whom they would be hired, they used their bodies and their work as leverage, withholding both in order to secure the conditions they desired. In the negotiations that took place between owners and their slaves, an awareness of profit and the market was always at the fore.

Husbands and Wives

"Come up on the block!" For many slaves these sharp words began their hiring transactions. A former slave from Alabama remembered that the auctioneer then called out to the white faces in the jostling crowd, "Here's a good nigger to be hired out. What you give for him?" The auction block, with all its haggling and inspection, was as much a part of slave hiring as it was of slave selling. Measy Hudson, for example, recalled that "every

New Year's Day, we was put up on the block and hired out to the highest bidder." Wintry temperatures rarely kept would-be hirers away from the countless public squares and courthouse steps where they could examine and place bids on slaves for rent. January 1 stood out on Southern calendars. Hinton Helper, notable for both his antislavery and his racist beliefs, was affronted by hiring day—"New Year's Day . . . is desecrated in the South"—because, for him, it was one more aspect of the slaveholders' conspiracy against white laborers. But for many more white Southerners, hiring day was a time to see friends, collect debts, and acquire labor. Former slave Plomer Harshaw remembered that whites in his county referred to hiring day as "a nigger show." And Sister Harrison, whose brothers were routinely enlisted to play music for the occasion, recalled that "the hirin' grounds was always lively." The easy sociability that whites enjoyed contrasted bleakly with the experience of slaves, however. Harriet Jacobs emphasized the palpable anxiety of "the Slaves' New Year's Day"—the title of the third chapter of her narrative—when enslaved men, women, and children could be found on hiring grounds across the South, "waiting, like criminals, to hear their doom pronounced."[7]

Contemporary accounts of hiring day commonly made note of the surprisingly large numbers of slaves assembled to be hired out. A Virginia teacher, for example, recorded in his journal the scene he witnessed at the 1841 hiring day in Drummondtown: "There were a great many people . . . More black ones than I ever saw together. The street was literally filled with them." A Boston newspaper reporter covering the 1860 hiring day in Alexandria, Virginia, noted (with the brute racism of the age) that there were "congregated all the hiring hands in the adjacent country; men, women, and children, mechanics, field hands, dining-room servants, cooks and house servants, of every color from the Octoroon . . . to the real wooly-headed Congo." Most owners brought their slaves to hiring day themselves, but many, especially in large cities, retained specialized hiring agents to carry out transactions for them. A few slaves would have come on their own, having been given by their owners the dubious privilege of choosing their own masters for the year. Hirings and sales often occurred on the same day, and the rituals that attended the two transactions were remarkably similar. Auctioneers "cried off" the slaves to be hired, reading stipulations set down by owners and driving up bids with smooth-tongued commendations. Hirers played both inquisitor and inspector, examining slaves for "flaws" in character and body. At the same time, slaves identified those in the crowd they knew to be cruel or humane, trying as best they could to steer the deals being struck. A former slave interviewed in 1910 remembered that certain inquiries were invariably put to hired slaves on the block: Will you work for this man, obey his orders, and not run away? "If you didn't want to go to the man that bid for you," he recalled, "they'd tell you to talk and say so."[8]

Such questions opened the way for slaves to influence hiring transactions even before the ink was dry on the contracts that bore their names. "The slave is sure to know who is the most humane, or cruel master, within forty miles of him," Harriet Jacobs observed. On hiring day, she added, it was easy to determine "who clothes and feeds his slaves well," for he would be "surrounded by a crowd, begging, 'Please, massa, hire me this year. I will work *very* hard, massa." Ingratiation, though, was just one tool slaves could use to shape the transactions. Effrontery had much to recommend it as well, especially when slaves were trying to dissuade rather than persuade prospective hirers. In the late 1850s, a young girl named Nancy Williams, no more than thirteen or fourteen years old, went with her owner to hiring day in Virginia. Once there, she was put on a raised platform to be cried off before a crowd of white men, men she later described as "poor white tobacco-chewing devils." Williams made no effort to mask the disdain she felt for the gazing men, yelling as loud as she could, "I don't want no poor white man get me! Ain't want to work for no poor white man." This bold protest no doubt startled the potential hirers, but it failed to discourage at least one poor white man in the crowd. "As the devil would have it," she lamented later, "one got me." As Williams' experience attests, slaves could let their views be known, but it did not always do any good. In fact, slaves who refused to leave the hiring grounds with their new masters, Harriet Jacobs pointed out, were whipped and then jailed until they promised "not to run away during the year." Those slaves who had run away the previous year were often, as one Alabama owner wrote in 1855, "corrected upon hiring day as a warning to the others."[9]

Hiring day was just one arena in which hiring transactions were carried out and in which slaves asserted their interests. Hiring agreements were just as likely to be hammered out privately between neighbors, acquaintances, or business associates. Rather than attend hiring day, many white Southerners simply wrote to friends who were large slaveholders to inquire whether any of their slaves might be for hire. Newspapers were also a hub for those looking to hire or hire out slaves. And large cities had multiple hiring brokerages that functioned like slave pens, where slaves were sent by rural owners to be hired out. In Richmond, Frederick Law Olmsted found a number of such establishments clustered together, each with signs advertising slaves for hire and some with slaves lined up in front. Lucien Lewis, whose offices were in Richmond's Metropolitan Hall, devoted himself "exclusively" to slave rentals, so that he could give his "personal attention" to those who had "servants to send to the city to be hired out." When they wanted to hire out slaves, owners could hammer out the details themselves, or they could entrust the process to men who had made the business their profession. Regardless of the manner in which hiring transactions were initiated and carried out, slaves always did what they could to make their voices heard. Three separate intentions, three separate wills —holding, of course, unequal sway—characterized every hiring arrangement.[10]

Whether they voiced their intentions from the auction block on hiring day or from a hiring agent's back office, slaves reinforced the deeply political nature of slave families in the South. What little power slaves could amass they deployed in the service of a stable family life. But slaves about to be hired out who wished to keep their families together faced an ambiguous situation when they initially approached their owners on the subject. For owners who were focused on the bottom line, and few were not, the financial benefits of hiring out families together were dubious. First of all, renting out families was complicated by the fact that hirers usually balked at maintaining small children not old enough to work, especially if they required attention from their mothers during the day. "Isaac and his family I don't think would do well to be hired out," a Mississippi hiring agent advised an owner in 1843. "There is the 2 children to be fed and clothed," he explained, "to which is added a third one (girl) no expense—save in the time &c. of the mother." Second, hiring out families was less lucrative, for owners almost invariably had to accept less money than they would receive if they hired out family members individually. "Single men and women are very little trouble to dispose of and at regular rates," hiring agent R. H. Adams wrote to an owner in 1855, "but with families you have to take whatever you can get." At the owner's request, Adams did hire out Old Sam along with his wife, his daughter, and his eight-year-old son, but Adams was offered fifty dollars less than he had expected to get for them. Sometimes, guardians or estate administrators were entirely stymied in attempts to hire out slave families, and then they were left supporting the families themselves. John E. Jones, for example, tried to hire out his uncle's slaves in Alabama in 1855, but he ended up paying the hire for two families himself, probably because he could find no one else to do so. Slave owners encountered the same problems when they tried to sell slaves. The intractable reality of the auction block was that slaves sold or rented for more when they were "unencumbered," as the contemporary phrase went, by children or spouses. In his study of South Carolina court sales, for example, Thomas D. Russell found that slaves auctioned off in groups sold for about 40 percent less than slaves offered individually. Slaves determined to hold their families together faced imposing obstacles, not least of which was an owner's financial interest in seeing them hired out individually.[11]

Conversely, both owners and hirers knew that the profitability of hiring transactions rested to a great extent on the consent, however grudging, of the slaves involved. Nothing sundered a hiring transaction more quickly than a slave determined to make life difficult for owner and hirer. Their use of slaves limited to a year's time, hirers had little patience for slaves left torpid by anger or depression. Many owners and hirers thus concluded that keeping slave families together made good economic sense. "I have always had them hired in family, and reference to a choice of masters made either by themselves or my agent," Joseph Anderson, a Virginia slave owner, informed a friend interested in hiring out slaves, "and never extracting the largest prices that c[oul]d be obtained." Anderson recommended the policy for its ultimate prudence and profitability, for he boasted that by following it he had "lost few and perhaps fewer than any person of my acquaintance." Anthony Trollope was told while traveling through Kentucky that "care is taken" when hiring out slaves "not to remove a married man from his home," and if this was indeed true on occasion, it was only because, by forestalling disputes over "lost time," it made life easier for owners and hirers. "The time lost by them going to their wives houses at all seasons," a Virginia hirer complained in 1854 of the slaves he had rented, "caused a serious interruption to business." Through such trials, many hirers learned that it made eminent sense to keep husbands and wives at least in close proximity, if not in the same household. "I will hire Ann if her Husband is hired in this place" is typical of statements that abound in the correspondence between owners and hirers, statements that grew out of long experience with despondent slaves who refused to work. The man who hired Gilbert in 1849 in Virginia also hired his wife, Clara, even though he had "but little use for [her]," in order to "prevent Gilbert from having to leave his work to come see her." When James Cooke was deciding whether to hire Solomon and Fanny, who were married, for another year in 1853, their owner reminded him that "if Solomon is sound and continues in good health, he will pay a good percent on his costs, and again, Fanny will be worth to you a good deal more by having Solomon, than if you separate them."[12]

Even though owners had the right to break up slave families whenever they desired, they understood that in exercising that right, they risked arousing the deepest hatred, and the most determined resistance, in their slaves. And that meant less profit. Consider the example of George Young, who hired out the slaves on James McDowell's Mississippi plantation in the 1840s. He swore by the inherent virtue of hiring husbands and wives near each other. Young often allowed men who had wives on other plantations to canvass the neighborhood for potential hirers, setting a price for each and sending them on their way. The policy saved Young the trouble of searching out hirers on his own, but it also dramatically increased the likelihood that the slaves would be satisfied with their placements. "I have hired out John to the owner of his wife for $150," Young reported to McDowell in 1842, adding that "Moses could get no one near his, with whom he was willing to live to offer for his hire more than $125." Moses continued to have difficulty finding hirers. Young reported two years later that "Banks would not hire Moses at more than $100, and no one else near his wife would hire at all." Young no doubt devised his strategy in part to parry accusations of bad faith from slaves like Moses, who, Young could claim, had been given the opportunity to find a hirer himself. As more of the McDowell slaves got married, however, and as hiring them out in situations that satisfied them became more difficult, Young tried to convince their owner to put them to work on the home plantation rather than rent them out. "The objections to hiring are increasing with them," Young wrote in 1845 to McDowell, revealing the extent to which slaves' convictions could influence transactions. "George, Henry, Susan &c.," he noted, "will be marrying and making their disposition more painful and embarrassing." "Embarrassing" certainly had multiple meanings here, from the social to the financial: separating families gave the lie to paternalist pretensions, sparked conflicts with hirers, and inevitably proved deleterious to the value of slave property. All these implications figured into Young's assertion to McDowell that "already Henry has a wife and must be hired hard by, else running away and ill usage are the consequence." Slaves like Henry who grew sullen or angry over separation from a spouse—and in turn provoked hirers to abusive punishments—could subvert otherwise promising transactions for both hirers and owners.[13]

Even though many slaveholders recognized the benefits of hiring out husbands and wives together, slaves knew that a consistent pattern of behavior could never be expected from those who owned them. If slaves wanted to keep their families together when hired out, they could not rely on their owners to make it happen. They had to come up with strategies of their own. Those strategies constituted an important aspect of the history of slave resistance. In particular, slaves used to their own advantage the fact that their bodies, their work, and their subordination were all forms of property that their owners expected to transfer temporarily to another person. By threatening to impair any of those three forms of property, slaves transmuted their owners' financial interest from an obstacle to family integrity into a source of leverage. If slaves made clear that they would harm themselves, run away, or flout authority if hired out, most owners thought twice. In such "negotiations" between slaveholders and slaves, there could be no mistake that the master-slave relationship was suffused with a thorough awareness on both sides of property, profit, and the market. Capitalism's defense of private property rights may have armed slave owners against abolitionist assaults, but the exaltation of property also gave slaves opportunities to exploit their value toward insurgent ends. It at least allowed them to make some demands about when, where, and to whom they would be hired.

For instance, slaves often made it clear to their owners from the outset of hiring transactions that they expected to be able to visit loved ones once established in their new positions. That their owners hearkened to such demands is reflected in the stipulations agreed to by owners and hirers in countless hiring contracts. Thom, for example, was allowed by his hirer to visit his wife and "stay with her a week in every two months." His hirer even furnished him with a horse to ride when he went. The contract that transferred Warner from Mary Timberlake to C. J. Faulkner in the 1830s had an addendum recording a "deduction made in hire for lost time in going to see his wife every other Saturday evenings." Most owners insisted that their hired slaves be free from work on Sundays, so on Saturday evenings Southern roads were alive with slaves traveling short and long distances to see loved ones. Leonard, for example, while hired out in Louisiana in 1853 went every Saturday evening to see friends and family at his owner's house, and the hirer had no objection "provided he returns in time for his duties on Monday morning (5 o'clock)." When Joe was hired out as a sawyer in Louisiana, his hirer agreed that every two weeks Joe should be allowed to return to his owner's plantation "to visit his wife." When Thom, Warner, Leonard, and Joe learned that they were to be hired out, they in all likelihood went directly to their owners and made clear that they wished time to be allotted for them to see their spouses. Most owners knew that if these demands were not met, slaves would simply leave hirers' places anyway, and such behavior inevitably led to punishments that made owners cringe at the treatment of their investments. Recall, for example, George Young's insistence that because Henry had married, he "must be hired hard by, else running away and ill usage are the consequence."[14]

Scheduled weekly or fortnightly visits were rarities, and they were especially difficult for slaves hired out at great distances from those they wished to visit. As white Southerners moved westward, expanding the geographic reach of their slave regime, and as they began to rely more on hiring agents to rent out slaves to strangers in far-flung counties, slaves found it increasingly difficult to maintain contact with friends and loved ones. But even slaves hired out at great distances made demands when they could. As with other hired slaves, their contracts often stipulated the timing of visits, although their visits were arranged at much longer and more irregular intervals. When Andrew Johnson hired Jim in 1852, for example, Johnson agreed in the contract "to permit him to be absent twice during each year for the space of three days each time (once early in July and once at Christmas) to go see his wife in Marengo County." If separated from his wife while hired out in 1851, Gilbert was to "be allowed to come to see her three times in the year, with an allowance of nine days at each time." When J. P. Aylett sent James and John to Richmond hiring agent Lewis Hill in 1853, he asked Hill, "Please bargain that they should come over twice in the year . . . besides Xmas" to see their wives. Owners and hirers could not avoid the demands made by slaves who were hired out because those slaves had too many opportunities to avoid work, to run away, to spark confrontations between owners and hirers, and generally to undermine the social and economic benefits envisioned by the whites involved.[15]

Of course, many owners hired out their slaves without a moment's thought to breaking up marriages. Henry Bruce's parents were split between two separate hirers in 1836 when his owner died and the estate was divided among the heirs. "Then it was," Bruce recalled, "that family ties were broken, the slaves hired out, my mother to one man and my father to another." In 1854, C. J. McDonald strongly advised his sisters to hire out their slaves in Macon, Georgia, even though the men would be separated from their wives. "It is useless to attempt to get them and their wives together," he told his sisters, reminding them that "a negro preacher" had "married them for the union to last as long as they live or until it is the pleasure of their owner to separate them." For every hiring contract that explicitly stipulated time that a hired slave be allowed to visit his or her spouse, there was another in which family life went unmentioned.[16]

Even when their wishes went unheeded, however, slaves formulated strategies of their own to overcome long-distance separations. These strategies reveal the ways in which slaves relied on their own resourcefulness rather than their owners' ostensible paternalism to keep their families together. Some slaves who were literate, for example, were able to exchange letters with loved ones as a means of staying in touch and pass on messages of continuing care and concern. While hired out, Osborne Copes wrote his owner to thank him for sending him a letter from his wife and then enclosed "one to her in reply which I hope you will please forward to her for me." In 1850, after having been hired out with several of her owner's slaves in Texas, Giney wrote her children to tell them to "*beg* Mas Jule to let you come up" at Christmas; she added that they should "tell Scott and Tabby their children are very anxious to see them and look for them too on Christmas." Slaves who were hired out in Southern cities sometimes wrote to their owners to inform them of the work they had secured and how they were faring, and they usually added messages to be passed on to friends or family whom they had left behind on plantations. "Give my best love to my mother for me," William Henry wrote in 1862 from Wilmington, North Carolina. Anderson F. Henderson also wrote his owners from Wilmington: "Please give my love to Mother and all the children and tell them I want to see [them] very much but must wait until next Christmas," he wrote in the summer of 1857, adding "my wife and children is all well and join in love to all my relation and friends." Bella DeRosset wrote to her mistress in 1862, asking her to "give our love to . . . Marriah and Fanny and Peggy, and tell them if I never see them in this world again I hope to meet them in heaven where parting will be no more." Letters were a feeble substitute for close contact with loved ones, but for those slaves who had achieved literacy they were a crucial element in determined efforts to keep loving ties from snapping under the strain of separation.[17]

When they learned from their owners or someone else that they were going to be hired out, many slaves either ran away or flatly refused to go. Without a hint of equivocation, for example, Beverly notified his owner in 1845 that "if he be hired on the Canal above Lynchburg or on the Rail Road he will be compelled to run away." When faced with such obstinacy, owners were often forced to explain to would-be hirers that the deals were off, or that they should be, given the determined opposition of the slaves concerned. It was not uncommon for letters to contain such simple statements of fact as "my boy Austin will not go out" or "Toby found out he was to be hired and run off." Running away was more difficult for women because they shouldered the overwhelming burdens of child-rearing, but women were just as likely as men to defy orders they could not bear. In 1838, the man who had hired out Clarissa reluctantly wrote her hirer to inform him, "She is extremely unwilling to go to Wilmington." The letter added, "She also suggests that she was deceived," an indication of the kinds of negotiations that occurred between prospective hirers and slaves: "She thought that you lived over the River near Mrs. Purdies, who owns her husband." Owners who forced slaves to go against their will often regretted doing so. In 1838, Peter's owner wrote to explain why Peter never showed up at the hirer's place, even though he had been sent there. As it turned out, the owner learned "from one of my negroes that [Peter] said that he could not live so far distant from his wife, perhaps not to see her over half a dozen times during the year." Many owners and hirers judiciously hesitated before pushing slaves too far against their will, especially when slaves' families were at stake. Explaining why he could send only some of the slaves for which a hirer had contracted, M. W. Ransom wrote in 1856 that "the rest have wives at home or are unwill[ing]." Ransom added, "I cannot in justice to you or myself send them," a laconic reminder of all that both owners and hirers had bound up in these transactions—profit, mastery, honor, respect—and that runaway or defiant slaves could quickly undermine.[18]

Some slaves, when ordered into hiring situations they could not abide, threatened to do bodily harm to themselves. Joseph Copes's hiring agent wrote to inform him in 1849 that Edmund, whom Copes wished to hire out in Baton Rouge, "had gone so far as to intimate that he would kill himself before he would separate from his wife." Some slaves progressed beyond threats and actually harmed themselves in order to avoid being hired out. In 1851, Henry "was opposed to going with Mrs. Michael," the woman who had hired him, wishing instead to be hired out in Mobile, where he could earn money in his free time doing odd jobs. Henry eventually broke out in a suspiciously virulent case of poison oak. "Dr. Ashe thinks he rubbed the poison oak upon himself on purpose," the owner noted, for Henry "wanted to live in town, as he said, where he would make something for himself." Aware of the hire money that his body could bring, Henry used this occasion to remind his owner that he was a piece of property that could make demands. Hired slaves and their owners often did not know each other well enough for such demands to be grounded in a sense of mutual obligation between masters and slaves; rather, the demands grew out of slaves' understanding that they in many ways could dictate their own worth. Like slaves who threatened to run away, slaves who threatened to harm themselves were using their market value as a weapon in the skirmishes that arose with owners determined to hire them out against their will.[19]

Rubbing poison oak on oneself and threatening suicide were most likely impulsive reactions to unwanted hirings, and they contrasted with other stratagems to forestall transactions that required more calculated planning. It is possible, for instance, that some slave women planned for their pregnancies to begin to show at the end of the year, when most hiring deals were sealed. Ultimately, we will never know what Katy, who was pregnant, was thinking in 1855 when her owner's agent decided that she was "not in a situation to hire out for several months yet." Nor can we read the mind of Harriet, who continually stymied her owner's plans to hire her out by getting pregnant. While the intentions and motivations of these women

must necessarily remain elusive—it is possible that the timing of the pregnancies was mere coincidence—we do know that getting pregnant was a
form of resistance often pursued by slave women who hoped to secure
smaller work loads or better food rations. If they wished to avoid being
hired out, women like Katy and Harriet could time their pregnancies so
that they began to show by December or January, when they would be in-
spected by prospective hirers inclined to want, as one hirer did in 1826,
"such young women as . . . are not likely from appearances to be breeding
in the course of the year." Being pregnant did more than disenchant hirers,
though. It also led owners, who had vested interests in protecting slave
women's reproduction, to hesitate before renting out such women to other
people. Reproduction was a tangle of desire, coercion, love, and property
in the South, and for slave women it could be at once a cause of deep anguish and a source of substantial leverage. It was no doubt deployed by
some women as a means of avoiding unwanted rentals.[20]

If hired out against their will, many slaves simply made life as difficult as
possible for their hirers and refused to provide the submission to which
hirers felt they had legal and social entitlement. Some slaves, for example,
"misbehaved" in the hope that exasperating behavior might prompt hirers
to relinquish their claims and transfer slaves back to their owners. "Hester
has not only been almost useless herself to us . . . (not wishing to remain
here I presume from now having a husband who is now out of Mr. Beards
employment)," Emma Beard wrote to Joseph Copes, Hester's owner, in
1855, "but so incites Parthenia to disobedience that it will be impossible
for me to keep her." Sly disobedience was manifest in petulant scowls,
dragging feet, and botched tasks, but some slaves went further, brazenly
threatening to run away from their hirers if not released from the hiring
contracts. "Lewis says he will not live with me, but will run away if I
attempt to keep him," wrote John Walker Tomlin in 1809, insisting to
Lewis's owner that the slave was so "impertinent" and "obstinate" that
Tomlin was "willing to have nothing to say to him." Hirers like Tomlin did
not have time to deal with fractious slaves, and slaves like Lewis knew it.

For the most part, slaves antagonized their hirers because they wanted
to be somewhere else, usually someplace closer to family members. Indeed,
one way that slaves frequently exasperated their hirers was by stealthily
prolonging the time they had been allotted to visit their spouses. According
to the stipulations made by his owner in a contract with a canal in 1855,
Cambridge was supposed to be able to see his wife for four days after
working three months. Cambridge did get to go see his wife, but there was
still no sign of him ten days after he had left. In 1852, Ellen was given permission by her hirer to leave "on a visit" with "the promise of returning in

ten days," but nearly two weeks later she had "not yet made her appearance." Still other slaves simply left to see wives or husbands even though forbidden to do so. Threatened with a "severe flogging" and a "ball and chain," for example, Ned ignored the orders of both his owner and hirer and at least twice made the twenty-five-mile trip to see his wife. Hirers trying to get work out of slaves who were worried about their families learned that submission was something that could be neither bought nor transferred with a piece of paper. Owners and hirers blamed recalcitrant behavior as much on each other as on slaves, and the recriminations went a long way toward fracturing white solidarity on how slavery should function.[21]

The efforts by husbands and wives to keep in close contact were probably the most significant way that slaves participated in shaping hiring transactions. Their beliefs and desires had to be acknowledged by owners and hirers alike, or arrangements were likely to be shattered by the calculated listlessness of dissatisfied slaves. Even in laying down austere conditions, the most hard-nosed of hirers could betray the negotiations with slaves that lay behind most hiring agreements. John Gamble, hiring slaves for a canal in 1825, averred to their owner that "if these men have wives they must understand that they cannot visit them before Xmas." Gamble added, though, that married men could stay two weeks with their wives before their work began in January, and that this was the "bargain" he had made with all other slaves he had hired. As an added inducement for the slaves, Gamble noted that "their food and clothing and treatment will give them perfect satisfaction." In these implicitly three-way negotiations, slaves used leverage they may not ordinarily have enjoyed to keep loved ones close to them, and for many slaves, the stakes were highest when those loved ones in question were small children.[22]

Children

A durable image in histories of slavery is that of the large plantation where elderly slaves tended small children while their parents worked in the fields. The image may reflect the reality on some farms and plantations, but it leaves a misleading impression of childhood under slavery. Most slave children did not lead idyllic lives, isolated for a time from the work to which they would eventually be put. Rather than playing in the quarters, in all likelihood the children on that archetypal plantation would have been rented out to neighbors who were willing to pay for their upkeep in exchange for whatever work they could perform. (The same would have applied to elderly slaves.) Children, in the eyes of many slave owners, were natural candidates for hiring. They had to be clothed, fed, and sheltered, yet the work they could perform on a fully staffed farm or plantation was often negligible. In the account-book calculus that structured the thinking of so many large and small slaveholders, children were consumers rather than producers; their debits almost always outweighed their credits. For instance, on a plantation where there were already enough slaves to pick up trash and stones, tote water to the fields, and scare birds away from gardens, many children could be superfluous even into their early teens. Many slave owners solved the problem by sending children to neighbors who were too poor to purchase their own slaves but who could afford to provide for the children's food and clothing in exchange for their work around the house or the fields. The children's owners, freed from the cost of maintaining otherwise idle slaves, augmented their returns on slave capital. "I sure was worth my weight in gold those days," John A. Holt remembered of his days as a small child hired out.[23]

Very young children were usually hired out with their mothers, although these women, especially if they were also pregnant, were more difficult to place than other slaves. Hirers were reluctant to take women with infants or small children because they feared that child care would limit the women's work hours, and because it meant more mouths to feed. "Servants with families and with young children are difficult to find suitable homes for and good masters where the children are properly attended to," wrote hiring agent R. H. Adams to Mary Gilliam in 1855. "Those [women] with children were not at all desirable," another plainspoken agent observed in the same year, "and such as had children with prospects of others ahead were with great difficulty hired." The preference of hirers was always for "women without encumbrances," and as a result owners and estate administrators often had to hire out women and children for simply their "victuals and clothes." The pinch of such parsimony was felt above all by slave mothers. Women hired out with small children probably encountered more severe material deprivation than other hired slaves, for they had to share their allotment of food and blankets with their children. Hirers were reluctant to provide more to slaves than was absolutely required, so more mouths inevitably meant smaller portions.[24]

It was not uncommon for hirers to receive money from an estate or an owner if several children had to be maintained or if a child was born unexpectedly. Frequently, women and children were hired out for "low bids"— that is, bids for the smallest amount of money hirers would accept in return for maintaining the slaves for the year. As Moses Grandy remembered it, when a woman had many children, especially during estate probate proceedings, it was "customary to put her and her children out yearly to the

person who will maintain them for the least money." Thus, in 1803, John
W. Perrin paid Thomas Crew "five pounds" for the yearly "maintenance"
of Lucy and her four children. Payments had to be increased if women
gave birth again during the year they were hired out. William Campbell,
for example, hired Chaney in 1860 but felt "deceived" when she had to be
"confined to her bed" while pregnant. "I cannot raise young negroes that
does not belong to me without pay," Campbell wrote to Chaney's owner.
Campbell had the force of custom on his side in his complaint. Testimony
in a court case resolving a hiring dispute in 1853 revealed that in Edge-
combe County, North Carolina, it was "a long and well established custom" that an owner of a woman who became pregnant while hired out
should "allow the hirer . . . ten dollars." Even though they were not paying
anything to rent these women and their children, hirers were free to extract
as much work from the women as they could, and perhaps even from their
older children as well.[25]

Children were separated from their mothers and hired out alone as soon
as they could command a price, however small. Noah Perry was straightforward in his 1824 will: he insisted that his youngest slaves be "hired out
as soon as they will bring anything." The year at which such remuneration
could begin differed for individual children and according to the whims of
individual owners. Only three states—Alabama, Georgia, and Louisiana—
had laws that prevented the separation through sale of slave mothers from
children under ten years of age. Yet only in Louisiana was the law enforced
with anything approaching regularity. Furthermore, the letter of these laws
pertained to selling, not hiring, so conscience and custom were the only
recognizable restraints on an owner's decision to hire out young children.
As slave mothers could attest, however, "custom" was a flimsy and unreliable check on slaveholders' behavior. Owners' decisions about when to
hire out children apart from their mothers were based not on law, custom,
or the age of the children, but on when those children could start bringing
in their own wages. As little as fifty cents was enough of an incentive for
some owners to hire out children away from their mothers.[26]

Slave owners had to look no further than their daily mail for reminders
of their slave children's potential rental values. Virginia slave owner J. H.
Cocke, for example, regularly received letters from neighbors or associates
who wished to hire "a boy or girl" or "some little negroes." "Should you
have any small negroes, either male or female, that you would put out for
the present year," wrote Juria B. Fariss to Cocke in 1831, "I would be extremely glad to get one." Fariss did not make clear why he wanted to hire
such young slaves, but he did promise that "they shall be well treated."
Cocke received a similar letter in 1837 from Martin B. Shepherd, who in-

quired "about the probability of your having any small girls or boys that you would put out for a term of years for board & clothing." Shepherd explicitly asked for a child who "might be taught pretty easily to do house business." Jesse Bowles told Cocke in the same year that it would "confer a favour" if Cocke would let him "have a small girl for the house & nurse for my baby." Ordinarily, whites preferred older, more adept slaves for household service, so the fact that these requests were explicitly for very young slaves strongly suggests that the white families involved were poor ones. But there may be an additional explanation for such requests for small children. Perhaps white women—who usually made the decisions about hiring domestic slaves, though their husbands wrote to owners in their stead—preferred very young slaves for the same reason that they sometimes preferred very old ones: these slaves were less likely to prove sexually appealing to sons and husbands.[27]

The painful reality of children separated from their mothers as soon as they could earn a little money is evident in the lists that owners kept of the slaves they hired out each year. On these routine lists, owners recorded from top to bottom the names of individual slaves, each one followed by the hirer's name and the price paid. Women with small children were invariably listed last. The lists document the inexorable movement of children's names from beneath those of their mothers up into the ranks of the wage earning. Sooner or later the children were listed individually, alongside the name of a hirer and a pitifully small price. In 1846, John L. Clifton, as administrator of an estate, began to hire out "the Negroes belonging to the children of Benjamin and Molsey Rivel." In that year, Raney and her four children were placed with Benjamin Rivel, who was paid fifty-nine dollars from the estate "to keep them." A year later, one of Raney's children, Eliza, was hired out to Thomas Ward for four dollars and ten cents, while Raney remained with Benjamin Rivel. In 1849, Raney lost another child, Clarisey, who was hired out to Thomas Ward for fifty cents. Clifton followed the same pattern of hiring out children as soon as possible when administering the slaves "belonging to the minor heirs of Joshua Craddock." In 1842, Peggy and her four children were placed with Mrs. Craddock, who agreed "to keep them for $30." Three years later, Peggy's son Jim was hired away to Clifton himself, who agreed to "feed and clothe him," and this situation continued for two years, until 1847, when Jim was hired to Samuel Raines for eight dollars and twenty-five cents. Peggy's son George was then taken from her in 1849, when Matthew Casey agreed to pay "for his victuals and clothes," an indication itself of George's young age. Needless to say, the loss of a child, even if the child was placed just a few miles away, could be heartrending for slave parents.[28]

Slave mothers like Peggy and Raney never would have seen the pieces of paper that so neatly recorded the removal of their children and the breakup of their families. But they understood better than anyone else the patterns that those papers revealed. With a parent's visceral certainty, each mother would have known that her children would be snatched from her as soon as they were old enough to work for their own keep, and perhaps bring home a nominal wage. Lavina Bell, a self-hired slave interviewed by the American Freedmen's Inquiry Commission in 1863, used images of theft and violation to explain the inevitable loss of children to hirers. "The white people have got two of my children over eleven years old," she told the interviewer—"soon as my children grow up, they take them." "That one," she said, pointing to a little boy aged nine or ten, "is about big enough to go." The separations were especially painful because slave mothers, as slave narratives and interviews attest, prized behavior among women that assertively and resourcefully protected black children from white power. If there was a "slave female principle" in the South, Brenda E. Stevenson has argued, it was "the protection and procreation of black life in the face of white opposition." Slave mothers fought hard to keep their children near them even when hired out, because those efforts were part of how they defined themselves as women and as mothers.[29]

Boys and girls were equally likely to be hired out, but gender shaped the work they performed once they were. In regions where the industry prevailed, boys were especially likely to be sent to work in tobacco factories. Henry Bruce, for example, beginning at age ten, spent much of his youth hired out to Missouri tobacco factories. In 1854, planter Farish Carter sent ten boys to work in a Georgia tobacco factory, and all were under the age of twelve. Four of them were only eight years old. Owners sent their young slave boys to tobacco factories for one reason: the work paid extremely well. Gilley M. Lewis, who got word that J. H. Cocke tended to "annually hire out a number of young negroes," applied in 1840 to get six or eight boys "from 10 to 14 years old to work in a tobacco factory." As an inducement, Lewis professed that "sprightly boys," after a year's practice, could earn yearly "from 70 to 100 dollars" for Cocke. In addition to factory work, boys were also hired out to do fieldwork or to learn skilled trades. "Plough boys" were a common fixture on fields across the South, and they were hired by small farmers and large plantation owners alike. The "small boys in the neighborhood" that Isaac Riley remembered being rounded up every year to be hired out in Missouri were probably working as plough boys. With an eye toward the future usefulness or profit of slave artisans, owners hired out boys as apprentices as well. James W. C. Pennington was hired out at age nine as an assistant to a stonemason, and his brother was placed with a pump-maker. Since hiring was such a frequent part of their early lives, slave boys did not necessarily spend their youths in the slave quarters to which they were born. Though "nothin' but a kid," Harry Johnson remembered being "just hired out from place to place" as a boy. "I was small," he averred, "but I done everything they was to do."[30]

Slave girls were also hired out, and their jobs were most likely to involve domestic labor. At age nine, Bethany Veney was hired out to "an old woman," who provided her with food and clothes in exchange for "whatever work I could do for her." For most girls, that work would have included looking after ("nursing") white children and performing various chores around the house. Millie Simpkins was hired out as a "nurse girl" at age seven, and she began to cook for white families at age ten. Margaret Davis was also hired out as a nurse before she turned ten, and she was so small that "she stood on a chair to wash." Owners often required that hirers pay only for young slaves' food and clothing, so girls were frequently hired out, as Mary Edwards was, "to do nursing for people who didn't own slaves." Because they worked primarily in the house, slave girls were more likely than boys to serve out their hiring terms under the constant supervision of whites. For poor white men and women, such girls were often the sole claim to public inclusion in the slaveholding ranks, not to mention the sole audience for private displays of mastery.[31]

Like the young boys sent out to learn artisanal skills, these girls were part of a modest apprenticeship system. Owners who wanted to train children in housekeeping, either for future work in their own homes or for later hiring, would rent them out for next to nothing to those who would instruct them in the domestic arts—in everything from building fires and making soap to serving meals and ironing clothes. "I should like to place [Mariah] where she would learn to make herself handy as a waiting girl, and I think she would be much improved with Mrs. Stockton," wrote one owner in 1851. "I sometimes think I will never let any of them go from their mother," he added, "but it might be better to get them off as early as possible." In 1855, hiring agent R. H. Adams hired out a "little girl" belonging to Mary Gilliam to a doctor's wife "to keep in the house," where the woman was "instructing the girl in sewing & house work generally." In sending requests to owners, hirers frequently mentioned the "training" they would provide to slave children placed under their control. William Randolph received a letter in 1857 from a hirer who wished to "have a little girl for the balance of the year, for her victuals and clothes, . . . to nurse and wait about the house." Not concerned "whether she has had any training or not," the hirer asserted that he would "endeavor to make her useful." The children sent out in such arrangements could be very young. In 1838, Peter Nevins and James McDowell, a future governor of Virginia, agreed that Nevins and his wife would hire McDowell's slave Matilda, who was, to her owner's hazy recollection, "about 5 years and upwards old." McDowell stipulated in the contract that Matilda should be "strictly managed and taught by Mrs. Nevins, as well as she can be taught, to be cleanly, active, and useful in the performance of all household business." Though the evidence is not conclusive, it is possible that slave girls were hired out at even younger ages than boys because their owners considered the work they would do less strenuous. In any event, hiring formed a quasi-apprenticeship program in domestic labor for the youngest slaves, especially girls. Hirers agreed to teach slave girls the rudiments of house-work, and in return they got as much labor as they could eke out of their small bodies.[32]

Harriet Tubman suffered through just such an exchange. In her narra-tive, she remembered that one day in her youth "a 'lady,' for so she was designated, came driving up to the great house . . . to see if she could find there a young girl to take care of a baby." Tubman placed "lady" in quota-tion marks to suggest that the woman was of the lower classes, and indeed it turned out that the woman "wished to pay low wages." The future "Moses" of her people, who was considered rather dull after having had her skull fractured as a child by an enraged master, "could command less wages than any other child of her age on the plantation," and so she was turned over to the woman. The woman intended to get as much work out of the young Tubman as she possibly could. Though initially engaged to mind the woman's baby, Tubman "soon found that she was expected to be maid of all work by day, as well as child's nurse by night." After sweeping and dusting all day, she was made to keep the baby quiet while her hirer slept, and every time the baby cried, the girl felt the sting of the whip that the woman kept "on a little shelf over her head." Countless children surely faced situations similar to this one, where hirers were determined to work children to their absolute limits. Tubman's hirer, in particular, "intended to get the worth of her money to the utmost farthing," an intention that left Tubman at the end of her stint "a poor, scarred wreck, nothing but skin and bone." The impoverished white Southerners whose only entrée into the slaveholding classes was to hire slave children in exchange for their maintenance could be some of the most exacting and stringent masters.[33]

Children separated from their parents by hiring were in dire straits, suf-fering the anxieties that any child would feel when torn from friends and family members. First, there were the children separated from parents who were hired out. "The practice of separating children from their mothers, and hiring the latter out at distances too great to admit of their meeting, except at long intervals," wrote Frederick Douglass, "is a marked feature of the cruelty and barbarity of the slave system." Second, many slave children were themselves hired out. These children faced the prospect not only of having minimal contact with their parents, but also of being separated from the community of slaves that had been part of their youth. Girls hired out to learn domestic work and boys bound out to learn a trade often found themselves all alone, surrounded by only white faces. James W. C. Pennington and his brother, for example, were separated from each other and then each hired out to "a family where there was no other negro." Because they were so young and could not travel long distances, children had to rely on their parents to make any efforts to visit.[34]

Historians have long recognized the predominant role slave women played in raising children, and they were indeed largely responsible for the heroic efforts that kept slave children, even once hired out, in close contact with family members. When Mourning was hired out in 1836, she was worried that her child, already "large enough to be put out," might be separated from her. Mourning therefore searched out a potential hirer for her child on her own, looking in particular for someone in the proximity of her own hirer. She eventually found a miller who wished "to get a girl for her board and clothes" and who was "willing to warrant her good and humane treatment." Through a proxy, Mourning then presented the option to her owner. Another slave woman, Ciller, faced a comparable situation in 1844 when her hirer began to grumble about continuing to feed Ciller's young child who did no work. Ciller, however, objected vehemently enough to induce the hirer to write to her owner that "if you will send as much corn as you think will be sufficient for her she can stay with her mother." Similarly, in 1842, California "made quite a to do" that she be able to live at Waverly, one of her owner's Mississippi plantations, because her children had been hired out within a few miles of the place and she wanted to be able to keep an eye on them. And in 1828, when Polly was hired out, she "requested for her child and nurse to go with her." Acceding to "the entreaty of this woman," the owner "hired her in that way." The actions of Mourning, Ciller, California, and Polly were examples of the kind of behavior that slave women considered fundamental to their roles as mothers and nurturers. The effect on their children was no doubt extremely powerful, for when slave mothers went to such lengths to keep their children nearby, they reminded the children that they had a value that was not calculated in dollars and cents, that white people's conception of the terms of their enslavement need not be their own. That reminder was critical to socializing children into the antislavery perspective of the slave quarters.[35]

The historical record on hiring is heartbreaking in its account of small children torn from parents so that they could make a few dollars, even a few cents, for owners. Slave parents knew that no child was exempt. Sarah Grant remembered that her mother would return from her hirer's place during Christmas week and that she would "cry when she had to go back to work" because she could never be certain that her children would still be there the next time she returned. It was while hired out at such a young age that slave children often realized for the first time the harshest implications of their enslavement. "I was taken away from my mother," Henry Bibb remembered in his narrative, "and hired out to labor for various persons, eight or ten years in succession . . . It was then my sorrows and sufferings commenced. It was then I first commenced seeing and feeling that I was a wretched slave, compelled to work under the lash without wages, and often without clothes enough to hide my nakedness." As long as there was a demand for even the smallest slaves, hiring would continue to ravage the childhood of young slaves and their parents' peace of mind. But slave parents, particularly mothers, did everything they could to bridge the distance that hiring opened up between them and their children. Those efforts did much to teach children that there was a stark difference between the beliefs of their parents and those of their owners, that slaves were unwilling participants in the world of their oppressors.[36]

A Resource for Slaves

In addition to finding ways to counteract the separations from spouses and children that hiring caused, slaves also used hiring to serve their own ends. The temporary movement of slaves from master to master was an expedient for slaves as well as for white hirers and owners. By using that resource, slaves helped to define a conception of master-slave relationships that was distinguished especially by its fluidity.

The extant family papers of Southern slaveholders abound in letters from people to whom slaves had appealed to hire them. In 1854, for example, W. W. Baldwin, a railroad superintendent, wrote to Farish Carter to inform him that Carter's slave Cyrus had come to the railroad office and made clear that he was "very anxious" to work for Baldwin, rather than continue in his current situation on the Macon and Western Railroad. Cyrus could have had any number of reasons for wanting to work on a different railroad: it may have been safer; he may have had friends already working there; or it may have been closer to family members. Whatever the reason, Cyrus was determined enough to approach the superintendent and propose that he get in touch with Carter. Excerpts from other letters suggest that similar appeals were made by other slaves: "Your man Nelson is disposed to remain with me the next year;" "Your man Aron is desirous to live with us the ensuing year;" "Your woman Hannah wishes me to hire her;" "Your boy Preston . . . wishes to be hired to me."[37]

These approaches by Cyrus, Nelson, Aron, Hannah, and Preston to prospective hirers offer important insights into the ways that hiring affected master-slave relationships. Given the existence of widespread hiring, slaves knew that the positions in which they found themselves were only temporary. The next year could find them working for virtually any other free person in the South. That thought no doubt inspired fear in some, but it also disposed slaves to view master-slave relationships as inherently fluid. The fundamental changeability of these relationships encouraged slaves to rely on themselves—as Cyrus, Nelson, Aron, Hannah, and Preston did when they sought, by acting first, to winnow the field of potential masters to those at least marginally in their favor. That same sense of self-reliance would pervade other aspects of their lives as well. It would be crucial, for example, in slaves' subsequent attempts to play owners and hirers off each other. It was also extremely important in their efforts to keep families together when separated by hiring. Given the perpetual contingency of their circumstances, slaves relied on themselves, not inconstant masters, to keep their loved ones nearby. Hiring kept slaves moving about, and that mobility meant that they rarely identified with a single master. By inhibiting individual bonds between masters and slaves, hiring made it less likely that slaves would fall into paternalist relationships that reinforced their dependence on white masters.

When slaves asked white Southerners to hire them, their motive was most often to keep families together. From the first years that hiring became a common practice in the Chesapeake, slaves tried to use the novel arrangement to their own benefit. Argy, one of Landon Carter's slaves, asked his master in 1789 that he be "hired to Mr. Richd Neale of Loudoun who has a Negro woman, his wife." And in 1792 Carter also felt "very much inclined" to satisfy Samson Robinson, a free black man who had appealed to Carter to hire his wife, Rose, and "his two Children of tender years." By the end of the antebellum period, slaves were still using hiring as a means to influence where they worked and lived, and thus to stay close to husbands, wives, and other family members. Sometimes, though, slaves went initially to hirers rather than owners, and these were potentially touchy situations. A slave's prevailing on another white person for intervention was itself an assault on an owner's honor and mastery, but, in addition, what slaves said to convince hirers to take them—anything from "my owner is moving" to "my owner will split up families"—could create public knowledge of information that owners did not necessarily wish divulged. "Adeline has applied to me to hire her," Walter Paine wrote to Adeline's owner in 1856. "She says you are going up the country," Paine explained, "and she does not like the idea much of going up there and leaving her husband." When Florilla heard that her owner, Farish Carter, was contemplating sending his slaves to be hired out in Milledgeville, Georgia, in 1850, she asked a Macon resident to hire her again because, as the man noted to Carter, "she says she wishes to be with her husband." When Mary Gilliam considered moving from Alabama to Virginia some slaves she had inherited, the slaves approached the hiring agent and asserted that, because of local family ties, they were "not disposed to return to Virginia." Some of them had already found hirers in the region willing to take them for the year. Hiring thus offered slaves a last-ditch means to keep their families together, a useful trump card in the negotiations they carried out continuously with their owners.[38]

There were other ways that slaves could use hiring to the advantage of their families. Many, for example, recommended the services of their loved ones as soon as they arrived at hirers' places. When John Faggart hired Tom as a miner in 1853, Tom immediately suggested that he hire his wife as a cook. And when Edward was hired out in 1857 and learned that his hirer also needed someone to hew wood, Edward immediately suggested his father ("'Papa would suit'"), promising he would help "when the lumber is heavy." When Julius was hired to Wilson Cary in 1822, he did not even ask Cary if he might want to hire the rest of his family; Julius simply took them along. Cary later remarked to his wife, Virginia, that he was "astonished at Julius's impudent attempt to fasten his wife and children upon us," and he ordered Virginia to have the wife and children "removed without delay." Insisting that he could not abide "supporting other people's negroes," Cary explained that, if Julius's owner wished the wife to remain, "it must be expressly understood that he provides corn &c. for her at his own expense." Israel, a slave blacksmith, also turned to hiring as a means of keeping his wife, who was owned by a man who Israel knew would never agree to sell her, as close as possible to him. Israel asked the men who owned him to approach his wife's owner, Elisha Barksdale, about hiring her out in their neighborhood. Noting that they wanted "very much to accommodate him if possible," Israel's owners notified Barksdale that they "would take pleasure in hiring her for you to some person near here who would treat her well, if you . . . will permit us to do so." Tom, Edward, Julius, and Israel all found that hiring, while an initial cause of family separations, could be used to counteract those same separations. Often, the best way to get the better of the omnipresent necessity in slave life to move around was through even more movement.[39]

The experience of Edmund and Sally, two slaves belonging to the extended family of Joseph Copes in Louisiana, exemplifies why slaves felt ambivalent about the practice of hiring. They were separated and then reunited precisely because hiring was a possibility for their owners. In 1849, Edmund was hired out to work in Baton Rouge, a move that entailed a separation from his wife, Sally, and his children. Edmund had already threatened to kill himself if he was hired out away from his wife, but apparently Copes did not take his threat seriously, for Edmund was eventually sent away. But Edmund did not give up his attempt to use what little leverage he had as a hired slave. He sat down and wrote a letter to Copes in his own hand, a letter that detailed his anguish and, in a strategic move, the way that anguish was impeding his work:

> I am not very well at present on account of being separated from my wife I cannot scarcely account for the uneasiness of my mind I could get along much better if you would be pleased to send her here to me or to let me go to her. My mind is so distracted on her acct. that I scarce can tend to my work as I ought to have done I hope you will take it into consideration and send for her without thinking hard of me in letting you know my present state of mind & situation.

Meanwhile, Sally, owned by Joseph Copes' son-in-law Gran B. Davis, was also working toward reunification by prevailing upon Davis to hire her and her children out in Baton Rouge. Her efforts were successful. Davis wrote to Copes in December 1849 to tell him that he wished "to bring my negro woman Sally, and her children, down to Baton Rouge." "I want her to be with her Husband," Davis wrote, "which you have got hired, at said place, and would like for you to remove her wherever you remove your negro man." It is unclear how Sally convinced Davis to hire her out in Baton Rouge, but it is evident that she made it clear to him that it would ultimately be in his interest. "I think it would be best for them, and all concerned in them," Davis wrote to Copes, "for them to be together."[40]

Self-hire offered the greatest opportunities for using hiring in the service of family integrity. Old Fanny, for example, agreed in 1851 to pay the fifteen dollars that her owner's agent had set as her monthly hire so that she could live with her husband. "They promise to pay the hire," the agent reported to Fanny's owner, though Fanny did send word that she thought the hire was "too much," asking her owner not to "deal so hard with her." In 1860, Lewis wrote to his mistress, Lucy Goulden, to ask her "a very important question, one that concerns me very much." Noting that he was "getting old and can't at best expect to live long," Lewis requested that his mistress allow him to "choose a home for the remainder of my life." Lewis had already spoken to the woman who owned his wife, who agreed to hire him, and he asked Goulden "to write to me at once and say on what terms you are willing for her to take me." "My reason is to be with my Wife," Lewis explained, "the balance of my days." Alfred Steele also took up a pen himself to present a plan to his mistress that would allow him to be near his wife. "I hope you will grant me the privilege of hiring my own time," Steele wrote in 1835, "and . . . will give you as much or more than anybody else." "I wish to live in Raleigh," Steele explained, "so that I can be close to my wife."[41]

For slaves, hiring could be both a blessing and a curse. That statement is, admittedly, a schematic rendering of very complex emotional reactions that slaves had toward the practice of hiring. The important point, though, is that hiring was more than an ominous possibility hanging over the lives of slaves. To be sure, hiring was for many slaves a threat to the integrity of their families, a hateful experience that tore children from their parents and spouses from each other. But for other slaves, hiring was a resource for negotiating with owners. Such was the case for Thom, whose owner agreed to hire his wife, Cate, and children in 1822 because "Thom is so importunate on the subject." Both these experiences of hiring—as a blessing and as a curse—are important to understanding the practice from the perspective of those who had the least control over it. It is incontrovertible that, as Barbara Fields has argued, "hire arrangements worked vast mischief in the personal lives of slaves," but it is equally true that hiring opened new avenues for slaves determined to keep their families intact.[42]

Slave families evinced a remarkable adaptability in overcoming the separations caused by movement from hirer to hirer. Slaves made all sorts of demands of their owners and hirers with respect to the time that should be allotted to them for visits with family members. They also made life very difficult and unprofitable for owners and hirers who ignored such demands. The assertive and ingenious ways slaves found to use hiring to their advantage partially explain the abundant evidence of strong slave family ties even amid the increasing mobility of slave life from the Revolutionary period onward. (In 1865, when freed slaves trekked along Southern roads to reunite with separated family members, they were doing, in different circumstances, what they had been doing for decades.) The triangularity of hiring arrangements crystallized when slaves' dogged resourcefulness in shaping transactions was joined by the even more powerful assertions, intentions, and desires of owners and hirers.

Slaves' convictions, desires, and emotions were all an essential component of Southern life. It is an unmistakable truth that slaves, who were deprived of personal freedom, could be acted *upon,* but it is also true that their wishes had a formidable, or at least unavoidable, force in daily life. Though overpowered, slaves were able to influence the social and economic life of the South. To put it simply, slaves had to be reckoned with.

In the process of hammering out hire transactions, owners were perpetually trying to discern the intentions of their slaves. The letters of both hirers and owners testify to the conventional wisdom that it was foolhardy to ignore the will of a slave about to be hired out. A simple statement from an owner to a hirer—something like, "I asked the girl if she was willing to go to Wilmington, and she said she was"—could reveal the decisive role of the slave in a hiring transaction. Slaves had to be negotiated with because the success of hiring arrangements for owners and hirers alike rested on whether the slaves were willing participants. But owners and hirers learned quickly that a slave's apparent willingness could often hide other, truer feelings. Alexander McDowell, for example, was surprised to hear from Peter's hirer that the slave had not arrived at the hirer's place, since Peter had "seemed satisfied as far as I could perceive." And G. S. Gillespie wrote in 1848 to the owner of the slave he had hired to inform him that the slave was missing, a surprising state of affairs for Gillespie since the slave had "appeared perfectly contented." Owners' decisions about where to hire their slaves thus had to be carefully thought out, and those decisions often hinged on a slave's willingness or unwillingness to be hired in certain places or to particular people. William Staples, for example, intended to hire his slave Isaac to William Weaver for another year in 1830, but he was forced to abrogate the contract when Isaac "expressed such an unwillingness to return." In a letter of explanation to Weaver, Staples reasoned that, should he send Isaac over his objection, "he would run away, and perhaps be of little or no service to you during the year." Staples hired Isaac instead to a place where Isaac was "willing to stay." If owners were going to view their slaves as individual units of investment, it would come at a price. Slaves found that the very value that their owners hoped to extract from them provided a source of leverage.[43]

Proslavery apologist Edward Bryan deluded himself in insisting that hiring in a slave society took place "regardless of the will of the individual hired," that slaves were always, without exception, "the material upon which others operate." Slaveholder William Drennan, for one, would have laughed nervously at the thought that slaves were no party to hiring transactions. Drennan had sent Rose to a hirer even though she "disliked to go there," and she ended up burning down the hirer's kitchen. "If she would do that," Drennan mused in his diary, thinking he might be next, "she would burn my house to spite me." He concluded with an apprehensive testimonial to slaves' powerful presence in the mental world of white Southerners: "I thought of her twice last night." Consider as well the difficulties that Iverson Twyman had with his slave Beverly, who wished to be hired out to work on a boat rather than on a railroad or canal, either of which would have paid Twyman significantly more. "All of us are of the opinion," Twyman wrote in 1849, "that Beverly *might* stay on a Boat and *will not* on public works." "But with such a rascal we are sure of nothing," he complained; "I say in short, Damn him." Twyman had similar difficulties with Gilbert: "As the negro wishes to go to Spencer, he will be less likely to run away from him, and consequently less trouble and vexation." Similarly, Rebecca Yongue's husband planned to hire out his slaves in order to make some money before striking out for the West in the 1850s, but "his plans were defeated" when one of the slaves "became so enraged at the idea of being hired out and moving next year from the place, he said if we did not sell him he would run away from us."[44]

As these ruminations on willful slaves suggest, white Southerners could not, as hard as they tried, make their slaves into perfect commodities, lacking beliefs and intentions of their own. Slaves, even from their position of limited strength, found ways to insinuate their views and wishes into the hiring contracts that kept them on the move from master to master. The inescapable presence of slaves who were determined to press their own demands fashioned the unique triangularity of hiring transactions. Neither hirers nor owners could get what they wanted from the transactions without to some extent incorporating into their own perspectives slaves' determination to shape their own destinies.

Risks and Returns

I was very successful last year in procuring good homes and good
prices for the Negroes.

R. H. Adams, hiring agent, to Mary Gilliam, 1855

ON THE docket of North Carolina's Supreme Court in 1852 was *State
v. Levi, a Slave*. At trial the year before, Levi had been convicted of
grand larceny. Levi was owned by George Williamson, but at the time of
the theft he was hired out to John F. Wagstaff. North Carolina law provided that whenever a slave was arrested for a criminal offense for which
the punishment "may affect life, member or limb," the local sheriff was to
serve the slave's master with notice of the trial, so that the owner might
"have an opportunity of defending said slave." If the slave were convicted,
state law also required that the master pay the cost of the slave's prosecution. In this case, the sheriff had apprehended a slave with two masters, so
he notified both Williamson and Wagstaff to come forward to defend Levi.

Levi's guilt does not appear to have been in dispute. Rather, the novel
question raised by the case was whether the owner or hirer should pay the
court costs of a hired slave convicted of a crime. North Carolina's attorney
general argued that the hirer should be held responsible. He pointed to
State v. Mann, the imposing North Carolina precedent holding that hirers
enjoyed all the same rights as owners when punishing slaves under their
control. If hirers had the same rights as owners over hired slaves, the attorney general's argument went, they should also have the same responsibilities, including paying for a slave's criminal defense. The trial judge apparently agreed, for he ordered Wagstaff to pay the cost of Levi's prosecution.

Wagstaff appealed to the state supreme court. The court reversed the
judgment and, in so doing, got to the heart of what separated owners and
hirers: self-interest. The court concluded that when a hired slave was accused of a crime, the owner should be served notice because the owner was
"certainly the one who has the greatest interest in the life, member or limb

of the slave who is about to be tried." By contrast, a hirer's interest in the accused slave might be "so slight" that he or she would be "unwilling to incur the trouble or expense of a defence." The ruling gave legal recognition to the fact that hirers had little compelling incentive to protect the lives and limbs of the slaves they rented. The North Carolina supreme court's conclusion in *State v. Levi* was essentially the same as that reached by owners across the South: hirers could not be trusted to safeguard the long-term health, well-being, and value of slaves they rented.[1]

A tension thus rested at the heart of every owner's decision to hire out a slave. On the one hand, hiring presented promising possibilities for the deployment of slave capital. For some owners it was a means to train slaves as carpenters, house servants, and cotton pickers. For others it was a means to punish slaves, or simply to banish them. More than anything, hiring was a resource for efficient slave management. Slaveholders were managers of capital as well as managers of slaves, and that dual role made them see in hiring an opportunity to secure returns on slaves they could not themselves put to work. But the promise of such returns was balanced by some peril because hiring, like all forms of speculation, was inherently a gamble. In particular, slaveholders transferred valuable bodies into the hands of people who had no apparent incentive to protect those bodies against debilitation, disease, or even death. More than one owner regretted, as George H. Young did in 1844, that when hiring out slaves, "truly it is difficult to have them clothed and treated as they ought to be." A slave mistreated by a hirer could become a serious financial loss for an owner because severe abuse or neglect could easily render a slave unable to work for months or even years. Prudent management of slave capital during hiring out thus meant finding the balance between short-term returns—"good prices"—and the humane treatment—"good homes"—that would guarantee that slaves were returned at the end of the year in hirable condition.[2]

Distrust pervaded owners' every interaction with hirers. A healthy skepticism, owners found, was the best way to avoid the improvident, stinting, and abusive hirers who, by failing to pay, could make needed wages disappear or who, by ruining a good slave, could instantly obliterate the profits of future hiring years. To protect their human property, owners' first step was to seek out men and women they considered humane, inquiring among neighbors and family about the character of prospective hirers. But, true to the market culture of the time, owners took the subsequent step of invoking the force of law to protect their slaves' value. They reduced each hiring transaction to a legal contract, stipulating therein the quality of food and clothing their slaves would be furnished, the nature of the work their slaves could perform, and the locations to which their slaves could be taken. Owners' distrust of hirers led them at every turn to attempt to circumscribe the mastery they temporarily transferred. Those efforts created serious potential for discord with hirers, but not enough to blind owners to the profits promised by this form of speculation. Battles over mastery might ensue, but hiring transactions generally began on an optimistic note.

The Promise of Hiring

Owners had many reasons to hire out some or all of their slaves. Most commonly, they decided to hire out slaves they considered superfluous to their own labor needs. Edmund Taylor explained to a hiring agent in 1852 that he wished to hire out one of his Richmond house servants "simply because I have no use for him at home." Taylor's predicament was played out innumerable times across the South whenever some unpredictable change in climate, shipping, industry, or European politics affected the price of the region's cash crops. Slaveholders adept at rationalizing and regulating the productivity of their farms, for example, were always subject to the whims of nature. Freak storms, sudden droughts, infestations—all could destroy a crop and bring productivity to a standstill. When such events occurred, slaveholders moved quickly to hire out their slaves to any industry or individual that had not yet suffered a setback, in hopes of cutting their own losses. In 1845, with caterpillars eating through his cotton crop, Louisiana farmer Edwin Epps had little work to keep his slaves busy, and he found them "idle half the time." Epps had heard, however, that "wages were high, and laborers in demand on the sugar plantations," so he decided to "make up a drove of slaves" and send them to the sugar-producing parishes of Louisiana to be hired out for the season. Solomon Northup, one of the slaves in that drove, remembered that "our number decreased as we advanced—nearly every sugar plantation requiring the services of one or more." To efficiency-minded slaveholders, this was an auspicious sight in the wake of a natural catastrophe: unneeded slaves being shed one after the other to those willing to pay cash for their temporary labor.[3]

As Edmund Taylor and Edwin Epps would attest, hiring out slaves was a way to cut losses—whether those losses derived from a single unneeded house servant or from an entire slave force sitting idle for lack of work. Owners reduced their expenses significantly when they hired out redundant slaves who consumed more than they produced. Robert Fogel and Stanley Engerman estimate that the cost of feeding, clothing, and housing an average adult male slave in 1850 amounted to roughly forty-eight dollars. Property taxes and doctor's visits—inevitabilities both—would have

added even more to the yearly investment in a slave. Owners hoped to recoup these costs when they hired out excess slaves. Lewis Mason, managing an estate held in trust for several orphans, hired out the estate's slave
women and children in 1860, and referred to them as "the unproductive
consumers." North Carolina slave owner George Johnson determined that
Henry, a young slave whom Johnson thought was "large enough for the
business," should be hired out to learn the craft of blacksmithing, a job
that would not only guarantee Johnson large profits in the future but
would keep Henry from eating "idle bread." Owning a slave was a major
investment, not only because of the initial cost but also because of the
significant expenses incurred from year to year. Profits on that investment
stemmed from the fruits of the slave's labor. Hiring promisingly expanded
the possibilities for keeping slaves at work all the time, even when their
owners had nothing for them to do. Idle slaves were a financial loss, so
owners relied heavily on hiring to ensure that their slaves always brought a
return on the investment.[4]

For many white Southerners, hiring became a slaveholding cure-all, a
way to use slave capital to meet the different financial exigencies they encountered at every stage of their lives. For the newlywed Robert Taylor
Scott, who may not yet have owned a farm or plantation of his own, hiring
out his slaves offered a chance to make "something considerable" as an
economic foundation for later pursuits. He bragged to his wife after hiring
day in 1861 that he was "beginning the year pretty well for a youngster."
The entrepreneurial Daniel Pinson, waiting patiently in New Orleans for
an opportune moment to head for gold-rush California in 1849, hired out
Perry to work on the city levee because "he just about pays my board by
his labor." William Shields Reid, who had settled down to a career as a
boarding-school headmaster in Virginia, hired out his slaves as a way to
supplement his yearly income. Likewise, James Chaney added to the wages
he earned as an overseer by hiring out the two slaves he owned to the
planters who engaged his services. At the end of his life, with work behind
him, H. P. Womack hired out his slaves as a way partially to fund his retire-
ment. For all these Southerners the risks and vexations that hiring often
entailed were well worth it. Hiring out their slaves brought them closer—
at least financially—to realizing their ambitions. They would have echoed
Thomas Jefferson's sentiment that hiring was "a hopeful prospect."[5]

Hiring held out a gleam of hope even for those who were looking to escape the past rather than meet the future. Indebtedness was a state few
white Southerners failed to encounter at some point, and for cash-strapped
slaveholders hiring was an expedient means of discharging debts. For situations in which loans were too large to repay through in-kind exchanges of

milk, corn, or pork, slaveholders could dispatch slaves to serve their credi-
tors until all was considered even. Slaves, their value measured by the
amount of work they could do in a week or a month or a year, became
walking and talking banknotes, transferred from place to place by owners
who needed to pay off doctors' bills, accounts at dry goods stores, loans
from neighbors, and other arrears. Exchanging slaves as commodities was
of course a regular affair in the South's slave pens, but hiring made slave
capital even more fungible. William Grose was hired out for a month to
a New Orleans gambling saloon, perhaps to make good on losses incurred during his owner's bad night at the poker table. Similarly, in 1856,
a woman hired out Frank and Angeline to Mississippi planter Joseph
Embree for three and seven months, respectively, "for the horse that Joseph Embree sold her." In 1828, Charlotte Lewis wrote Farish Carter to
ask him to take a recently purchased slave and "let him work out what I
am owing you." "He shall work until you are fully satisfied," Lewis assured Carter, admitting that this arrangement would be advantageous to
her because it would "enable me to get out of debt without having to sell
one of my negroes, which would ruin me." Refigured in endless possible
valuations according to their skills and the duration of their promised labor, slaves were goods to be bartered and trucked. Frank and Angeline's
owner, for example, had done some simple arithmetic: three months of
Frank plus seven months of Angeline equals the cost of one horse.[6]

Hiring continued to offer expanded possibilities for using slave capital
even after slave owners had died. Many provided in their wills that their
slaves should be hired out, usually to pay off the debts on their estates. In
this way, hiring often ensured a family's continuing presence in the slaveholding class. Just as slaves often worried that they would be sold following an indebted owner's death and separated from their loved ones, so too
did white heirs worry about the same set of events, except that for them
the impending threat was a fall from the slaveholding ranks. Hiring reassured anxious heirs that they could discharge debts without losing ownership of slaves. Thus, as early as 1754, James Wallace ordered his executors
to "hire out annually as many of my slaves as shall exceed one hundred
pounds per annum, which sum I desire may be applied toward the discharge of my debts." In a similar way a century later, William Bullard directed his executors in 1852 to hire out his five slaves "for the purpose of
getting money enough to pay off all my debts, defray expenses that may
occur during the winding up of my estate, and make up for the payment of
the money directed to be paid to any of the legatees." For slave owners
who took the role of patriarch to heart, hiring allowed them to continue,
even in death, to provide for the dependents in their households. Joseph

Dickson stipulated in his 1804 will that Virgil should be hired out for ten years because the money could be used to educate and clothe Dickson's three sons. Likewise, Sion Smith's will required that his children "should be kept together, and schooled upon the hire of the negroes, til they come of age to demand them." Occasionally, white Southerners freed slaves through their wills, and they used hiring to offset losses incurred by their radical plans. In his 1835 will, John L. Poindexter ordered that his slaves be freed upon his wife's death and that "they be hired out until a sufficient sum is raised to defray their expenses to a land where they can enjoy their freedom." Similarly, Hugh Kelso's 1843 will directed that his nineteen slaves be emancipated once they reached the age of forty, and that the returns on their hire be used to pay for transporting them to Africa.[7]

Hiring allowed slaveholders to shape not only their legacies, but their slaves—to mold them into the house servants, cotton pickers, and expert blacksmiths they could see in their mind's eye. In 1839, Brisco Baldwin hired out his slave to William Shumate because he believed that the slave "would be considerably improved" by Shumate's "instruction." An especially sanguine owner could embrace the hope, as Baldwin did, that the slave who was sent away to a hirer would return somehow "improved." Owners hired out slaves, even the youngest they owned, to learn all manner of crafts and skills, from housework to carpentry. Henry Watson hired out eleven slaves to W. L. Lyon in 1842, describing the slaves as "new hands unused to cotton picking," with the stipulation that Lyon "have an account kept of the quantity of seed cotton they respectively pick daily." Edward Ware wanted his slave to be hired out in 1859, perhaps to an upholsterer or a hotel, because he had a "preference for him to learn painting or paper hanging." Selina Powell wanted to hire out Margaret again in 1849 because, though somewhat "improved" after a year hired out as a household servant, Margaret was "still too slow for me to be willing to take her back yet." "I am in hopes another year will be a great improvement to her," Powell explained in a letter to her daughter. Similarly, in 1806, Henry, a slave who (according to his owner, a biased witness) had been "brought up tenderly and never been used to hard work," was hired to a canal because his owner simply "wished him to be taught how to work." Many owners used hiring to bring their vision of what slaves should be—from the skills they should possess to the diligence they should display—ever closer to reality. This was the enduring promise of a hiring transaction, that at year's end an owner could retrieve the upholsterer, blacksmith, cotton hand, or house servant always hoped for—a reverie invariably interrupted by either a resistant slave or a contemptible hirer.[8]

Hiring held a different kind of promise for owners who took a darker view of their slaves. It was a convenient means for exiling irksome slaves whom owners were reluctant, unable, or not yet prepared to sell. George Washington was so exasperated by his slave Tom that he finally concluded that the plantation was simply not big enough for the two of them. He hired Tom out to put an end to what had become inevitable, daily clashes between master and slave. Mistresses, too, had reason on occasion to want certain slaves banished. In the close physical and psychological quarters of Southern households it was not uncommon for mistresses and slaves to have personality clashes, and these clashes were exacerbated when it appeared that a female slave was becoming sexually attractive to a husband, a son, a brother, or a suitor. Henrietta King, a former slave, remembered that she lived in the same household as a slave named Mary, and that Mary was prettier than their mistress, Josephine. One day Josephine's "feller" came to the house and treated the light-skinned Mary decorously, thinking she was "some white gal." The sight enraged Josephine, who insisted that Mary be taken immediately to Richmond and hired out. Abolitionist Levi Coffin described a similar situation that had been recounted to him by a slave named Rose, a woman "so nearly white that a stranger would never suspect that there was a drop of African blood in her veins." A "favorite house servant" of a Kentucky family, Rose was "seduced" by her master. When a child was conceived, Rose was hired out in distant Louisville, banished "on account of the disturbance . . . created in the family." For many owners, hiring allowed them to achieve some soothing distance from vexing slaves.[9]

Hiring out was also a way for owners to distance themselves from slaves they considered not just vexatious but unbearably insolent. In 1840, William Spotswood Fontaine sent Aggy to a hiring agent in Richmond with a note insisting that the slave had "disappointed me by bad conduct." The conduct was nothing "criminal," Fontaine took pains to note, but rather "a continual disregard to my orders." For such insubordination he wished Aggy hired out for three to four months, even if only for her victuals and clothes. In addition to being exiled for their recalcitrance, slaves were also hired out for violating, in their owners' eyes, the peace of their households. Virginia resident Socrates Maupin was "so much incensed" when his slave Marshall "got into a fight with the wet nurse" that he had Marshall hired away "at once." Theft also ranked high among the reasons for hiring out disobedient slaves. In 1852, Iverson Twyman advised Thomas Austin to hire out Henry, who had been "pretty deep into your corn for the support of his friends in the neighborhood." Twyman assured Austin that hiring out Henry "on the railroad"—which could bring twelve dollars per month—would be a "better business" than allowing Henry to continue his depredations. Twyman admitted that Austin might "not make *quite* so much corn without him as . . . with him," but this loss could be offset by "the sum of his hire, finding, &c." Also, Twyman reminded Austin, under Henry's tutelage, other slaves might get "in the habit of stealing from you and thus your losses will be double what they are now." For each of these owners, hiring out was a better strategy for dealing with recalcitrant slaves than was sale, at least for the time being. Hiring allowed owners to wait out sluggish sales markets. Still on the subject of the thieving Henry, Iverson Twyman advised that "the scoundrel ought to be sold, but he will bring in *little* in the way of sale and *much* in the way of hire." Similarly, William Fontaine informed the hiring agent to whom he had sent Aggy that he would hire her out only for a few months, noting that "if negroes rise I will sell her."[10]

Sometimes owners hired out refractory slaves whom they wished not only banished but punished. In these cases, they cared little about how much money they made, intent solely on putting unmanageable slaves into the harshest and most punishing situations possible. Thomas Auld, in a famous example, hired out Frederick Douglass to the notorious Edward Covey to have Douglass "broken" of his impudent habits. Similarly, in the 1840s, Jesse Deloach hired his slave Isaac to R. R. Turner "to break him from running away." No money changed hands in this transaction because Deloach conceded that Isaac "was so habituated to living in the woods, that his hire was not of much value." Elijah Fletcher, a Virginia planter, boasted that he had so many slaves that he could afford to hire out some to work on canals "without interrupting the usual course of plantation work." He added that he liked to "make it a sort of punishment too to those who do not please me at home." Charles Montague urged his aunt in 1845 to hire out Phil to the Richmond coal pits—work so dangerous that many owners refused to hire out their slaves to do it—because "his conduct for the whole time you have owned him, in my opinion, most richly deserves such a punishment." James L. Smith recalled in his narrative that when his owner suspected that he was making money for himself as a shoemaker, the owner hired him out "to a man considered by everyone to be the very worst one in Heathville, . . . advising him 'to keep me very strict, for I was knowing most too much.'" White Southerner Edward J. Thomas remembered that when a group of runaway slaves returned to his father's plantation, his father told them that he could only "wish them in hell." What the slaves got was indeed bitterly infernal: they were hired out the next day to a railroad contractor "for the balance of the winter." Rather than cash, the promising return these owners hoped to secure through hiring was duly chastised slaves—slaves who, they hoped, no longer talked back or ran away.[11]

Though owners had any number of reasons for hiring out their slaves—

from learning skilled crafts to being ruthlessly punished—the predominant motivation was to increase returns on their slave capital. Hiring could indeed be very profitable, and its profits encouraged owners to think of their slaves as individual units of investment. In 1826, Hannibal Harris, whose farm was stubbornly resistant to growing any crops of real value, weighed the two options open to him—continuing to work the land or hiring out his slaves to others—and settled quickly on the latter. "By renting [the land] and hiring out," Harris concluded to a friend, "I find I can make more than six percent on my capital." No more "inducement" was needed, once he realized that he could make more money by hiring out his slaves than he could by working his land "as I have done." Similarly, Henry Mandeville, a resident of Adams County, Mississippi, kept careful records of the slaves he purchased, the attendant costs, and then the subsequent rates at which he hired them out. In October 1850, for example, Mandeville purchased Alfred and Rachel for nine hundred and seven hundred dollars, respectively. He noted in his account book additional expenditures for life insurance, notary's fees, and clothing for the slaves, all of which added another forty dollars to the cost of each slave in the first three months that he owned them. Beginning in March and April of the following year, he hired the two slaves out—Alfred to a steamboat for twenty dollars per month, Rachel to Allen Tucker for ten dollars per month. At these rates, Mandeville earned a 26 percent annual return on his investment in Alfred and a 16 percent return on Rachel. By way of comparison, James Henry Hammond estimated a 9.5 percent return on the capital investment he made in his South Carolina plantation during the first year he managed it. Hiring out slaves made good economic sense, by providing returns that could rival those on other business ventures in the South.[12]

With the potential for profit so high, owners kept closely attuned to vagaries in hire and sale markets alike. Careful attention to market conditions was critical to success in maximizing returns on slave capital, so owners kept studiously abreast of variables that might elevate or depress the wages for hired slaves in particular regions. The arrival of the railroad in a region, for example, was a sure sign to owners that hiring rates would increase there, for contractors would rent neighborhood slaves to fell trees, blast rock, and lay down track. In contrast, a reliable sign that the hiring market in a region would soon fall into a lull was the failure of a corn crop—hire rates went down as the cost of feeding hired slaves went up. To facilitate their detection of such market trends, slaveholders frequently corresponded with each other on the state of hiring markets in different counties or states. "What are boys hiring at in S[outh] C[arolina] this year?" began a typical query in 1853. In exchange for the information he solicited, the author proffered an account of conditions in his own locality: "We pay $150 dollars by the year or $20 per month and can't get enough at that. Wages [will] be high here for some time to come. It is a cotton region and there is lots of R.R. building."[13] This economic reconnaissance was vital to the endless pursuit of high returns on slave capital, just as vital as the weekly bulletins that slaveholders scrutinized for "prices current" in cotton, tobacco, rice, sugar, and other commodities. "As a man sometimes alters his plans," John Austin wrote to Iverson Twyman in 1851 from Buckingham, Virginia, "I will tell you something about prices over here, that you may not act in the dark." His counsel was clear: "Negroes will hire very high over here this year." Conversely, Charles Montague advised his aunt in 1845 that her county was "the very worst market that could be imagined" for hiring out her slave Phil. All of this attention to market variations—the necessity of acting, that is, as a manager of capital as well as a manager of workers—tired the Virginian Robert Taylor Scott, who found slave hiring "a troublesome and tedious business." He admitted, though, that the travails were worthwhile, for hiring did "pay well." In fact, it often paid better than selling slaves. A Richmond firm that specialized in hiring and selling slaves advised Robert Carter in 1846, for example, that his slave "would doubtless hire for more in proportion to his value than could be obtained for him were he offered for sale." Under similar circumstances, John Taylor, Jr., asked his Richmond hiring agent to hire his slaves out again in 1842, because slaves were, at the time, "too low" to justify putting his up for sale. By encouraging owners to move their slaves about as commercial pawns in the South's local labor markets, and by keeping owners constantly aware of the capacity of their slave property to produce valuable capital returns, hiring discouraged master-slave relations predicated on a sense of mutual obligations, duties, and rights. Hiring kept the pursuit of profit the focal point of master-slave relationships.[14]

When slaves hired at high prices, slaveholders often tried to make do with as few as possible on their own farms, so that they could earn some extra money by hiring out. Making money was a powerful incentive in the South, and for those with slaves to spare, vibrant hire markets were an auspicious place to indulge that passion. "Negroes . . . continue to hire very well, notwithstanding their low prices," Wilson Cary wrote to his wife in 1823, "and I think . . . we might be able to spare a good number for hire from the plantation, without materially reducing the chance of the crops." Given the temptation to earn extra money when prices were high, vigorous hire markets had an almost gravitational pull, drawing in those slaves cast off by enterprising slaveholders who were determined to winnow their forces to the utmost, for the sake of extra cash. "Negroes are hiring very high this year," Virginian Patrick Catlett wrote in 1847, "and for that reason I wish to make out with as few as I can conveniently." Like coming into a large inheritance, elevated hire prices set white Southerners to imagining the alluring changes that such money might effect in their lives. Rebecca Yongue explained to a friend in 1858 that her husband had decided to hire out his slave men, keeping only "the two women and children at home," because he had thought that by doing so, "he could settle up his business early in the fall and move west where we might stand a chance of making something for our children." Hire markets, especially when thriving, underwrote white Southerners' dreams of financial success.[15]

The most lucrative way to hire out slaves in the South was to send them to public works projects. The construction of turnpikes, canals, and railroads required huge amounts of labor, and in the South the heightened demand sent the prices of hired slaves soaring. "Public work and the iron mines . . . have raised the hire of negroes more than twenty percent in this country this year," wrote Jonathan McCalley in 1849. Iverson Twyman was sure that the hiring market in his region of Virginia would be strong in 1852 because "the Virginia and Tennessee Railroad is still going on, the Danville Road is in progress, the Canal will probably go on further, and it will be a better year for the Boatery than the present has been." Though internal improvements could be grounds for political debate in the South, slaveholders who hired out their slaves found them to be a financial boon. Of course, public works were notoriously dangerous. Slaves working on canals and railroads performed such risky tasks as felling trees or blasting rock so that the land could be appropriately graded for future travel. In addition, slaves were able to use to their advantage the very mobility afforded by the internal improvements they were constructing. Escapes to free states were a common occurrence, especially among those slaves hired out to work on the waterways of the South. In 1835, a free black woman in New Orleans hired out her slave Eliza to the aptly named steamboat *Freedom,* and she later sued the boat's owners after Eliza escaped in Cincinnati. Robert Beverley, who sued when his slave escaped from the steamboat *Empire,* again in Cincinnati, probably learned nothing new when one of the witnesses in his case testified that there was a "great risk" in hiring slaves to steamboats because "it is a matter of almost absolute impossibility to prevent them from being run off." That was the danger in placing slaves on the steamboats heading north out of New Orleans. But the boats that skirted close to free territory also paid a dollar or more per day for hired slaves—about three times the rate owners could otherwise secure by renting their slaves out to artisans, farmers, and other more conventional hirers. For many owners, such a payoff was worth the risk.[16]

Though white men monopolized the public traffic in slaves, white women were not mere bystanders, especially in markets for hired slaves. They, too, recognized the promising possibilities presented by hiring. Slave hiring was a crucial source of income for single white women and for widows, and they often carried out the business for themselves. In many families as well, particularly those in which husbands were frequently away, wives hired out the household's slaves. White women were thus prominent participants in the communities of owners and hirers across the South. Their names show up with regularity on extant hiring contracts, and there is still more evidence that female owners followed prices in regional hiring markets, drove hard bargains, confronted hirers, and sued for damages with a vigor and deftness equal to that of their male counterparts. By contrast to sale markets, where slave pens were virtually off-limits to white women, hiring markets were more accommodating of female participation, because these markets could, in a sense, come to women. White women could conduct hiring on their own if they desired, either in the confines of their own homes or through correspondence.

Whether widowed or single, white women who lived alone relied heavily on income earned by renting out their slaves. Often, the annuities produced by slave hiring were the only source of financial support these women could claim. "Christmas is an important time to Frances and Grace," Virginia slave owner Iverson Twyman wrote in 1851, "as all their little income arises from the hire of their negroes." "This is their *crop*," he explained, employing a metaphor any Southerner would understand, "and if they pitch it badly they reap a sorry harvest." Just as a crop could be botched by poor management, so too could one hire "badly." Women like Frances and Grace could ill afford to miss out on maximum hire rates or to send slaves to untrustworthy hirers. L. M. Walton, for example, informed a friend in 1837 that she could keep her slave Ben working at home for only a few months. "I cannot do without his hire," she explained, "as my income this year is two or three hundred less than it has been." Ann Smith lived alone in North Carolina, where she used her slaves to raise a small cotton crop, but in 1829 her daughter warned her that her "crop this year will be a mere pittance." Since the slaves would have "no ginning to employ them," Smith's daughter urged her to hire out her slave men in Charleston for a few months so that "something may be got in this way to assist you." Women who owned a sufficient number of slaves—ideally adult male slaves—could earn enough hiring income to support themselves well. One Virginia resident noted in 1847 that just three-fifths of the hire of the slaves belonging to "Mrs. S." would be enough to educate her son and "maintain" her "like a Lady." James Redpath, an antislavery newspaper editor on a tour of the South, found no lack of people living comfortably off the hire of their slaves. "I once got myself into hot water," he quipped, "by calling a lady who lived on the hire-money of her slaves, a kept woman—kept by negroes!"[17]

Married white women hired out household slaves when their husbands were unable to do so. When they did, they could get as caught up as men in the thrill of slave speculation. Lucy Battle, whose husband spent a good deal of time riding around his North Carolina judicial circuit, carried out the hiring of the family slaves from her home in Chapel Hill. She held negotiations with men who came to her home, and she haggled over prices, a subject on which she made it a point to stay well versed. "I have had three applications for Peter," Battle wrote her husband in 1852, noting that everyone who came by seemed to think that her thirty-dollar asking price was "too much for him." But Battle stuck to her guns, for she had been attentive enough to the hiring market to "hear that fellows go at about $50 this year," and for even more if they were hired out to railroads. She drove a hard bargain, perhaps even harder than her husband would have. In 1854, for example, she sent Hal off to a hirer for his victuals and clothes, even though she was sure that "we ought to have demanded something more." Battle understood that hiring transactions could be prickly affairs, and she knew how to avoid future disputes with hirers who believed that a slave's abilities or character had been misrepresented. When she hired Maria to Mr. Wolff in 1854, for example, she "neither praised nor dispraised her"—later joking with her husband that "he therefore took *her*, as you did *me*, for better, for worse." Lucy Battle was adept at the hiring business, and she relished her success at hiring out her slaves for the highest prices and at the least expense. "So you see, old man," she bragged to her husband at the culmination of one year's hiring efforts, "that they are all disposed even without an advertisement."[18]

Margaret Brooke, a resident of Staunton, Virginia, also hired out slaves while her husband was away from home. Like Lucy Battle, she thoroughly understood the laws of supply and demand and refused to be taken advantage of. She demanded high prices for the slaves she hired out and waited until she got them. "I hold Joe at 120 dollars and expect to get it," she explained to her husband in 1842. Joe worked at the local hospital, and Brooke knew that "they can't do without him." She was determined to make the hospital "*pay* for him." Other slaves belonging to the Brookes—including John, Beverly, May, Ann, and Charlotte—were slated to be hired out in 1842 as well, but Brooke insisted that she "never had as little anxiety about hiring servants" as she did in that year. In fact, she boasted that she "never did better." The patriarchy of Southern households was not under threat when women like Margaret Brooke and Lucy Battle assumed the delegated powers of a household head during their husbands' absences. Nevertheless, their activities brought them increasingly into the market life of the South, and these women found that experience deeply affecting, even intoxicating. Standing out in the letters of both Brooke and Battle is the relish these women took in stewarding their families' slave capital through the hire market. They were good at it, and they knew it.[19]

Not surprisingly, some women did feel that their sex placed them at a disadvantage when dealing with hirers. Elizabeth Chowning hired her slave Thom to Edgar Montague in the middle of the Civil War, but when Montague tried to shave money off the agreed hire price by deducting money he lost while Thom was sick, Chowning responded with a letter expressing her dissent, noting that, as a woman, she was "liable to be imposed upon." Octavia Bullitt hired out slaves for Richard Smith while he was away from home, and she had trouble with one hirer who thought she had overstated the price for a slave named Ben. Bullitt wrote to Smith that it seemed to her that the hirer "expected to get him for nothing." Imploring Smith not to let the hirer "have him for one cent less," Bullitt recounted that the hirer had "remarked that he knew *you* would not ask him that price." Octavia Bullitt did not shrink from her antagonistic encounter with the hirer, and other white women were equally resolute when managing their slave property in hiring markets. Sarah Brockenbrough hired out her slaves through an agent in 1841, but she learned in early 1842 that the hirer did not have enough money to pay all the owners from whom he had rented slaves. A compromise was reached by which each owner would receive a portion of the money proffered by the hirer, but Brockenbrough, thinking she was being taken advantage of, demanded all the money due her under contract. She fired off a letter to her Richmond hiring agent in April 1842. "I must say," she asserted, "that I am not willing to lose any part of mine, as my hands were always allowed to be better hands than the others." "Arrange matters in such a manner," she concluded, "that I may get all instead of a part of what is due me." White women had a more difficult time in the male-dominated public world of the South, but when their livelihood was at stake, they were as adamant in protecting their property rights as other slave owners.[20]

The men and women who hired out slaves in the South were, for the most part, trying to make money. This deceptively simple motive had important implications for how owners viewed their slaves. As we have seen, slaves were a source of income on which owners based not only their economic security but also headier dreams of financial success. Frances Austin aimed to use the 1849 hire of her slave Beverly to pay "a *little* account at Mr. Brown's store." But Henry Alderson Ellison probably had more grandiose plans for the $15,500 that made up his combined earnings on hired slaves in 1858 and 1859. To understand how the effort to maximize returns on slave investments influenced relations between owners and slaves, we need only look at how owners discussed those slaves who for some reason were not hirable. In a tone of evident disgust, Frederick Kimball informed his niece and nephew in 1806 that his slave Harriet had "another child." As a consequence, "she is gaining nothing here," he complained, "for she is hardly ever employed and when I have had a chance to hire her out I am obliged to take anything I can get for pay." Lewis Mason, as administrator of an estate in 1860, hired out every slave child over the age of seven as a "nurse for negro children"; all those under seven he tersely recorded as "expensive." Similarly, in the 1860 inventory of hired slaves belonging to Dabney Carr's estate, the slave Alfred was listed as "diseased and worthless—dead expense." Worth, value, profit, and expense—these were the criteria by which slaveholders judged their slaves. As a result, slaves and owners approached each other on ground thoroughly shaped by the market, in particular by the potential returns for owners in the hiring market. Owners found that the necessary first step in making a profit through hiring was to be diligent about searching out hirers who were reputable, judicious, and solvent.[21]

In Good Hands for Good Wages

In 1852, George Cummings hired out his slave Warren to Robert Bell, who kept a livery stable in Nashville. Sometime midyear, Bell decided he no longer needed Warren's labor, and he subhired Warren to a third person, to drive a dray along the city's wharf. Cummings protested that he had no wish for Warren to be exposed to the dangers of the crowded wharf after he had specifically chosen to place his slave at the livery stable, a comparatively safe business. His protests unheeded, Cummings eventually sued, contending that the courts should outlaw the subhiring of slaves. As this was "a question so closely connected with the every day transactions of men in slave States," the case soon reached the Tennessee supreme court. In the decision handed down there, Judge Caruthers held that subhiring should be prohibited, primarily because owners protected their property by making careful initial choices regarding where, and with whom, to place their slaves. "When the master's interest requires him to commit, for a season, the use and control of his slave to another for hire," Judge Caruthers noted, the owner's "prudence" dictated that he "not subject his slave to the hazards of dangerous employment, nor to the power of an unfeeling temporary owner." Assuming the perspective of such an owner,

Judge Caruthers explained that if hirers were permitted to subhire, then "there is no advantage in the right of choosing who shall be trusted with my slave; my right and duty to save him from the control of a cruel and unfeeling man, a hard master, is unavailing; my right of selection is nugatory; . . . the very man I would avoid may get him the next day." As did so many legal rules governing slave hiring, the rule against subhiring rested on a commonplace distrust of hirers. Whereas it could "well be presumed" that owners would manage their slaves in ways that guaranteed their safety and well-being, Judge Caruthers concluded, "it is the interest of the hirer to get all the labor he can out of the hired slave, without regard to his comfort, or the effect upon his permanent health and value." The rule against subhiring was designed to counter "the influence of this selfish feeling" on the part of hirers, and thus to ensure "the protection of the owner and his property."[22]

The law thus recognized that owners' first step in safeguarding their slaves must be carefully to locate "good hands" into which to place them. Selecting hirers was a delicate business, driven by two basic, and sometimes competing, aims: to make as much money as possible and to ensure that slaves were well treated while hired out. Owners were always thinking at least a year ahead. They knew it would be difficult to get good prices later for slaves who had been run down through overwork and undernourishment by previous hirers. Indeed owners often worried less about the work to which their slaves would be put than about the men and women who would actually be putting them to work. One Tennessee judge put it simply: "An owner of a slave might be very willing to hire his servant to A. to drive his wagon, and at the same time would by no means agree, that he should be employed under B. to drive his wagon."[23]

Separating A. from B. was the first step for any owner about to hire out slaves, and the effort began with inquiries to determine the "character" of potential hirers. White Southerners subscribed to the notion that masters made their men. Thus, when James Knapp approached Mrs. L. M. Young in 1861 about hiring her slave Cupid, the first thing Young did was write to a friend to inquire, "Do you know what kind of a master he is?" Good slave masters were those whose strictness did not verge on abusiveness, and whose humanity did not verge on indulgence. Iverson Twyman received assurances from a friend in 1861 that a potential hirer was "a man of excellent character" and that Twyman need not "have the least fear trusting your hands to him." The friend assured Twyman that the hirer would "not abuse them in any way but [would] make them behave themselves and attend to their duty." Owners like Twyman firmly believed that bad masters made bad slaves, that a hirer's bad character could rub off on his slaves. As one resolute owner wrote of a hirer in 1841: "I am astonished at Mr. Sharp. It seems to me that any man of common perception would have known from my conduct that I had no idea whatever of hiring him the negro. I would not under any consideration be willing that the negro should remain another year with him . . . I have no doubt, it would be a serious injury to him, owing to the habits of laziness and drunkenness which he would certainly contract." Skilled managers of slave capital kept their slaves out of such hands. As one slave owner warned from the pages of *DeBow's Review,* slaves, "like any other property," could lose value through "unskillful usage." By inquiring into the character of hirers, owners hoped to preempt this "great pecuniary evil."[24]

Hiring day presented special difficulties for owners trying to determine the character of potential hirers. The owners' inspections often rested on no more than quick scrutiny of a hirer's appearance. In large cities like Richmond, Charleston, and New Orleans, hiring day brought a jumble of strangers from inside and outside the city, but even at smaller countryside auctions potential hirers unknown in the community would arrive looking for slaves. For wary owners, these unfamiliar, and sometimes shady, characters caused some anxiety. At a hiring day in Bertie County, North Carolina, in 1824, Robert Jones began to worry when "a bystander of very indifferent appearance" entered the bidding for Patty and her six children. The unknown bystander put in the lead bid, and Jones was faced with a dilemma. On the one hand, "judging from his appearance," Jones determined that the man "would be a very unsafe hand to trust such a family of Negroes with." On the other hand, he felt "some delicacy to refuse his bid" because he "did not know him." Jones, like so many other owners, had to engage in a careful calculus on the bidding ground, trying to make a profit while ensuring good treatment for his slaves. He also had to avoid stepping on the toes or impugning the character of a potentially touchy white man. The "delicacy" of the hiring ground prefigured the precarious conflicts that could subsequently arise between hirers and owners.[25]

In contrast to Robert Jones, Martha Battle made no pretense of propriety at a North Carolina hiring day in January 1846, when her female slave eventually went to the highest bidder, Dickerson Ricks. After the auction, Ricks met Battle nearby and tried to give her his signed note for the hire of the slave, but Battle refused to take it and refused to hand over the woman to him. Ricks and Battle continued their standoff in county and state courts over the next year. In the North Carolina Supreme Court, Battle eventually explained that, even before the hiring had taken place, she had said to Ricks that "he should never have any negroes, over which she had any control." She justified her actions by noting to the court "that he was a

cruel man, that she was afraid he would kill them and that he was poor
and unable to feed them." Battle insisted that Ricks "had the character of a
cruel man to negroes, and that he was unfit to have any control over
them." In effect, Battle had based her refusal to hire to Ricks solely on the
grounds of his character.[26]

As Martha Battle's behavior toward the impoverished Dickerson Ricks
attests, concern about the character of hirers could easily merge into class
snobbery. George Young, who hired out James McDowell's Mississippi
slaves while McDowell was governor of Virginia in the 1840s, had a raft
of grievances with impoverished hirers. "The class who hire negroes,"
Young explained to McDowell in 1844, "are pretty much the same in all
communities: persons generally who are hard run and poor besides." Indeed, earlier that same year, Young had written to McDowell to lament the
fact that he was not able to hire the slaves "into any hands save broken
down overseers, who were renting any place they could live on." Young
worried that such men were, by virtue of their class condition, unfit to be
proper slave masters. Their unfitness was exacerbated, he knew, by the dis-
dainful views that many slaves held of poor whites. Of the slave Moses, for
example, Young wrote that, though "the best negro in the world," he was
"rather too heroic and impulsive to be governed by the *small fry* who generally hire." For these reasons, Young was convinced that poor whites
lacked the requisite character to be trusted as good slave masters.[27]

Distrust of poor hirers grew as much out of a fear of nonpayment as out
of a fear of improper treatment of slaves. George Young got to the heart of
the issue for most owners when he declared in 1843 that "those persons
who are to be found hiring are generally speaking both bad paymasters
and bad slave masters." Owners avoided whenever possible the tribula-
tions inevitably generated from dealings with impecunious or improvident hirers. Thomas Clement Read refused to let a particular hirer have
his slave Ephraim for another year in 1847 because "it is impossible to
get money from him unless you sue him every time." Similarly, Iverson
Twyman advised a relative against hiring out to a certain neighbor because
he made "a rather sorry paymaster." Owners often had other financial
pursuits hedged against anticipated hire income, so their difficulties were
compounded when hirers were not forthcoming with payments. "I find . . .
I shall not be able to collect a single dollar of the hires now due," William
Terrill lamented in 1839, "a circumstance truly provoking as I have several
engagements predicated on the prospect of collections here, which must
consequently be materially affected by the failure." "Money *I must have,*"
John Grasty growled to his brother in 1860; "will you just let me know at
once," he pleaded, "how far I can depend upon hires in Danville." Grasty

so disliked dealing with dilatory hirers that he decided in the future to "hire to *prompt* men even at prices not so large."[28]

Requiring "security"—a cosigner on the hiring contract responsible in case of a hirer's default—was a frequent tactic of owners to ensure prompt payment. But it was also a surefire way to raise a hirer's hackles. Demanding security could be an affront to hirers whose republican sentiments led them to believe that a signed and sealed contract was sufficient guarantee of payment between people of honor. In 1815, William Brent agreed to hire three slaves to David Rees and to wait until the end of the year for payment. But Brent required "security for the payment," a condition for which he asked Rees to excuse him: "were it not for the *uncertainty of life*, I would not ask it, as be assured, sir, I have as much confidence in you as in any man living, but it is a method which I have determined to pursue and which I know you will not refuse." As hiring became more prevalent over the antebellum period, and as more transactions were carried out between strangers, requiring security became increasingly common, and by the 1850s it was virtually compulsory. Affronts to honor were ultimately less troublesome than unpaid hiring contracts. None too careful, the administrators of Thomas Bennett's estate in 1852 required that hirers present notes "with two approved securities." Such demands for security are good evidence that slave hiring was not part of a "social economy" in which rich planters provided various services—from cotton ginning to hired slaves—in return for the political support and respect of their less wealthy neighbors. Although there may have been a sense of social reciprocity, slave owners wanted their money—on time and in full—and they took all means to ensure that they received it.[29]

Most commonly, owners worried that their slaves would be treated too harshly while hired out, but many were as alert to lax supervision as they were to brutal treatment. These owners wanted to ensure that their slaves would not be "indulged" while on hire. They feared that any such license would be exploited by their slaves in ways that could ultimately prove detrimental to their "morals," their lives, or both. One estate administrator, fully aware that the slaves he was hiring out had a penchant for racing each other on horses, conditioned the slaves' rental on the hirer's promise that he would prohibit them at all times "from riding horse races." Other owners went further, demanding that hirers be vigilant and rigorous disciplinarians, not simply that they avoid leniency. Lewis Hill, a hiring agent in Richmond, often received admonitions from owners that he should search out hirers who would not be too permissive. Andrew Leslie sent his slave Letitia, whom he described as "smart and active, but obstinate," to Richmond in 1843 with instructions for Hill to obtain for the slave "a *strict* but *humane* master." James Govan sent Dave, who allegedly had been "much indulged" by his former mistress, to Hill with a note asking him to "endeavor to get him a situation where he will be properly attended to." Edmund Taylor sent his slave William Giles, noting that he wished Giles to be hired out to someone Giles was unacquainted with, and "the *stricter* the manager the *better.*" With such instructions, owners pursued the same end they did when they admonished Hill and other hiring agents to keep their slaves out of the hands of overly harsh hirers. Owners wanted their slaves returned to them in the same condition in which they had been furnished, and in the eyes of many owners, lax governance was as much a threat to slaves' future value as were the scars left by brutal whippings.[30]

Owners were especially apprehensive about the effect that cities and towns might have on their slaves' "morals." Owners were always worried that "good" slaves might somehow be compromised—in either body or mind—while under the control of other people, but they reserved heightened suspicion for urban hirers, for many slaveholders considered the South's cities to be unquestionable sources of degeneracy. When owners conjured up images of Southern cities, they pictured shady worlds of grog shops and, worse, free black people. They feared that such an environment would leave their slaves' "morals"—which included, in the ideal, faithfulness and tractability—irremediably impaired. In 1821, North Carolina slaveholder Isaac T. Avery was disquieted by the fact that one of the slaves he had hired out was "still in Morganton where his morals I suspect are not improving much." In 1809, Elkanah Talley urged the hirer of his slave Nead to give the slave "a pretty severe correction every time he is caught in town of a Sunday evening." "There is too many negroes resorting [in] that place of a Sunday," Talley wrote, "and I think there ought a stop be put to such conduct." No doubt for the same reason, the slaves belonging to Francis Harper's orphan children were forbidden to "go to Brunswick" when they were hired out in 1848. Trying to convince his aunt to hire out her slave Antony in Richmond, Charles Montague insisted in 1845 that the city's vigilant police force would ensure "less danger of vicious practices than in a country place" and thus give Antony the "least opportunity for learning vice," but his aunt was still "afraid his morals will be corrupted there." Despite Montague's defense of Richmond's supervision of its slave population, most owners in fact worried that their slaves would be exposed in cities to people and experiences that would ultimately make them less valuable.[31]

Southern courts agreed that a slave's morals were as much an owner's property as were the slave's body, health, and labor. Owners were justified in safeguarding that property against the actions of negligent hirers—that is, the law sanctioned owners' efforts to prevent hirers from turning their slaves into liars, cheats, or thieves. In November 1841, for example, an Alabama slave owner who is identified in court records only by his last name—Willis—enlisted the help of several friends to take back, in advance of the contracted return date, a slave he had hired out to a Mr. Brantley. In court, Willis would justify recovering the slave by insisting that "Brantley was employing him to steal property." Willis had been outraged when he had learned that the hirer ran a grog shop "about which negroes resorted" and where "an unlawful traffic with slaves was carried on." He pointedly described Brantley's behavior as a threat to his own property rights. Willis's lawyer argued to the judges that "employing the negro to steal, was not only impairing his morals, and thereby his value to his owner, but was also putting his life in danger." The Alabama high court agreed. According to Judge Ormond's decision: "When a slave is hired, it must be implied that he is to be employed in some honest pursuit, and if the hirer should incite him to steal, or compel him to become the receiver of stolen goods, it cannot be doubted that the owner would be authorized to rescind the contract of hiring . . . It would be difficult, if not impossible, to admeasure by damages, the amount of injury inflicted on the owner, by debauching the morals of his slave." Everyone involved in the case considered the benchmark of injury to be the value of the slave. Through disputes such as this one, owners reinforced their conception of slaves as investments. The law that governed hiring transactions impelled them to transform even their slaves' "morals" into a property interest that could be protected in court. Hirers were liable when they "debauched" slaves, because they thereby imperiled those slaves' potential to create wealth for their owners in the future.[32]

In their worries about hirers, owners provide insight into their perspective on master-slave relationships, revealing their relations with slaves to have been mediated by profit, property, and the market. Their prime concern was to safeguard present and future profits earned by the slaves they hired out. As Mississippi slaveholder Frank Hawkins maintained in 1849, "They will work a negro in this county just as hard whether they give $50 or $150." From this observation, he concluded that "the main thing is to get them where they will not be abused and to men punctual to pay." To a brace of concerns—"humanity" and "interest"—slave owners joined questions of treatment, the character of a "good" slaveholder, and speculation on slave capital. Profit and treatment were rarely uncoupled. Ebenezer Cooley instructed his son in 1829 to hire out his slaves "where they would be humanely treated, and apparently where I should be punctually paid, without delay or difficulty, when their hire should become due." George Taylor urged his agent in 1833 to get his slaves "into good hands upon the best terms you can." In 1838, Edward Garlick hoped to hire out his slave to the Richmond factory run by Mr. Myers, because "I understand he is punctual in paying the hire, and treats his hirelings well." John Taylor told his Richmond hiring agent in 1842 that he expected "good prices from good men." William Starke hired out Lawrence in 1844 and wished only that the agent "get a good home for him and good pay." These are the words of men whose first concern was profit: short-term returns on slave hiring depended on placing slaves in the hands of good paymasters; long-term returns required that slaves be placed in the hands of good slave masters.[33] In the search for good masters, owners never relied solely on their own ability to discern hirers' good character. Ensuring short- and long-term profits required that the "good homes" in which slaves were placed actually remained good throughout the hiring term. To secure that outcome, owners made sure they had the force of the law on their side.

Contracts

The law of slavery hovered over every hiring transaction, from the moment the deal was struck to the day the slave was returned. Indeed, the slaves hired out on courthouse steps could easily be the center of disputes raging inside the very same courthouse just weeks or months later. Owners were not loath to sue when hirers put slaves to forbidden work, took slaves to distant counties, or showed negligence in attending sick slaves. This constant threat of liability separated hirers from other slave masters, the vast majority of whom could expect to manage slaves free from virtually any official oversight.

As a general matter, it was extraordinarily rare for the law to intervene in master-slave relations. Southern judges and legislators refrained whenever possible from imposing legal constraints on slaveholders' treatment of their slaves—a legal reticence based in part on a republican respect for independent householders, in part on liberal respect for property rights, but largely on the commonsense expectation that prudent slaveholders, if left alone, would treat their slaves humanely. The law intervened between masters and slaves only when slaveholders' behavior threatened the property rights of other slaveholders. Thus the laws of most Southern states prohibited owners from emancipating or wantonly killing their slaves, because these two extreme actions, left unchecked, could ostensibly undermine the system of slavery as a whole. In the ordinary course of affairs, only when one owner imperiled the property rights of another did Southern judges and legislators invoke their regulatory powers to proscribe or punish specific slaveholding behavior.

Hiring arrangements, by virtue of their triangularity, fell outside the ordinary run of affairs between masters and slaves. Courtrooms were thus never far removed from everyday hiring activity. The law was always present while slaves were hired out, because property rights were shared rather than absolute, and thus constantly implicated. A hirer purchased short-term control over a slave and so gained that slave's labor and subordination as his temporary property, but at the same time his every action—issuing work orders, inflicting punishment, distributing food and clothing—potentially threatened the property rights of the slave's owner. Owners protected their interests by searching out hirers of good character, but they understood that this was a limited safeguard. Ultimately, owners needed the law to fill the gap normally filled by prudent paternalism. Hirers could not be trusted to regulate themselves; wary owners could see that hirers had every incentive to work slaves long into the night, feed them inexpensive food, and inflict on them more severe beatings. So owners who determined that hirers were treating their slaves improperly went to court to seek legal redress for hirers' neglect or brutality.

To resolve such disputes between owners and hirers, Southern judges searched common-law precedents for analogies to the triangular hiring transactions. By the 1830s, courts in nearly every slaveholding state had resorted to the law of bailments, a category of property law, as the legal standard to govern hiring transactions. It was the same standard that governed the rental of horses and plantations. The crux of the law of bailments is the temporary transfer of goods from one person (the bailor) to another (the bailee) for reasons that are beneficial to both. Those reasons are always codified in contracts, the sine qua non of the law of bailments. These contracts, whether express or implied, cover the use of the transferred property, the redelivery of the property, and, significantly, the duty of the bailee to exercise "due care" in his use of the property. Because they fell under this category of common law, hiring transactions were always reduced to paper; every one began with a signed contract. The mere existence of a contract—a legal instrument—made it impossible for the law to be absent from the day-to-day relations of owners, hirers, and slaves.

The law's oversight of hiring transactions had a powerful effect on master-slave relationships, for the law of bailments reinforced the notion that hired slaves were property, not people. As a Florida judge explained while presiding over a hiring dispute in 1835, "in all relations, and in all matters, except as to crimes, the slave is regarded by our law as *property;* and being so considered, the case before us is governed by the law of bailments." And if the practice under the law was to conceive of hired slaves solely as property, then owners would have to do the same. Given the legal focus on slaves as property, for example, owners could not indulge in paternalist fantasies in which their slaves were persons with whom they shared reciprocal rights and duties. To secure the protections of the law, to protect the health and well-being of their slaves while hired out, owners had to define their slaves' very humanity as their own property. In that way any harm done to slaves through neglect became a violation of owners' property rights—which could be given a remedy at law—rather than a transgression of implied personal rights in a paternalist relationship. By turning to the courts to police hirers, owners shifted questions of slave treatment from the realm of individual conscience and prudence to the realm of law and market. When governed by law and contract, rather than personal rights and duties, master-slave relationships were necessarily more impersonal, more detached, and more commercial.[34]

Hiring contracts were tangible artifacts of the law's oversight, and as such they varied little in form or content. By the 1850s it was possible even to purchase pre-printed, standard-form hiring contracts, although for the most part they were penned by the parties on handy half-sheets of paper. Apart from slaves' names, it was only the details of particular transactions that changed. Owners and hirers hammered out those details in any number of ways: neighbors could haggle in front parlors or over backyard fences; acquaintances often bargained through an exchange of letters; strangers usually conducted their transactions through an auctioneer. However its terms were arrived at, the contract—once signed by the hirer before a witness—memorialized and cemented the deal that had been struck. It laid out the working components of the agreement: the hiring price, the method of payment, the day the slave was to be returned, and the work the slave would perform. It stipulated whether owner or hirer would pay for the slave's food, clothing, doctor's bills, and taxes. And nearly every hiring contract required that hirers treat slaves "with humanity"—a phrase as vague then as it is today. Despite their uniformity, however, these contracts, as mundane and matter-of-fact as any others, were charged documents. They were at bottom owners' attempts to put strict limits on the mastery of hirers. As one Tennessee judge noted, when an owner and hirer signed a contract, "the owner of the negro may limit the power of the hirer," who would then have "no other right than such contract conferred." Of course, there was usually some ambiguity about the contours of the power transferred to the hirer. Signed in optimistic moments to seal mutual benefit, hiring contracts could quickly become instruments of disagreement, exhibit number one when owners and hirers resorted to Southern courtrooms.[35]

Prominently placed in a contract's upper left-hand corner, the first item to catch the eye, was the price. Matching a price to a person was an activity that set the slave South apart, and with every transaction owners and hirers negotiated the reckoning of an individual slave's age, sex, and skill, among other factors, into a dollar figure. Hiring contracts did more, however, than simply record the agreed-upon sum. For owners, setting the price was often an easier business than actually collecting the amount negotiated. Indeed, owners were as precise about the form and method of payment as they were about the prices themselves. Owners worried in part about the instability of financial institutions. Special complications could arise, for example, when hiring transactions spanned state borders. Because banknotes could lose value outside the state in which they were issued, many owners specified that they should be paid in "current money of Virginia" or "Tennessee banknotes." The issue was especially salient after Andrew Jackson's "specie circular" and the demise of the Second Bank of the United States. As one owner complained in 1837, "I find some difficulty in collecting all my hires due now, as Genl. Jackson's '*better currency*' does not answer my purposes. The salt makers here have plenty of money on the Western Banks and but little of any other kind. I shall have to leave here deficient in several hundred dollars . . . rather than receive Western money." More often, problems with payments resulted from hirers' being men or women of limited means. Owners constantly worried about hirers' lack of promptness in making payments, or even complete default. As a safeguard, especially with poor hirers, owners often required that hirers pay on a monthly basis. In 1851, Virginian Iverson Twyman, cautioning Thomas Austin about a particular hirer whose "circumstances" were "somewhat doubtful," advised Austin to "bind him to pay the money monthly." Twyman added, though, that "good security would be best."[36]

Owners also wanted their slaves back at the appointed time, so contracts stipulated in the opening lines the length of the hiring period. Across the South and throughout the antebellum period, slaves were customarily hired out from January 1 to December 25, but there were countless possible variations on this norm, depending upon the needs of hirers and the work to be done. Contracts clearly noted the specific dates on which slaves should be returned to their owners. Such specificity, especially in contracts that stretched from New Year's to Christmas, was driven by several concerns common to most owners. First, all slaves, including those hired out, expected to have the week between Christmas and New Year's to themselves, free from the burdens of work and free to visit and celebrate with friends and family. According to Solomon Northup, Christmas was "the only time to which [slaves] look forward with any interest or pleasure." Depriving slaves of their Christmas holiday would invite disgruntled resentment, and bitter slaves were poor candidates for immediate rehiring at New Year's. Second, owners specified return dates so clearly in order to ensure that their slaves were back in their possession before hiring day for the next year. It was vital to owners that confusion over the length of hire not delay the return of slaves, because timing was everything in hiring markets. Of hiring out his slaves, Iverson Twyman wrote on Christmas Day in 1851 that "*about this time* is the all important one in the whole year." Another owner regarded the week between Christmas and New Year's as "the most vexatious season of the year." His vexation resulted from the knowledge that if he did not have his slaves in hand during this crucial period, he risked incurring serious financial losses. He knew that it was increasingly difficult to find good hirers, and good prices, as January progressed and labor needs were filled.[37]

Once owners and hirers had contracted a price and a precise length of hire, they moved on to clothing, food, and shelter. Owners hoped to ensure that their slaves would be returned both on time and in good health. Because hiring periods spanned several seasons, owners gave particular attention to clothing when drafting contracts. As they saw it, warm clothing for winter and loose, dry clothing for summer were precautions against slaves' ill health or even death. Owners justifiably suspected that hirers would be tempted to skimp on clothing. Most slaveholders, apart from the wealthiest and most self-sufficient planters, purchased slave clothing and shoes that had been manufactured in northern or English factories. Thus, clothing hired slaves, unlike feeding them, required actual cash outlays—a painful activity in a world where cash was scarce and debts grew quickly. Cautious owners therefore left little ambiguity about the quality and quantity of the clothes that hirers should furnish to their slaves. In 1862, Thomas B. Montague directed that his slave "be returned well clothed with an outside suit of summer clothes, an outside suit of winter or woolen clothes, a pair of yarn socks, a pair of heavy brogan shoes, two good cotton shirts, a hat, and a blanket." In 1805, Nathaniel Burwell was even more specific, insisting that his slaves receive: "Two shirts of German Ticklenburg, coat and breeches of good kersey, new shoes and stockings, and a good Indian blanket. The former suit to consist of, for the males, trowsers of German linen; for the females, petticoat and jacket of ditto." Not all owners were this fastidious, and in the absence of special requirements hirers were governed only by custom; most promised, for instance, to return slaves to their owners "with such clothes &c. as hirelings usually have" or "with usual summer and winter clothing." No minor issue, clothing could easily prove a point of contention between owners and hirers: outfitting a slave for a year could average fifteen dollars or more, a sum

that would have added twenty percent to the cost of a slave hired for sev-
enty-five dollars. Maryland resident Susanna Warfield ultimately refused
to hire a slave to her neighbor because the two could not agree on the
yearly cost of furnishing the slave with clothes. The triangularity of hiring
arrangements ensured that points of contention were not simply confined
to the white principals. Slaves made themselves aware of the contents of
the contracts on which their names appeared, and they demanded the
clothing to which they were entitled when they did not receive it. "Those
negroes want their clothes for last year," William Danieley wrote to John
L. Clifton in 1858 regarding a group of hired slaves, "and you will have to
get them yourself as I don't want to have anything to do with the matter."
Such complaints were common enough that, in 1850, a hiring agent in Alabama recommended his services to a client by claiming that "at the end of
this year you will hear no complaints from the negroes that they did not
get their clothes."[38]

If owners did not trust hirers to clothe their slaves well, they did not
trust them to feed them well, either. Given that hirers had a year to extract
as much work as they could from slaves, they had an incentive to feed
those slaves inexpensive foodstuffs that were high in calories—and thus
good sources of energy—but that lacked the nutrients necessary for pro-
moting long-term health. As with clothing, owners' stipulations regarding
diet were an effort to safeguard their valuable human property against
misuse, neglect, and debilitation. For this reason, the hiring agent who
leased Samuel Smith Downey's slaves to a Mississippi railroad in 1836 required that the slaves be furnished "with plenty of good and wholesome
food." Some owners realized that their understanding of "good" or
"wholesome" might not exactly match that of hirers. The Wyche family
therefore carefully qualified "the meaning," as they put it, of the phrase
"sufficient and wholesome diet" in the contract that transferred their
slaves to a Louisiana firm in 1829. That phrase, according to the Wyche's
clarification, indicated "plenty of meal and bread, and occasionally molas-
ses, milk, vegetables, &c." Prudent owners like the Wyches circumscribed
the hirers' latitude in providing food because malnutrition would jeopardize future hiring contracts. But it is entirely possible that contractual
specifications about diet resulted as much from slaves' demands as from
the owners' self-interested calculations. Diet was among the most critical
changes that hired slaves faced in new living and work environments, one
that had direct bearing on comfort and well-being. It would not be surprising if slaves asked to receive certain foods while hired out.[39]

Knowing that it was foolhardy to expect hirers to be forthcoming providers for slaves' material needs, owners also used contracts to ensure salu-

brious living conditions. Samuel Smith Downey's 1836 contract with a Mississippi railroad directed that the line's superintendent "provide good and comfortable houses for said negroes to live and sleep in" and that he "pay strict attention to keep them comfortable." For slaves working from sunup to sundown, sleep was a prime consideration with respect to their living conditions. Contracts invariably provided that each slave would receive at least one blanket during the year, but many owners went further in arranging the conditions in which their slaves would be sleeping. Both Sanford Rainey and Elizabeth Allstadt, to make certain that their slaves would not be left with only a blanket on a cabin's dirt floor, directed in their contracts that hirers furnish their slaves with "comfortable bedding." Catherine McKenney stipulated that her slave Alice, perhaps at Alice's insistence, should receive a pillow along with her customary blanket. Owners knew that only such precise contractual stipulations as these could guarantee the food, clothing, and shelter that they wanted their slaves to receive while under the domain of other Southern householders.[40]

After owners had precisely stipulated price and length of hire, and guaranteed that their slaves' material needs would be met, they went on to place contractual bounds on the work to which hirers could put their slaves. Partly, this was an effort to preempt hirers' natural inclination to put slaves they had hired, rather than those they already owned, to work on tasks that were especially strenuous or especially dangerous. And partly it was an effort to prevent slaves who had pre-existing injuries or specialized skills from being put to work in ways that would aggravate those injuries or jeopardize the skills. Rhoda Stevenson required in 1855 that her slave Jefferson was "only to be worked as a farm hand," forbidding the hirer from working Jefferson in ditches, shingle swamps, stave plantations, or public works projects. Similarly, Mary Claiborne insisted in 1859 that her slave Henry Corbin "must not be hired in a brick yard or anywhere tote bricks." And when David, a carpenter, was hired out in 1855, his hirers expressly agreed "not to put him in or hire him to be put in a harvest field."[41]

Restricting *where* slaves could be worked as equally important. Many owners specifically forbade hirers from working their slaves near water. Because most slaves never learned to swim, work on or near rivers, streams, and ponds placed them at risk of drowning. For just this reason, Edmund Pendleton Barbour agreed under contract when he hired Edwin that he would "specially in no case suffer him to cross the mill pond at liberty mills, or water course when high." David Outlaw, an owner who was influenced by the law's tendency to conceive of slaves as property rather than individuals, required by contract in 1847 that his slave "not work by water except at the risk of the hirer," meaning that the hirer was free to put the slave's life in danger so long as he assumed any liability for the slave's full cost if he drowned. Water was just one danger that could take the lives of hired slaves. Owners were equally worried that their slaves would be exposed to contagion. At a time when smallpox and other diseases emerged unpredictably in particular locales, owners often deemed it wise to restrict hirers to working their slaves only in a single county. J. F. Alexander, while hiring out several slaves in 1851, stipulated that the slaves not "be worked on any internal or public improvement," but also that they not "be hired out of the bounds of this county." Restrictions such as this one on the movement of hired slaves were frequent, and they were intended, as were all contractual stipulations, to delimit the mastery that hirers enjoyed.[42]

A distinguishing characteristic of the law of bailments is that those entrusted with temporary control over another's property must exercise "due care" in using that property. Hiring contracts were not complete, therefore, without some reference to how slaves were to be treated by their temporary masters. The word to which owners nearly always resorted was "humanity." Thus the Wyche family hired out its slaves to a Louisiana firm in 1829 only after guaranteeing by contract that the hirers would "promise to treat said slaves with humanity." And in 1853 the executor of Thomas Bennett's will hired out the estate's slaves on the condition that hirers "treat them with humanity." Likewise, when Edmund Pendleton Barbour hired Edwin, Barbour agreed that "in consideration of his services," he would "treat [Edwin] with kindness and humanity." In 1854, Sanford Raney hired out his slave Mary and her infant son Thomas, but only after the hirer had agreed by contract "to treat said negro woman and her said infant child in a human manner." As a linguistic referent, "humanity" was no more clear-cut in the slaveholders' world than it is in our own. But owners employed the word despite its ambiguity because, however hazy "humanity" might be as a contractual term, it best captured what "due care" entailed when rented property happened also to be human property.[43]

By using the word "humanity," owners managed to create a cause of action—that is, a basis for suing another person—out of "inhumanity" to slaves, a subject to which Southern courts otherwise rarely turned. Southern judges ordinarily operated on two somewhat contradictory assumptions: first, that slaves did not have any humanity that could be violated and, second, that slave owners' natural discretion and prudence checked any inhumane behavior toward their own slaves. But through hiring contracts a slave's humanity was made the legal property of a white person, not an inviolable natural right held by the slave, and this perception forced judges, when an owner sued, to determine whether inhumanity had actually been shown to the slave. "Inhumanity" has an elusive meaning in any context, and in relations with slaves it carries a warped irony that is difficult to ignore, yet Southern judges grappled with such ironies of a slave society every day, and they did their best to clarify the legal meanings of "humanity" and "inhumanity" in the context of hiring. The Texas high court, like those in so many other Southern states, held that "the hirer of a slave is bound to observe towards the slave the same care which a discreet, humane, and prudent master would observe in the treatment of his own slaves." Hirers, then, were held to the standard of the imagined "prudent master." The prudent master was humane and self-restrained because he had the foresight to recognize that his slaves were lifelong investments. The inevitable conflicts between owners and hirers over the bounds of mastery and the prudence or inhumanity of particular treatment of slaves made hiring contracts charged documents. The charged nature of divided mastery stemmed, in the end, from the claim to control that both hirers and owners had over the bodies of the same slaves. As everyone in the South knew, a master's power was manifest in his ability to control the bodies of the people he owned; dominance, honor, respect, and whiteness were substantiated through the prerogative of determining how slaves were clothed, fed, sheltered, worked, and punished. Such control was precisely what owners wanted to limit, because the more latitude hirers enjoyed as masters, the greater the threat to owners' long-term property rights. Yet, of course, it was just such latitude that hirers demanded, thinking that they had rightfully purchased full mastery over the slaves they rented—without at every turn having to prove that they were acting "humanely" or "prudently." Conflict was virtually inevitable.[44]

The battles that ensued between owners and hirers were unique in that the slaves involved were not silent onlookers. On occasion, slaves actually instigated these conflicts by making complaints or allegations about their hirers, but even when their role was less proactive, slaves necessarily participated in the disputes unfolding between their two masters. Because their bodies were at issue, it was unavoidable that slaves would figure centrally in the legal division of mastery between owners and hirers. Indeed, slaves were often the only witnesses to whether the terms of the contracts were being lived up to, and their owners thus relied heavily on their reports. "John has been to see me several times," Hez Ford alerted John's owner in 1849, "and begs that you will not hire him to Mr. Foster and says he has not given him a rag of clothing or attended to him during the year." J. F. North wrote to the hirer of his slave John in 1853 to tell him that John had run away, returning to North "in a most exhausted condition," in or-

der to protest the fact that "he had been over worked and not well fed." "I
regretted very much to hear it," North continued, "as tis my wish that my
negroes should work faithfully for those who hire them—and on the other
hand tis equally my wish and I will say my expectation that those who hire
them will see that they are taken proper care of in every respect." North
got to the heart of every owner's basic demand of a hirer: "To you I look to
have my negroes taken care of, and return them next Christmas in good
condition." The triangularity of hiring arrangements ensured that slaves
would play a crucial role in the social relations between slaveholders.
Slaves leveraged that role whenever possible, doing what they could to
achieve their own aims by bringing their white captors into conflict.[45]

In conclusion, it is important to note the influence that slave hiring had on
the way that owners viewed their slaves. Not surprisingly, the language of
the market that owners used to describe the transactions they carried out
with hirers also shaped the way they perceived their slaves. Owners frequently resorted to the notion of risk—part of the grammar of investment,
speculation, and the market—when describing relations with hirers and
slaves alike. In 1838, when the slave Peter failed to reach his hirer's place
on the appointed date, Peter's owner and his hirer both assumed he had
run away. Peter's owner perceived the situation in a way that was deeply
influenced by the market. "If you choose to risk him," the owner wrote,
"complete the bargain and sign the note yourself according to the agreement . . . If you choose not to risk you can destroy the note." Like Peter's
owner, other slaveholders clearly saw negotiations with hirers as financial
endeavors that wavered between potential risks and desired returns. Farish
Carter was willing to hire out a slave to Thomas Grimes in 1824 for a hundred dollars, with Grimes "risking [the slave's] life and all accidents that
may happen to him by disease or anything else," or for two hundred dollars "if I risk his life." To a female relative who was worried about hiring
out her slaves to unreliable hirers, Iverson Twyman wrote straightforwardly, and patronizingly, that "in all business we have to run *some* risk."
Significantly, this language of risk and return also shaped the way owners
talked about their slaves and the relationships they formed with them.
John Austin wrote in 1851 that, although his slave Cambridge preferred
being hired to urban blacksmiths, he would "risk the hiring of Cambridge
in some country shop." Similarly, Iverson Twyman suggested in 1849 that
rather than sell the recalcitrant slave Beverly, it would be better to "risk
him for hires."[46]

   How owners dealt with the risks attendant on hiring out their slaves is
telling. First, they sought out "good" hirers, men and women they thought

more likely to be humane. Then they invoked the power of the law, using contracts both to restrict hirers' mastery and, sometimes, explicitly to shift risk to hirers (recall, for example, that David Outlaw permitted his slave to be worked on water "only at the risk of the hirer"). Last, for situations in which these two safeguards might for some reason be insufficient, owners took out insurance. Life insurance, by protecting the long-term value of a slave, served much the same functional ends as did prudent paternalism. Take, as an example, the hiring of slaves to railroads. Trying to secure "paternalist" behavior—meaning simply "due care"—from the diverse array of superintendents, contractors, and overseers that made up railroad management was a futile task, so most owners instead required as part of public works contracts that their slaves be insured for their full value. Samuel Drewry hired out his slaves to railroad contractor John Buford in 1854, but he demanded "an insurance on them for $1000 each," just in case "any accident occur so as to leave any hand injured permanently so that his value was seriously impaired." Buford, who always had a tough time getting enough slaves to work on his railroad, asked Drewry to prevail upon others in his neighborhood to hire out their slaves to the railroad as well. Drewry informed Buford that owners were reluctant to hire out to public works because the work sites were usually "too far off," because there seemed to be a large number of "deaths by accident," and because too many "escapes have been made to free states." The owners' reluctance, however, was not intransigent opposition. Like Drewry himself, these owners were perfectly willing to sign contracts in which there would be "a guarantee for the value of the slave in case he should come to his death by being on such work, and further a guarantee for the safe delivery of such slaves at the end of the year." Hiring reinforced an impersonal view of slaves as capital assets whose interest-bearing capacity needed to be protected by whatever means available.[47]

Hiring worked against the formation of paternalist relationships—relationships based on a sense of mutual rights and duties—between masters and slaves. As Eugene D. Genovese argues, paternalism was "encouraged by the close living of masters and slaves." It was difficult for hired slaves to form paternalist relationships with owners (or hirers) from whom they were continually separated by stints working for other people. Henry Bibb was hired out, beginning in his childhood, for "eight or ten years in succession" and to "various people." William Wells Brown, in his narrative, recounts experiences with at least six different hirers. And evidence from extant estate inventories, guardian accounts, and hire lists reveals that slaves often moved from one hirer to the next, year after year. Owners and slaves alike recognized the effect of such mobility: some were likely to know each other only slightly. Regarding a slave she had hired out for many years in a row, Tennessee resident Etta Kosnegary told her family in 1862: "Allen knows nothing about me. He has never lived with us since we were married." When asked years later by an interviewer to describe his owner, former slave Henry Clay replied that, having been hired out "a long, long time," he didn't "know much about Old Master Dyson Cheet." And Henry Atkinson, interviewed in Canada, noted that as a result of being hired out in Norfolk, Virginia, until the age of thirty-four, "I never saw my owner, but when I was a little boy."[48] Owners and slaves still negotiated with each other in ways that are characteristic of paternalist relationships, but the leverage that hired slaves used in these negotiations was based not on the rights due them as dependents but rather on the value they represented as a profitable investment. If owners expected to reap hiring's promise, they had to heed their slaves' demands. Hirers, too, learned that lesson.

Compromised Mastery

In the Southern States, . . . there are three odious classes of mankind; the slaves themselves, who are cowards; the slaveholders,
who are tyrants; and the non-slaveholding slave-hirers, who are
lickspittles.

Hinton Helper, *The Impending Crisis* (1860)

*H*AD Fanny Kemble and John C. Calhoun discussed the institution of
slavery, they could have agreed on at least one point: slave hirers did
not fit neatly into the dominant proslavery argument, which held that self-
interest reined in a slave owner's great power. Proslavery author George
Frederick Holmes explained that because slaves were a lifelong investment, "the interests of the labourer and the employer of labour are absolutely identical . . . The consequence is that both interest and inclination,
the desire of profit and the sense or sentiment of duty concur to render
the slave-owner considerate and kind toward the slaves." The antislavery
Kemble perceptively observed, however, that the "extremely common"
practice of slave hiring was "very seldom adverted to in those arguments
for the system which are chiefly founded upon the master's presumed regard for his human property." Because they had only a "temporary interest" in the slaves they worked, Kemble insisted, hirers must have as their
chief aim "to get as much out of them, and expend as little on them,
as possible." John C. Calhoun, unsurpassed as a defender of slavery,
would have agreed with Kemble. Upon learning that his son-in-law
planned to hire out his slaves, Calhoun warned that the object of a slave
hirer was "generally to make the most he can out of them, without regard to their comfort and health." Those who rented slaves, Calhoun
maintained, would have no compelling reason to "take good care of
them."[1]

It is telling that two white Southerners with such opposing political convictions on slavery could find common ground here. The unlikely meeting
of the minds between Kemble and Calhoun was the voice of a conventional wisdom in the South: hirers lacked the self-interest that was funda-

mental to any slave system grounded in the absolute rights of property and the pursuit of profit. As one Kentucky judge opined in 1809, hirers were impelled to treat rented slaves well only by "the mere feelings of humanity," which, he noted, "we have too much reason to believe . . . are too weak to stimulate to active virtue." This conventional wisdom provided the context in which hirers attempted to exert control over the slaves they rented. Indeed, the experiences of slave hirers were shaped above all by the tension between, on the one hand, their desire for absolute mastery over slaves only temporarily theirs and, on the other, the common assumption—in neighborhoods and courtrooms alike—that hirers lacked the self-interested discretion required for "proper" mastery. In signing hiring contracts, hirers believed that they thereby purchased not only the temporary use of slaves' services but also the rights to complete mastery over those slaves. But their mastery was qualified by different parties at every step. First, owners placed all manner of contractual checks on the use and treatment of their slaves. Second, Southern courts circumscribed the mastery of hirers, for judges reasoned that restrictions were required to keep hirers from impinging on the property rights that owners retained even while slaves were hired out.[2]

Not surprisingly, hirers claimed that such limitations eviscerated their mastery by impairing the complete authority on which the complete submission of slaves rested. In a sense, they were right, for the third check on their mastery inevitably turned out to be the slaves they had rented. Hired slaves exploited the attenuated power of their temporary masters whenever possible, in order to manipulate situations to their advantage. They refused to go with certain hirers; they neglected work orders; they resisted punishment; and they demanded privileges previously granted them by their owners. The greatest obstacle to the mastery for which hirers pined was not owners' contractual stipulations, or even the restrictions placed on hirers by Southern courts, but rather the daily confrontations hirers faced with the slaves they had rented.

In such circumstances, slave hirers were justifiably ambivalent about the desirability of renting slave labor. On the one hand, it could be a rewarding experience: slave hiring offered cheap and flexible access to slave labor, and, for many hirers, it was the sole entry into the South's rarefied master classes. Entrée into the slaveholding ranks brought both cultural and economic rewards; in the South, the luxury of ordering slaves about was a way to enhance both one's social standing and one's production for the market. The South's slaveholding culture, however, prevented the transfer of mastery from being a smooth process.

Mastery

White Southerners had many reasons to hire slaves. Hiring was, above all, a way to acquire extra labor at prices significantly lower than outright purchase would require. For small farmers, just one additional slave could supply the labor they needed to produce a little more cotton, wheat, or tobacco for the market. For urban white craftsmen, hired slaves provided the added assistance that could enable them to take on a few extra jobs in a year. For those setting up tobacco factories, turpentine plantations, and other industrial enterprises, hiring was a way to acquire a sufficient number of slaves—dozens, or even hundreds, at a time—without huge capital outlays at slave auctions. The benefits of hiring slaves were not by any means limited to Southern men, for white women also profited from the labor of slaves whom they or their husbands hired. Poor white women, for example, could often be spared from working in the fields when their families were able to rent a slave or two to labor in the fields alongside husbands and children. For rich and poor women alike, a slave hired for domestic work was a boon that eased, for them, the drudgery of household management; to this extra pair of hands could be delegated such noisome tasks as milking cows and emptying bedpans. Hirers, regardless of class or gender, rented slaves to do *work*. But working slaves was as much a cultural as an economic activity in the slave South. Being a master was about more than producing for the market; for men, mastery entailed patriarchal honor, and for women, it often substantiated their claim to refined femininity.

From an economic perspective, hirers were especially drawn to the flexibility that renting slaves afforded them. Hiring arrangements did not always run for a full year, and indeed white Southerners frequently resorted to hiring when they needed extra labor for limited periods or to complete specific projects. "I understand you have Harkless to hire at 75 cents per day," T. G. Mitchell wrote to Iveson L. Brookes in 1838, adding that he would gladly pay that amount "until I finish a job, which is building a kitchen." Craftsmen like Mitchell, whose employment was likely to be sporadic and unpredictable, relied on hiring to avoid maintaining slaves when they were not working. "I cannot say definitely what length of time I shall want them . . . ," E. D. Williams wrote to Farish Carter in 1840 regarding several slave carpenters he hoped to hire, "but shall want the privilege of discharging them whenever I finish the job of work I have on hand." Planters, too, relied on hiring when they needed extra labor for a short period. In December 1844, a Louisiana sugar planter arranged to hire several slaves only for the duration of his "sugarmaking." "I expect to finish in 2 months," the planter stated in the hire contract, "but will not bind myself to return said negroes at the expiration of this time . . . if I have not finished or keep them any longer than the making up of my crop makes it necessary." When hiring slaves, craftsmen and planters alike often demanded the same flexibility regarding length of employment that they would have enjoyed if using free labor.[3]

But hirers did not want free labor. Whether rich or poor, hirers preferred slave labor, primarily because they wished to be masters as well as employers. White laborers, though not so numerous as slaves, were available to do much of the work to which hirers put the slaves they rented. Poor whites and immigrants, both male and female, could be hired to do everything from field labor to domestic work, sometimes at lower wages than would have been paid to owners for hired slaves. But hirers showed a marked preference for slaves, even when white laborers were readily available. "I prefer blacks to the white men who usually work on the canal," wrote a Virginia canal contractor to J. H. Cocke in 1825 as an explanation for why he wished to hire even more of Cocke's slaves to work as stonemasons, quarriers, and blacksmiths. In 1842, Louisiana resident W. H. Oram considered returning a slave he had hired from Joseph Copes for twenty dollars per month when he discovered that he could get "a good German Dutchman" to do the same work for half the price. Oram proposed, nevertheless, to pay Copes fifteen dollars per month—at this rate, fully sixty dollars more per year than he would pay the white worker—because he preferred keeping the slave. Daniel Jordan, who owned a North Carolina turpentine plantation, groused to his wife in 1845 that he had been forced to hire a white cooper and pressed her to look for a slave he could hire in the white man's stead. "I am very sorry you are compelled to hire another white man," his wife commiserated, regretting that she could not find "a negro cooper to get any where." "Could you not learn some of the boys?" she asked. Like Daniel Jordan and W. H. Oram, most hirers avoided white labor whenever possible, preferring to be masters, not just employers.[4]

Hirers' preference for slave labor sprang from their desire to exert mastery over the laborers they employed. Stripped of their freedom and individual autonomy, slaves could be controlled in a way that white laborers flatly could not. During his journey through the South, Northern newspaper editor James Redpath one day met a Virginian who informed him that Irish workers could be hired for ten to twelve dollars per month, the same price at which slaves could be hired from their owners. Redpath inquired why the man did not hire the Irish workers instead of slaves. "It's the custom," the man replied to Redpath, "and *you can order slaves about.*" As for the Irish, he added disdainfully, "when they come to this country, [they] get above themselves." North Carolinian John Wilkes, during the first laborious weeks of launching a new sawmill in 1856, wrote to his father to explain that he had successfully hired three slaves. The transaction was heartening for Wilkes because hiring these slaves allowed him to discharge several white laborers who had become an increasing source of vexation for him. "I at once dismissed two of my white hands who had been carrying on very independently," Wilkes declared to his father in a gratified way, "and have had the sawmill running night and day since." "Having 5 negroes now, they (the whites) see that the tables are turned on them," he concluded, "and I do not think I shall have any more trouble." Hirers like John Wilkes considered slaves superior to white laborers because they were subject to stricter governance and mastery. Though hired slaves could be irksome, defiant, and truculent, they at least lacked the freedom and independence that white workers so often made a point of displaying.[5]

Mastery appealed to hirers for reasons other than the ability to order slaves about. Hirers reaped some of the cultural rewards that naturally fell to masters in a slave society. Of course, many were already slaveholders when they hired and were merely looking to fill specific labor needs. For many others, however, hiring a slave represented their first or only entry into the slaveholding ranks. Sarah S. Hughes, for example, found that out of a sample of 57 hirers in Elizabeth City County, Virginia, between 1784 and 1786, 21 percent were nonslaveholders. Randolph B. Campbell, using a sample of 463 rural Texas hirers between 1848 and 1862, found that 41 percent were nonslaveholders during the year they hired slaves. The significance of these numbers is that far more white Southerners every year enjoyed the social, economic, and psychological benefits that derived from asserting mastery over slaves than census or tax records would have revealed. To some extent, hiring helped democratize access to slave labor and thus gave a taste of mastery to a wider cross-section of white Southerners. And because mastery was powerful, affecting the most mundane affairs in a white Southerner's life, hiring a slave could change an individual's social and personal identities overnight. But for hirers, those identities were precarious for two reasons. First, hirers might not have the money every year to continue their forays into slaveholding. Second, and more significant, mastery always rested on the willingness of others to recognize it, and for hirers that recognition was not always forthcoming—from owners, from the courts, or, more important, from slaves.[6]

Entry into the slaveholding classes was most dramatic for the poor whites—including tenant farmers, tavern keepers, and craftsmen—who hired a slave or two to work in their fields, their shops, or their houses. Southern whites of such limited means often had to resort to hiring slave children because owners would part with them for lower prices, often only for the children's "victuals and clothes." Unsurprisingly, many of the former slaves interviewed by the W.P.A. during the 1930s, who had been children under slavery, remembered having been hired out to work for their owners' more impoverished neighbors. Mary Edwards told her interviewer that her owner "hired me out to do nursin' for people who didn't own no slaves." Mary Reynolds, born a slave in Louisiana, remembered similarly that her owner would send his slaves "to work for trashy whites." She recollected being hired, along with an even younger boy, "to work for some ornery white trash by the name of Kidd." A master of slave children was, of course, a master nonetheless, and for lower-class whites, hiring a slave child meant the opportunity to play the role of master—handing out work assignments, issuing commands, and meting out punishments. Nancy Williams, who was eventually beaten brutally by her poor white hirer, remembered that as soon as she stepped foot in the man's home, "his ole woman told me to mind the baby, give it some toast; wash them dishes and git them 'tatoes peeled for cookin' dinner. Poor white trash gimme that bundle o' work to do!" To Edward Covey, the Maryland tenant farmer who became the bane of Frederick Douglass's life, hiring meant more than just temporary enjoyment of mastery over several slaves; he saw the practice as an opportunity to guarantee his position for years to come. Every night, Covey would lock up Bill Smith, a slave he had hired to work his farm, with Caroline, the one slave he owned, in hopes that Caroline would get pregnant and thus add to his slave capital. For a man like Covey, hiring was as much about reproducing mastery as producing for the market.[7]

Hirers had to be selective about the slaves they rented. In particular, hirers tried to choose slaves they thought would give them the least reason to doubt their positions of authority. Slave mastery entailed a rewarding and privileged status in the South, but the viability of that mastery hinged in large measure on the behavior of slaves. Mastery always rests, to some extent, on the consent of those mastered. While owners could devote time and energy to overpowering unconsenting slaves, hirers did not have that option. Beating slaves into submission exposed hirers to lawsuits, but it also ate into the finite period in which they could exploit hired slaves' labor. Even more than other slave owners, hirers could ill afford to fritter away valuable work time in feuds with intractable slaves. So hirers carried out extensive inquisitions of slaves on the auction block on hiring day. On occasion, they also agreed to hire slaves only after a brief "trial" period.

Most often, hirers carried out their reconnaissance by keeping their ears to the ground, listening closely to local talk about particular slaves for hire.

Indeed, most hirers found that the best information on hired slaves was to be gleaned not from newspaper advertisements, or even at public auction, but through word of mouth. While talking to an acquaintance at a country store or while serving on a jury, a man in need of labor could learn which neighbors were looking for ways to employ extra slaves. While visiting friends, women could learn which slaves their friends were currently hiring, or had recently hired, to do domestic labor. Slaves their acquaintances already knew, and perhaps had once hired themselves, were a safer bet for hirers than were slaves who were completely unknown to them. "Our friend Randolph Harrison, Esq.," John Gamble wrote to J. H. Cocke in 1825, "casually mentioned to me that you probably had some stone cutters whom you would hire out." "Having heard from a friend that you have a lot of Negroes to hire," a railroad superintendent wrote in a similar manner to planter Farish Carter in 1853, "I have taken the liberty to drop you a few lines to know if this is the case." Friends could also provide hirers with valuable information about local slaves who had special skills to recommend them. "I understand from Abram," E. D. Williams wrote to Farish Carter in 1840, "that you have some good carpenters and should like to know what you are willing to engage them at." Calling on the advice of friends was one of many means that hirers relied on to guard against getting stuck with slaves they considered "indifferent"—that is, slaves who might perform only mediocre work or be difficult to manage.[8]

For similar reasons, hirers frequently turned to their extended families when looking for slaves to rent. In December 1845, John Baird decided that he needed eight extra slaves to ensure that he could complete his work before summer, and he turned first to his uncle, who had already hired him a number of slaves. Likewise, George Johnson asked his brother William for slaves twice when he was trying to set up new businesses, first when he was setting up a blacksmith's shop, and then again when going into "the manufacture of tobacco." Relying on friends and family for information about hiring opportunities was a pragmatic choice for hirers. Hiring was as much a gamble for them as it was for owners. Because hirers had to pay the contracted price whether the slave they rented ever did any work or not, they took every available precaution to avoid engaging slaves who would end up malingering or running away. Resorting to slaves whom they, or friends, already knew was just one of those precautions.[9]

In selecting particular slaves to rent, hirers devoted serious consideration to "character," just as owners did in selecting hirers. Impudent or unruly slaves were a particular curse to hirers, considering that they had only a certain window of opportunity to exploit the labor of those slaves. Also, punishing slaves was a sensitive matter for hirers because observers, especially owners, could never be sure that hirers, given their lack of long-term interest in the slaves, were acting with sufficient "prudence" when they inflicted whippings and other beatings. Aware that unmanageable slaves would cost them time and money, the owners of Virginia's Mid-Lothian Coal Mining Company advertised for hired slaves in 1846 with the stipulation that "none of bad character should be offered." As a point of negotiation, hirers often considered slaves' character no less important than prices, and they placed it high on the list of variables incorporated into the calculus that structured their effort to translate individual slaves into dollar figures. In 1830, Henry Langhorne wrote to a Virginia slave owner to ask about hiring several stonemasons, and he requested that the owner specify "the number, price (per month), and their character." When George Foster wrote to Joseph Copes in 1855 to inquire about hiring a slave, he underscored that he wanted only a slave "*of good disposition and habits.*" When G. W. Mussfield hired a slave of Bowker Preston in 1835, he told Preston that he did not "by any means want a negro either of vicious habits or *religious* habits," probably because he thought that such a slave—running to the woods out of defiance or piety—would be more difficult to exert mastery over. Hirers had to get down to business with the slaves they rented, so they did not want to waste time with slaves who might run away, defy orders, talk back, or malinger. Hirers were partial to those slaves they thought would acknowledge the mastery to which the temporary users felt entitled.[10]

Conflicts could arise when a hirer thought that an owner's representation of a slave's character had been willfully false. These were just some of the situations in which the triangular hiring arrangements made white social relations vulnerable to resistance from slaves. In 1840, for example, a Mr. Womack hired Nancy in Louisiana in part because her owner, Mr. Nicholson, had attested to her being "a good and valuable field hand" as well as "humble, tractable, and healthy." Womack sued Nicholson when he came to the conclusion that he had been duped into renting a slave who was actually "insolent, disobedient, and in the habit of running away when able and well enough to do so." A slave like Nancy could embitter a hirer like Womack for two reasons. First, she refused to recognize his mastery. Testimony in Womack's support corroborated that Nancy had a "vicious and unmanageable character" that made her "stubborn" and in need of "more whipping than ordinary negroes." Second, Nancy cost him money. Womack sued not just for the money he had lost in hire, but also for five hundred dollars, "from the loss of his cotton and corn crop."

Womack had entered the hiring market expecting to purchase a mastery that entailed both cultural and economic rewards, and when Nancy obstructed both, he accused her owner of disingenuousness. The implication was that Nancy could not help herself—it was her "character"—and that her crafty owner had attempted to palm her off on an unsuspecting hirer.[11]

Hirers relied on owners' representations of slaves' abilities and conduct in order to imagine the work that those slaves could perform. They were angered, therefore, when slaves did not match what they had envisioned, and they blamed owners for exaggerating their slaves' skills or for passing over their shortcomings. In 1854, James Horner suggested that Iverson Twyman had been less than forthright about the slave John whom Horner had hired for fifty dollars "without knowing anything about his being injured." Horner felt his plans had been sabotaged by the concealment of this crucial piece of information. "I find he is not competent to do what I expected him to do," Horner informed Twyman. Georgia resident Samuel Griswold felt himself similarly deceived by Farish Carter, from whom he had hired a slave carpenter named Townshend in 1850. "You are probably mistaken as to his mechanical skill," Griswold declared to Carter; "he is an able hand, but never has been taught to do good work, and was too old before he came to me to make a fine workman." Hirers felt especially cheated, of course, when the slaves they hired did no work at all. In 1858, the Virginian Beverly Hutchison tried to return two slaves he had hired from Mrs. Hooe, because, according to Hutchison, the "negroes are both runaways and one of them has been gone some 6 weeks." Similarly, in 1860, William Campbell wrote to Caroline Foscue to complain that Chany, the slave he had hired from Foscue, was pregnant and unable to work. "I was deceived in her," Campbell maintained.[12]

When hirers complained that they had been given slaves of poor character, owners sometimes countered by intimating that perhaps it was the character of the hirer, rather than that of the slave, which was causing the problem. Thus, when slaves resisted, owners and hirers often pointed their fingers at one another, rather than at the slaves in question. For hirers who were already prickly about their authority, such intimations of improper mastery could put them over the edge; to impugn a white Southerner's mastery was to assault his personal identity, sabotage his claims to whiteness, and threaten his social standing. In 1857, C. G. Fulks complained to his friend William Massie that a Mr. Thompson, the owner of the slave he had rented for three years in a row, had suddenly, and without explanation, refused to hire the slave to him for another year. Fulks insisted that he had "fed and clothed [the slave] well," "promptly paid . . . his hire when due," "worked him moderately hard," and "kept a strict watch over his morals." He had been, as he saw it, a good paymaster and a good slave master. Fulks thus considered the owner's refusal to hire the slave to him a personal affront: "I do not think I deserve from Mr. Thompson or any other man such treatment. If he had given me his reasons for not hiring his boy to me it would have all been right; but merely to say he would not hire him to *me* without assigning any reason I think wrong." Fulks suspected that his mastery of the slave was somehow the cause of Thompson's sudden reversal in policy. "I am of opinion," he told Massie, "he thinks I am too tight with his boy." And he suspected further that the slave had put the notion in Thompson's head. "If the boy has complained to him about hard work, or a little switching for card playing, or running about at night," Fulks maintained, "this is not I think sufficient grounds for taking him away." When mastery became so much a part of a white Southerner's personal identity, so cherished a form of property and source of social prestige, dividing it between two people could easily result in such ill will and acrimony.[13]

Mastery was prized not only by men, and hiring brought white women into the slaveholding ranks as well. The effects could be momentous in the lives of these women. In a slave society like the South, as historian James Oakes has pointed out, "the ownership of even a single slave affected all the other relationships that made up the master's world." It could be argued that these changes in a white Southerner's life were more noticeable for a woman than for a man. Slaveholding determined a white woman's social standing, the work she had to perform, and her relationships with friends, neighbors, husband, and children. Women in nonslaveholding families or in those with few slaves were frequently compelled, out of necessity, to work alongside their husbands raising crops for market. In fact, an easy way to distinguish between classes in the antebellum South was to look for white women working in the fields. By hiring a slave, poor families could often afford to allow wives to restrict their labor to tasks within the household.[14]

Once a woman was able to stop working in the fields, she and her family reached the next level of refinement when she could avoid the most menial household chores by delegating them to a slave. Having slave labor *inside* the household was also a major distinction in the South. To have a slave in the house who could perform menial tasks at the bidding of a white woman was a Southern ideal. As J. D. B. DeBow noted in his essay on "The Non-Slaveholders of the South": "The non-slaveholder knows that as soon as his savings will admit, he can become a slaveholder, and thus relieve his wife from the necessities of the kitchen and the laundry, and his children from the labors of the field." Hiring slaves, even if those slaves were only children, made it possible for less wealthy white families in the South to achieve that ideal.[15]

White women of all classes played a decisive role in choosing when to hire additional household labor. On small and large farms across the South, white women were charged with overseeing and managing domestic operations, from kitchens and gardens to smokehouses and dairies. In the domestic sphere, they were often better attuned to the labor needs of the household than were their husbands. In letters that their husbands wrote to owners about renewing or initiating hiring transactions, it is clear that women were the decision makers, determining which slaves to hire, when to do so, and even what prices to offer. E. B. Weed routinely hired a slave from Georgia planter Farish Carter to "do some housework as well as take care of the child," and he always consulted his wife on the subject, letting her decide which of Carter's slaves would "suit better." In December 1852, as his contract reached expiration and as Carter pressed him to select a slave for the next year, Weed promised that he would write with his decision just as soon as his wife returned home from a trip. In the same year, the North Carolinian John L. Clifton wrote to William Darden to inquire about the conditions and price of hiring Darden's slave Emma because, as Clifton noted, "my wife wishes me to hire the Girl for her." In such situations, husbands served as proxies for their wives in the negotiations with owners. "My wife informs me that she . . . would be glad to hire your girl Margaret," R. W. Shaw wrote to Iverson Twyman in 1853, "and she says she would be willing to give you three dollars per month from this time to Christmas." Many white Southerners felt that propriety dictated that men act for women in public negotiations for slaves, even when the women themselves made all the decisions about the particulars of hiring domestic slaves.[16]

Women who were widowed, single, or married with husbands away from home regularly acted on their own in hiring the slaves they required for their households. For these women, finding a male proxy was not always possible, or perhaps even desirable. Emily Jordan, for example, hired the slaves her family needed while her husband was away from home managing his turpentine business. She wrote to her husband in 1845 to inform him that she had "not yet been able to hire any boys" but that she had not yet given up her efforts. She had her eye on several slaves whom she expected soon to be put up for hire by a bankrupt tavern keeper. "I will do all I can towards it," Jordan assured her husband, "and if there are any to be hired it shall be done." Like their male counterparts, women who hired slaves refused to be taken advantage of in the transactions they conducted. In 1856, for example, Archibald Henderson received a letter from Mrs.

Shoburn, the hirer of his slave Polly, in which Shoburn complained that
Polly was "not smart and active enough to do the work that a younger servant could easily do." Shoburn proposed, as a way of rectifying a situation
she found unsatisfactory, that Henderson let her "have another to assist
[Polly] to wait in the Dining-room." Additionally, she asserted to Henderson that she would consider it only fair that "the wages of this second servant ought . . . to be somewhat lower on account of Polly's deficiency or
. . . Polly's ought to be lowered to enable me to hire the additional one."[17]

Joseph Copes, a New Orleans slaveholder who routinely rented out his
slaves to work as domestic laborers, often received letters from women
dissatisfied with the slaves they had hired. "One day's trial with Harriet
has convinced me she will not suit," Mrs. Jeffers wrote to Copes in 1859.
Jeffers insisted that Harriet was "too old," and indeed it is likely that
Copes hired out Harriet as a way to eke a few more dollars of profit out of
her as she reached old age. "I have no work that Rebecca can do in the position that you directed," Mrs. M. S. Wolfe informed Copes in 1844;
"therefore I have concluded to send her home until you think she is able to
perform her usual work, which is cooking, then you will be kind enough to
send her back." "Mrs. Harris is sorry to trouble Dr. Copes," began another letter in 1853, "but finds it impossible to get along with the servant
Cloe without her being punished. For the last week she has been particularly negligent. It is now nearly dinner time, and she has not been seen
since twelve o'clock. Of course her work remains undone." In 1855,
Emma Beard flatly refused to hire Hester again from Copes because "she
complains and lays up so much that she costs us the price of two servants."
All of these women were directly involved in the slave market, presiding
over the conjunction of market and household. Their letters suggest that it
may have been easier for white women to participate in hire markets than
sale markets because hiring transactions could, by and large, be carried out
by correspondence.[18]

Once they had hired slaves under their control, white women were as
consumed by the exercise of mastery as were men. As with men, their concern for mastery found frequent expression in the abuse of slaves. Louise
Jones was hired out by her mistress to work for what she remembered was
the "meanest white woman in the world." The woman treated her "so
mean" while hired out that Jones "took and run away from her." Henry
Bibb was also driven to run away by a woman to whom he was hired. At
the woman's house it had reached the point that he "dreaded to enter the
room where she was" because "she was every day flogging me, boxing,
pulling my ears, and scolding." Similarly, the woman who hired young
Harriet Tubman, intent as she was to "get the worth of her money to the

uttermost farthing," kept Tubman working night and day, inflicting indiscriminate beatings. Women, like men, turned to slave labor precisely because it allowed them to assume the position of master rather than merely of employer. When newspaper editor James Redpath asked a Virginia woman why she hired slaves rather than Irish servants to do domestic work, she replied that "when you hire a slave, if *you* like *her*, you can hire her from her master for seven or eight years, or as long as you like; but, if you hire an Irish girl, if *she* don't like *you*, she will leave sometimes in less than a month." The rewards of slave mastery were as compelling for white women as they were for white men.[19]

Renting slaves had mixed blessings for hirers in many ways, not least of all because the practice engendered simultaneous, conflicting feelings of independence and dependence. Though hiring slaves could provide entrée into the slaveholding ranks, it could also leave many hirers with a disturbing feeling of dependence on another person for slaves. Such feelings of dependence only aggravated the difficulty of trying to manage slaves over whom hirers could never exert more than a limited mastery. Hinton Helper, the racist Southern critic of slavery, knew how to hit hirers where it hurt. He labeled them "a kind of third-rate aristocrats," despicable wretches left "in their false and shiftless pride, to eke out a miserable existence over the hapless chattels personal of other men." With similar sentiments perhaps swirling in his own head, Georgia soldier Alf Bell, off fighting in the Civil War, was pleased to hear that his wife had purchased two slaves, primarily because the purchases would end the couple's reliance on hired slaves. "I hope we now can get along without having any thing to do with Loves negroes," Bell wrote to his wife, referring to the wealthy slaveholder from whom they had hired slaves. "I do crave to be independent and unbeholding to any body." Poorer hirers, as they struggled to scrape together enough money to continue hiring, were especially vulnerable to distress over their dependence on other people. Thomas Grimes informed Farish Carter in 1824 that Carter's hire price for a particular slave was more than he could afford to give, "yet such is my unpleasant condition," Grimes admitted, that "I must submit to your rates; men situated such as I am must do as they can and not as they please." Similarly, Alexander Campbell knew in 1841 that the owner of the slave he had hired could surely "obtain more for his labor than we can afford to give." Though Campbell was "reluctant to change him" for another slave who might be cheaper, he knew he "must yield to the necessity of the case." For hirers, the thrill of entering the master classes was often tempered by an equally strong resentment of their dependence on another person for slaves.[20]

During the 1850s, slave prices soared in the sale and hire markets alike, and hirers' natural resentment was piqued all the more. George Scarborough Barnesley recorded in his journal in 1859 that there was a "great demand" for slaves at hiring day in his region of Georgia—so great, in fact, that "several white people [were] grumbling at [the] price of negroes hired—at $150." Hirers usually placed the blame for escalating hire rates on calculating owners. Henry McCormick, who was hiring slaves for Virginia ironmaster William Weaver, reported to Weaver in 1855 that "those who have negroes to hire are holding off to the last moment." "You have no idea of the trouble there is in hiring hands here," he complained: "At this day, there is all sorts of trickery and management. I don't expect to be able to hire more than thirty or forty hands. We may get fifty, but I assure you the prospect is very gloomy." As hire rates escalated, so too did the hidden costs of renting slaves, and the difficulty for hirers was only exacerbated. In 1850, J. H. Gibbon moaned that five years earlier he could "hire 2 good hands for the sum I am to pay this season for one," noting that "the prices of food and clothing are also advancing" since "our merchants are not backward in using the advantages of such impulse." In 1853, William Carrick was sure that even doctors were taking advantage of rising prices for hired slaves in Norfolk, Virginia: "They hire very high down here for the next year. Everything has taken a rapid rise. Even the doctors have struck for double what they have been getting." Hemmed in by vigilant owners and assertive slaves in the frustrating triangle of hiring arrangements, hirers considered their mastery vulnerable even in the best of situations. Paying high prices for that limited mastery added insult to injury.[21]

As prices rose in the 1850s, therefore, hirers became even more adamant that the slaves they rented be considered fully *theirs* for the length of their contracts. Rising hire rates reinforced the notion that mastery was itself a form of property. "I will give you two hundred and twenty five dollars for Tom," John Faggart wrote to Archibald Henderson in 1853, "in which I consider him mine for the next year." Similarly, in response to an owner who demanded that his slave be returned, John F. Glenn asserted unequivocally, "Sir, I consider him mine till the time is expired that I hired him for." "I do not intend to be imposed upon if I can help it," Glenn asserted. Hirers struggled to find a workable middle ground between their dependence on other people for slaves and the absolute necessity of being able to stand firm as a master before all the slaves who worked for them. Their mastery, though, as much as they tried to make it absolute, was under assault from all sides. Hirers exercised their mastery under the watchful eyes of owners, within parameters set by Southern judges, and over resisting slaves who understood perhaps better than anyone else the inherent contradiction of a slave with two masters.[22]

Hirers and the Law of Slavery

Hirers were a frequent subject of consideration in Southern courts. Central to the cases that arose was an unresolved question that plagued hirers incessantly: In purchasing the services of slaves for discrete periods, did hirers also purchase the right to complete mastery over those slaves, including, for example, the critical right to whip with impunity? The question was not an easy one for Southern judges, who were in the forefront when it came to crafting not just the legal but the ideological underpinnings of the slave system. In case after case, Southern judges had always ruled that mastery over slaves was virtually inviolable, that by rights the only check on it would be the self-interest of each slaveholder in his or her own property. But hirers did not fit this schema. They had no readily apparent self-interest in the slaves they rented. What was to stop them, many owners asked, from abusing their mastery to the point of working slaves to death, and in the process assaulting the property rights of owners? With the exception of North Carolina's Judge Ruffin, who worried in the famous case of *State v. Mann* that the submission of slaves would end if hirers were not given full and absolute mastery, Southern judges dealt with the anomalous position of hirers by placing restrictions on their rights of mastery.

The North Carolina case *State v. Mann* (1829) is, in fact, a good starting point for discussing the legal conundrum that hirers presented to Southern courts. This case established unequivocally the right of all slaveholders to absolute control over their slaves, which included the right to inflict any punishments not already proscribed by state statutes. Judge Ruffin insisted, in an oft-quoted line, that "the power of the master must be absolute, to render the submission of the slave perfect." Contemporaries and modern historians alike have turned to the decision as a manifestation of the brutal root ideology on which slavery rested. Harriet Beecher Stowe insisted in *The Key to Uncle Tom's Cabin* (1854) that no one could read the decision in *State v. Mann*—despite Ruffin's elegant exposition, "so fine and clear in expression"—without being struck with "horror for the system." Eugene D. Genovese has adduced the case as the most faithful discourse on "the logic of slavery" ever written. While Judge Ruffin's decision has received abundant attention from scholars, lost in most analyses is the recognition that the case grew out of a dispute over the rights of hirers, not owners, to punish slaves. In all likelihood, the case would never have appeared before the court if it had not been complicated by the anomalies inherent in the hiring process.[23]

The facts of the case—those, at least, reported in trial transcripts—were simple. Sometime in the 1820s, in Chowen County, North Carolina, Elizabeth Jones hired her slave Lydia to John Mann. One day, Lydia "commit-

ted some small offence," for which Mann attempted to punish her. But as
Mann tried to carry out the beating, Lydia ran off. Mann shouted to her to
stop, and when she ignored his order, he shot her. John Mann was subsequently charged by authorities with assault and battery. North Carolina's
attorney general, conducting the prosecution, argued before Ruffin that
the applicable precedent was a case involving criminal conviction for
"battery on a slave by a stranger." In effect, he argued that a hirer did not
hold the same power of absolute and total mastery over a slave—which
would have included the right to assault and batter—that an owner would
hold. A hirer, according to the attorney general's argument, was more a
"stranger" than a proxy in the master-slave relationship.

The issue of mastery thus immediately became the legal and cultural cornerstone of the trial. The question at stake was straightforward: What
rights did hirers enjoy when they stood as temporary masters over the
slaves they rented? Ruffin's decision on this question became so famous in
large part because he considered a satisfactory answer to be central to the
preservation of the system of slavery. Disagreeing with the state's argument
that hirers were analogous to "strangers," Ruffin insisted that hirers must
be allowed to exercise the same rights of mastery as owners, or slavery, as
a social and labor system, would crumble. Ruffin ruled that since both
hirer and owner had the same "object"—"the services of the slave"—both
also had to share "the same powers." Since an owner could not be charged
with assault on his own slave—or, at least, as Ruffin noted, no one had yet
been charged with such a crime—no hirer could either. Without absolute
domination, no master could keep his slaves in submission, and the same
fact held true for hirers. "This discipline belongs in the state of slavery,"
Ruffin wrote: "They cannot be disunited, without abrogating at once the
rights of the master, and absolving the slave from his subjection." Absolute
power lay at the core of the master-slave relationship, Ruffin noted, and if
the right to use force was taken from either owners or hirers, the submission of slaves and, as a consequence, the system of slavery were at an
end. It is important to remember that *State v. Mann* was a criminal case.
Though Ruffin ruled that John Mann, as a hirer, could not be charged with
a crime in his shooting of Lydia, he and other hirers might be subject to
civil action by the owners of the slaves they rented. Ruffin's ruling, however, showed him to be unswerving in his conviction that owners and hirers were on equal footing in relation to the slaves they shared. Ruffin conveyed to all hirers the same rights that owners enjoyed.[24]

Ruffin's categorical equation of owners and hirers was more easily rationalized in legal theory than implemented in practice. His decision would
not be the last word on hirers' rights of mastery, because the question was

actually more complicated than Ruffin acknowledged. As dockets swelled with cases involving the actions of hirers, judges across the South realized that there were in fact practical differences between hirers and owners, and that those differences were not easily resolved. Ruffin, in the name of preserving slavery as a system, had simply ignored the differences between hirers and owners, by considering them one and the same in the eyes of the law. Other judges would find that hirers were indeed anomalous slaveholders, not lightly, or even appropriately, to be overlooked.

Consider the case of *James v. Carper,* which reached Tennessee's high court in 1857. According to the statement of facts in the case, Jane G. James had hired out her slave Bill to work as a servant in a public house owned by a man named Champ. Sampson Carper was a guest at the house, and one morning he mistakenly left $120 under the head of his bed. As part of his usual round of duties, Bill made up the bed in the morning. Later in the day, Carper realized that his money was missing and appealed to Champ. Both men confronted Bill, who proclaimed his innocence. Champ and Carper then confined Bill to a horse stall and beat him with a martingale, one of the straps that make up a horse's harness. Almost immediately after the beating, "it was ascertained that a vagrant white man about the house had committed the theft." The man was arrested, and he soon surrendered the money he had stolen.

The issue at stake in this case in both the low and high court was, again, the rights of a hirer to exert mastery over rented slaves. The judge in the lower court instructed the jury that "the owner of a slave had the right to inflict chastisement on him, and that the law had made no provision to determine whether it was right or wrong . . . except that the master had not the right to take away life or limb." He added, significantly, that "any one to whom a slave was hired for a definite period would for that time be substituted to the rights of the owner, and have the same right to punish or chastise the slave that the master would." His instructions to the jury thus echoed the position that Judge Ruffin had taken in *State v. Mann:* owners and hirers were virtually the same person in the eyes of the law. He directed the jury to find Carper innocent if the members determined that the hirer, Champ, had sanctioned the beating of Bill. The jury found him innocent.

When the case was appealed, Judge McKinney of Tennessee's highest court disagreed vehemently with the instructions delivered by the lower-court judge, especially with the judge's equation of the owner's and hirer's rights to mastery. Whereas Judge Ruffin in *State v. Mann* and the lower court judge in this case had deemed the absolute right of mastery best safeguarded by transferring that right to hirers, Judge McKinney noted that dividing mastery in such a way between owners and hirers actually raised more troubling problems than it solved. He maintained, conversely, that the absolute nature of mastery made it imperative *not* to divide it between two people. On this basis, McKinney "wholly" dissented from the proposition that the right to inflict punishment was "by mere implication of law, delegated to the hirer of the slave." "A more startling proposition to the slave-owner," he stated, "can scarcely be conceived." Making "such a delegation of power to a hirer," McKinney noted, would be the "last thing that the owner of a slave would consent to do." "One of the greatest dangers to the owners of slaves," he explained, "is the recklessness and wanton disregard, on the part of hirers, of the safety of the slave and the interests of the owners." Hirers, McKinney suggested, lacked the self-interest on which slavery rested in a liberal capitalist world.

To McKinney, the difference between owners and hirers was clear and inescapable, and that difference issued from the absolute nature of master-slave relationships. An owner, for example, "in virtue of his absolute right of property," could "take the law into his own hands" when punishing the behavior of his own slaves. But, McKinney insisted, "it is very clear that this may not be done by the hirer of the slave, or by a stranger." He admitted that hirers had to be given the power to inflict "reasonable corporal punishment" to ensure proper subordination, but this right was conveyed "in a qualified sense and to a limited extent" because it was a right which should "properly belong only to the owner." According to McKinney, the right to punish could only be absolute in the owner by nature of the owner's property rights (the hirer had property only in "the services of the slave in the business or occupation contemplated by the contract") and by nature of the relationship between masters and slaves. He drew an analogy to parent-child relationships to show that "certain peculiar rights" were characteristic of particular relationships and "from their very nature, are not to be absolutely transferred." The right of an owner to punish a slave and the right of a parent to discipline a child were both "inherent in the relation" between the two parties, and neither could ever be transferred to another person.

McKinney's ruling, if followed to its letter, would have made hiring a practical impossibility, for hirers would refuse to rent slaves they could not legally force to do the work they wished. McKinney recognized that difficulty. Hiring was a remarkably popular practice, one that would continue despite his ruling and despite his fervent belief that it damaged the ideological footing on which slavery rested. Hirers, he understood, had to be given a "qualified" right of punishment in order to keep slaves. McKinney added resignedly, though, that "the difficulty of defining with exact precision the limits of this qualified right in the hirer to chastise the slave of another in his employ, is very sensibly felt." How could anyone define that nebulous middle ground of mastery that owners and hirers by necessity had to share if they were going to divide their authority and transfer control over a slave? As Judge McKinney understood, no satisfactory answer lay ready to hand. This elision was the weak point that so many slaves were able to exploit when they were hired out. By running away to protest abuse by a hirer, for example, slaves exposed the contradiction of divided mastery and made it impossible to ignore. The competing property rights that sparked disputes between owners and hirers—and bedeviled Southern judges—was just the leverage that slaves needed in order to exploit their own value for subversive ends.[25]

Recognizing the *sui generis* position of hirers, Southern judges issued rulings on a variety of issues that in effect restrained the prerogatives of hirers as masters. Courts across the South ruled, for instance, that hirers did not enjoy the same rights as owners in putting slaves to work. Courts ruled that hirers had to seek permission from owners before setting hired slaves to do dangerous work. In *Mullen v. Ensley* (1847), a case involving a hirer who put his slave to blasting rock, Tennessee's high court ruled that "a bailee, who has hired a negro for general and common service, has no right to employ him in such an occupation without the consent of the owner." According to Alabama's Judge Chilton, hirers should always follow the standard that they had only "the right to employ [hired slaves] in any business to which slaves are usually put by prudent owners." Such restrictions seem sensible on their surface, but they were insidious in a society where mastery was assumed to be absolute. They were also exasperating in their vagueness. Did chopping wood with an axe qualify as "dangerous" work for a slave? Was working hired slaves until late at night "prudent" or "imprudent"? These unanswered questions kept hirers perpetually guessing, but on one point the courts were clear: hirers could never assume they had rights equal to those of owners. It would be a "mistake," Alabama's Judge Walker explained in 1860, for a hirer to assume he had "all the rights of a master during the period of bailment," or that he could "use or employ him in any way, or at any place, where or in which the master could lawfully use or employ him." "A master may, if he chooses," Walker concluded, "set his slave to blasting rock, immure him in an unhealthy mine, or put him before the mast on a distant voyage; but the hirer, under a general contract of hiring, has no right to do any of these things." Hirers thus had to worry not just about following the stipulations owners made in hiring contracts but also about what judges might later determine to be an inappropriate use of slaves on their part.[26]

The limitations on hirers' rights to employ slaves as they saw fit were explicit in the Florida case of *Kelly, Timanus & Co. v. Wallace* (1856). The case involved a slave named Peter who had been hired to a sawmill in Jacksonville for fifteen dollars per month. Peter himself informed the hirer that he could not swim, but the hirer nevertheless put him to work maneuvering logs from the water pen to the mill. Peter eventually drowned, and his owner sued, arguing that the mill owners had no right to use Peter for such dangerous work, even if the owner had failed explicitly to proscribe that work by contract. Judge Baltzell agreed, ruling that a hirer was but "the assignee" of the owner, a master by proxy in the most limited sense. Baltzell began with some rhetorical questions: "Now what is the extent of this power and authority of the master? Is it absolute, unlimited, uncontrolled?" The judge's answer was unequivocal: "By no means." A slave was subject to the mastery of his hirer, Baltzell maintained, "to the extent of his capacity and power, mental as well as physical," and it was "a duty on the part of the hirer to inform himself of this capacity." A sawmill owner who hired a slave, Baltzell ruled, did not have the right to employ hired slaves for all the tasks such an operation required. Rather, he had to limit work assignments to those which slaves were capable of performing. Hirers' rights to work slaves as they saw fit were not absolute, unlimited, and uncontrolled, as so many courts ruled they would be for owners. Hirers always had to be conscious that they held the property of another person in trust. The property rights of owners dictated how slaves could be treated and what work they could do.[27]

Crystallizing the idiosyncratic problems of divided mastery was the question of liability in the event that hired slaves ran away during the period of their employment. "The question is one of interest in a State like ours," opined Judge Walker of the Arkansas Supreme Court in 1852, "where slaves are held as property, and contracts of hire are of common occurrence." Indeed, as Judge Walker perceived, the issue at stake in such cases when they arose was *property*. Should a hirer be held liable, courts were asked, for the value of a slave who ran away while under that hirer's control? Courts routinely ruled in the affirmative. "It is one of the risks, both in contracts of purchase and hiring," South Carolina's Judge O'Neall pointed out in 1838, "that the slave may run away, and hence the party buying or hiring must sustain the loss." Hirers had to sustain the loss primarily because there was no other way to ensure proper treatment of slaves while hired out. Thus, in cases revolving around the flight of hired slaves, the mastery of hirers, rather than the behavior of slaves, became the focus of trials. It was true, Judge O'Neall noted, that a slave's flight could have been occasioned simply by the slave's own "volition" or any number of other "accidental circumstances," but the court could never be sure of this. "For it may be," O'Neall maintained, "that it arises altogether from the act of the hirers, and that no proof to that effect could be obtained." The burden was on hirers, then, when the slaves they rented ran away, to prove that the escape had not been caused by the hirers' own behavior. The centrality of self-interest and the market to the institution of slavery was especially evident in these cases. Simply assuming that hirers had no self-interest in the case of the slaves they controlled was enough to shift the presumption of guilt in instances of slave flight from the slaves themselves to their hirers.[28]

Southern courts also addressed the question of whether hirers should pay the entire year's hire price if the slave died before the expiration of the contract. Strict adherence to the tenets of common law, one of which is that an "act of God" should penalize no one, would have led Southern judges to the conclusion that hirers should not have to pay the full price in such situations. In an 1806 case in Virginia, the judge held just that way: "The court understands the rule to be, where one hires a slave for a year, that if the slave be *sick,* or *run away,* the tenant must pay the hire; but if the slave *die without any fault in the tenant,* the *owner,* not the *tenant,* should lose the hire from the death of the slave, unless otherwise agreed upon. By pursuing this rule, the act of God falls on the *owner,* on whom it must have fallen if the slave had not been hired; from which time it would be unreasonable to allow the owner hire—Hire!—for what?—for a dead negro!"[29]

But in these cases hirers posed a difficulty identical to that posed when slaves ran away. How could the courts know, if the slave was dead (and, if not, could not testify anyway), whether the hirer was at fault or not? Lawyers for owners came into court with the argument that hirers must always be held accountable for the hire, or else they could literally work slaves to death. One such lawyer in a Mississippi case in 1852 argued that "considerations of policy would dictate that the hirer should be held responsible for the whole hire, notwithstanding the death of the slave, for then the hirer is directly interested in bestowing every care and attention upon hired servants; but if he be not thus responsible, this salutary check of self-interest is removed." The only way to ensure that hirers felt a personal stake in the health and well-being of the slaves they rented, owners argued, was to hold them responsible for the full hire price if slaves died while under their control.[30]

The way this issue played out in Georgia courts provides an example of how the mastery of hirers became a divisive issue, one deeply influenced by class. Georgia courts held firmly to the conviction that a hirer must pay the entire contracted price when a slave died. In *Lennard v. Boynton* (1852),

Judge Lumpkin ruled that both "principle" and "public policy" dictated that hirers be held accountable in such circumstances. First, principle dictated that hirers be held to the contracts that they had signed of their own free will. Lumpkin held no stock in the argument that the slave's death, as an act of God, should not fall on the hirer. By way of explanation, he pointed out that "owing to the high price of cotton and other produce," Georgia slaves had been hired that year "at the most extravagant rates." A drought, however, had caused most of the crops in the state to fail. A hirer could just as well claim that the drought was an act of God, Lumpkin noted: "If the death of the negro would entitle him to relief, why should not this other Providential visitation?" "In our judgment, neither should," he ruled. The hirer "expressly stipulated to pay the hire; and however hard it may be upon him to pay wages for services which cannot be rendered, let it be kept in mind that he brought this hardship upon himself. It was his own voluntary act, and he has no claims upon the justice of the Courts to be relieved."

Lumpkin could have left his ruling there. His logic was solid: the contract was entire; hirers assumed the risk of death when they rented the slave; they must pay. But he took his argument further to insist that public policy—specifically, the protection of slaves—necessitated this treatment of hirers. Lumpkin continued his ruling as follows:

> Apart from the principle involved, motives of public policy forbid a rescission of this contract. Humanity to this dependent and subordinate class of our population requires, that we should remove from the hirer or temporary owner, all temptation to neglect them in sickness, or to expose them to situations of unusual peril and jeopardy. We say to them, go, and they must go; stay, and they must stay; whether it be on the railroads, the mines, the infected districts or any where else. Let us not increase their danger, by making it the interest of the hirer to get rid of his contract, when it proves to be unprofitable. Every safeguard, consistent with the stability of the institution of slavery, should be thrown around the lives of these people. For myself, I verily believe, that the best security for the permanence of slavery, is adequate and ample protection to the slave, at our own hands.

In short, hirers could not be trusted with the full arsenal of mastery because they lacked the all-important check of self-interest. The only way to ensure the "stability" of slavery, according to Judge Lumpkin, was to hold hirers financially accountable in all circumstances for the valuable property they temporarily held.[31]

The decision outraged Georgia's hirers. They undertook efforts to get the legislature to change the law in their favor, but on several occasions their efforts met with opposition from lawmakers. In public discussions of the issue, class became a dominant consideration. An editorial in the Milledgeville *Federal Union* weighed in on the debate, asserting that Lumpkin's ruling was "signally oppressive to the poorer classes of our citizens—the large majority—who are compelled to hire servants." When the issue arose again in Georgia's Supreme Court in *Brooks v. Smith* (1857), Lumpkin acknowledged the public uproar, but stuck to his decision. "I am aware," Lumpkin noted in his ruling, "that hirers, who constitute a large class, especially in towns, cried out against the decision when it was made." That was a "natural" reaction, Lumpkin observed, but he nonetheless considered his previous ruling appropriate, given that many hired slaves were "the property of women and minor children," that slaves were powerless to defy the "bidding" of their temporary masters "no matter how hazardous the service," and that hirers needed "strong inducement to take care of the negroes entrusted to their care." "Several sessions of the Legislature have since intervened," Lumpkin pointed out to his critics, "without changing the law. It never should be. It is founded upon the principles of justice, as well as humanity." The law stayed in place for the next four years. Then, significantly, on the eve of the Civil War, as state authorities rallied popular support for states' rights and slavery, the legislature reversed itself and passed a law that prorated the cost of hire in the event of a slave's death.[32]

When hiring disputes reached Southern courts, weighty issues were involved. To many participants in these trials, nothing less than the future of slavery as a system of labor seemed to hang in the balance. Hiring was so troublesome in these cases because it raised circumstances in which absolute mastery and absolute submission were dislodged from their customary social and legal places. As Judge Ruffin understood in deciding *State v. Mann* in North Carolina in 1829, whenever mastery became an issue in Southern courts, so, too, did submission: "We cannot allow the right of the master to be brought into discussion in the courts of justice. The slave, to remain a slave, must be made sensible that there is no appeal from his master; that his power is in no instance usurped." The implication here was that if slaves, or their proxies, could bring masters into court on accusations of abuse, then the domination on which slavery rested would be undermined. Ruffin no doubt understood that the same problem would arise if hired slaves appealed to owners, who could in turn prosecute hirers, as had occurred in *State v. Mann*. In any event, Ruffin categorically equated hirers and owners in their rights and prerogatives of mastery because he feared that doing otherwise risked exposing chinks in the slaveholding armor.

But the problem was not so easily remedied as Ruffin had assumed, and judges in later cases and in other states could not avoid the legal and ideological difficulties that hirers posed. Despite their efforts, judges simply could not assign hirers self-interest in this species of property, and, as a result, they held in ruling after ruling that owners were *primus inter pares,* that their long-term property rights had to be safeguarded by restricting the mastery of hirers. Hirers, of course, argued that, with their hands thus tied by the courts, they lacked the absolute authority that slaveholding required. As one lawyer for a hirer argued, if courts insisted on limiting his client's mastery (and that of other hirers as well), then "the rule of the master is at an end, and the slave becomes a freeman." Torn between guaranteeing the absolute property rights of owners and the absolute submission of hired slaves, judges leaned toward the former—Ruffin being the exception rather than the rule. Whether judges gave any thought to how these decisions would play out in houses, fields, and factories across the South is unclear, but hirers were more than cognizant of the effects. When they could, slaves made the most of the contradiction of having two masters, using it to shirk assignments, to avoid punishments, and generally to thwart their hirers' best efforts to exert mastery over them.[33]

"A Servant of Mine, and a Slave of You"

In 1845, William B. Randolph received a letter from a fellow white Southerner who had rented one of his slaves. Referring to the slave as "a servant of mine, and a slave of you," the hirer's phrasing exposed the fundamental fact with which all hirers had to come to terms. The slaves they rented would never be fully theirs. Owners, recognizing this state of affairs, limited contractually the powers that hirers could wield over slaves. Southern courts, recognizing the same, reined in the mastery that hirers could exercise under law. Perhaps most important, hired slaves recognized that hirers occupied relatively compromised positions of mastery. It was with slaves, not owners or judges, that hirers found the most vexatious checks on the mastery they so wished to exert. In various ways, slaves exploited the anomalous position of hirers in order to frustrate the aims of their temporary masters.[34]

Rendering slaves submissive was never an easy process for any slaveholder—indeed it was generally futile—but hirers especially found it difficult. Their difficulties stemmed primarily from the awareness on the part of the slaves they rented of the straitened conditions in which hirers were attempting to exercise their mastery; slaves were wise to the quasi control hirers could claim, and that knowledge shaped slaves' behavior. Frederick Douglass pointed out that slaves could "readily distinguish between the birthright bearing of the original slaveholder and the assumed attitudes of the accidental slaveholder." "While they cannot respect either," he explained, "they certainly despise the latter more than the former." A former slave whose life story was published in *Putnam's Monthly Magazine* in 1855 recalled the ways in which an awareness of being a slave with two masters altered his behavior. "Not believing that I owed service to any but the master over the mountains," he wrote, "I neglected my duties, and, in truth, was unmanageable." That kind of behavior exasperated hirers far more than any strict contractual stipulations or unpopular court rulings ever could.[35]

Hirers' difficulties with slaves began as early as hiring day, sometimes before transactions had even been carried out. On hiring days, hirers, milling about amid the crowds of owners, hiring agents, and slaves, intermittently stopped to discuss with owners or agents the particulars of price and other conditions for slaves who had caught their eye. Slaves did not necessarily stay mum during these conversations. Many boldly asserted themselves in the negotiations carried out between their owners and prospective hirers. Sister Harrison, a former slave, remembered that her father "used to go to the hiring grounds and tell the man what bought his services that he'd run away and leave him if he tried to beat him during the year." In 1854, Alma Hibbard, a Virginia teacher, accompanied her friend Mr. Sowers to hiring day, where she was shocked by the brazen behavior of some slaves. On the hiring grounds, her friend Sowers spotted a slave, "standing by his master." Being interested in hiring the slave, Sowers approached the owner to make an inquiry. As negotiations began, the slave did not simply let the two white men haggle away his future. He stepped forward to express his unequivocal determination not to go with Sowers. "I don't want to," he avowed, "I won't work for him." The remark angered Sowers but also strengthened his determination to have the slave, despite his opposition. Hibbard, recounting the episode in her journal at day's end, noted that Sowers eventually threatened not to allow the slave to see his wife during the year if he continued his insolent conduct. Sowers' experience at this 1854 hiring day was indicative of the difficulties that so many hirers had with the slaves they brought home. As any slaveholder would, Sowers resorted to threats when he believed his mastery to be imperiled by a hired slave, but hirers were not always free to carry out those threats, especially when they involved physical punishment.[36]

Henry Bruce had a similar confrontation with a prospective hirer on hiring day. On New Year's Day in 1855, Bruce's owner conducted negotiations with a tobacco factory owner named Mr. Beasley, a man Bruce had strong opposition to working for. "I did not want to go there," Bruce recounted in his narrative, "and told my master in the presence of Mr. Beasley." Beasley asked Bruce why he was so reluctant to work for him, and Bruce responded straightforwardly that he had "heard that he was a hard man to please." A negotiation ensued between Bruce and Beasley, during which Bruce's owner "remained silent." Eventually, Bruce reported, "Beasley and I came to terms." Afterward, Bruce's owner pulled him aside and scolded him for "speaking so harshly" to the hirer, but Bruce was glad he had seized the chance to put Beasley on his heels. "That was my opportunity to make easy sailing that year with Beasley," he observed in his narrative. Even before any money changed hands, slaves could use the inherent triangularity of hiring arrangements to their advantage and shape —whether negligibly or substantially—their relations with prospective hirers.[37]

Mastery was no more easily achieved once hirers brought their rented slaves home from hiring day. Hirers often fired off letters to owners in the first days or weeks after signing contracts, to complain that slaves had run away, had been impudent and unmanageable, or had simply refused to do any work at all. In late January 1855, D. B. McLaurin wrote to the man from whom he had hired Will to complain that the slave had run off "after disobeying a plain and positive order, besides giving . . . a great deal of insolence." Just a few days after hiring Edmund from Joseph Copes in 1845, Thomas J. Hawkins wrote Copes to inform him that Edmund not only had been working indifferently at the tasks assigned to him but also had been coming and going as he pleased. "He has scarcely been here half his time this week," Hawkins complained to Copes, "and when here does but very little." Hawkins suspected that Edmund was trying to use the distance from his owner to wriggle out of his duties. "I think it likely he may be dodging about Town thinking you believe he is doing his duty," Hawkins explained. The difficulty of controlling a slave who knew how to exploit belonging to two masters was too much for Hawkins. "If Edmund can do no better than he has done," he concluded to Copes, "I don't want him any more."[38]

As Hawkins' contretemps with Edmund suggests, hired slaves, recognizing their temporary masters' somewhat compromised position, often found a way to ignore orders. Slaves were no doubt aware, for instance, of the contractual limitations their owners had placed on the permissible types of work to be performed. Bill Smith, a slave hired along with Frederick Douglass to Edward Covey, returned one Monday morning after visiting his wife to find Covey and Douglass in the middle of a rancorous fight. Smith disregarded Covey's order to help subdue Douglass. "My master hired me here, to work," he remarked to Covey, "and *not* to help you whip

Frederick." "*This is* your work," Covey insisted, but to no avail. F. B. Deane complained to J. H. Cocke in 1835 that Henry, a slave he had hired from Cocke, was causing Deane to lose money by his "occasional indisposition" to do the work he had been assigned. Deane thought that Henry, who, when "in the humor for it," was a good worker, was "often out of humor and then his good qualities [were] much *obscured,* to say the least." Henry's "occasional indisposition" to work might have been a bane to any slaveholder, but hirers like Deane were especially susceptible to such behavior. Deane felt that his ability to deal with Henry was cramped, as is evident from his having written a letter to Henry's owner about the problem rather than simply disciplining the slave, as an owner would have been free to do.[39]

The triangularity of hiring arrangements made it easier for slaves to appeal to the authority of their owners in dealings with the men and women who hired them. F. B. Deane's problems with the slaves he hired from J. H. Cocke, for example, did not end with Henry. Deane also complained to Cocke that he was losing considerable work time from several other slaves because they insisted on visiting their wives. Deane confronted the slaves about their visits, but "when spoken to," he explained to Cocke, "they usually replied that you allowed them time to go." When slaves made such appeals to the customs or expectations of owners, hirers were forced to clear up the situation in writing. "I should like to know your mind about Tom," Samuel Dixon wrote to James McDowell in 1844. "His wife has gone to Augusta he says it is about 46 miles which will take him three or four days to make a trip and I do not like to let him go with out consulting you about it as I have such a small force I dislike the idea of his going very much though it is very hard you will please therefore say whether you will allow him to go or not and if so how often and whether he shall ride or walk." In 1850, with a very similar problem, Samuel Griswold wrote to Farish Carter that "Townshand . . . begs to know if you allow him time to go & see his wife." "If so, how often," Griswold inquired, adding "I can't afford to loose his time at the present price—. . . he is the dearest hand I have employed." Such letters were no doubt difficult for hirers to write, but they were forced by the circumstances of their position to follow up on the appeals that slaves made to the authority of their owners. As historian James Oakes has pointed out, the essence of mastery was not so much treatment as it was "the master's power over the intimate details of slave life." Hirers could rarely enjoy such pervasive and intimate control over the slaves they rented, not least of all because their power was continually called into question by the irksome propensity of slaves to play their two masters off against each other.[40]

Hirers were especially plagued when the slaves they rented lived within a short distance of their owners. Lewis Stirling, a plantation owner in Louisiana, hired ten slaves from his neighbor Mary Rusker in late October 1854. Consider just some of the many entries that Stirling made in his daily journal of the slaves' comings and goings: October 29: "Alfred went home sick tonight"; October 31: "Henry went home tonight with a sore foot"; November 1: "Alfred returned this morning"; November 7: "Major went home this morning at 9 o'clock sick"; November 21: "Charles disappeared this morning." It is impossible to know whether these slaves were actually sick, but it would not be implausible that hired slaves used their owners' concerns for their well-being to extricate themselves for short periods from work assignments. Consider also the experience of the Georgian Mary Bell with two hired slaves, Tom and Liza, after her husband left for war in 1861. Her problems stemmed not from her gender, or even from wartime disruptions, but from the fact that Tom and Liza belonged to a nearby slaveholder, Dillard Love. Indeed, the proximity of Love's place was a source of great difficulty in Bell's attempts to exert mastery over both slaves." "Tom has been at Dillard's all week," Mary wrote to her husband, Alf, in 1862. "I do not know what he is doing or whether he intends coming back or not. He does as he pleases." Bell had the same problem with Liza. "It is a hard matter to get Liza to do her work, she always has to gad about with Dillard's niggers when they are in town, which you know is often." Bell later wrote that she had "concluded to send Liza home before long," since the slave "goes when she pleases and comes when she pleases." Eventually, she decided to give up on hired slaves and purchase them because she was convinced slaves would be easier to manage—that is, easier to exert mastery over—if she owned them.[41]

When confronting such difficulties with slaves, owners could always resort to punishment. For hirers, the issue was not a straightforward one. Courts, as we have seen, did not recognize them as having all the rights of owners. Central to the mastery of all slaveholders was the prerogative to punish, when and as they saw fit, any slaves they found recalcitrant or insolent. Submission was not freely offered by slaves; it had to be wrought, by continual infliction of ritualized violence. Thus, hirers' mastery was vitiated most severely by the limitations placed on their right to manage slaves through brute force. Many owners insisted outright that hirers refrain from ever laying a hand, much less a whip, on their slaves. Henry Bruce's owner always "notified the hirer that he did not whip any of his grown slaves, and would not allow it to be done by anyone else." He ordered that, in the event hirers "could not get along" without punishing the slaves, the hirers "should return them to him." Similarly, Frank Bell remembered that his owner would hire out slaves "in slack times" but that "he never let no one whip his slaves." "He always told the white man who hired his slaves that if they didn't do right he was to bring them back and he would handle them, but not to hit any of his property." Likewise, Frederick Douglass remembered that on Edward Covey's farm "the hands hired temporarily"—except, of course, Douglass himself—"escaped flogging," including Bill Smith, who "was protected by a positive prohibition made by his rich master."[42]

Hirers frequently refused to keep the slaves of owners who demanded such special treatment. They found it impractical to try to manage slaves they could not punish as they saw fit. When Walter Baylor hired several slaves in 1851 to work in his brickworks, he informed their owner that he did not think there was "a single very bad negro in the whole lot." Such slaves he would refuse to tolerate. "If they cannot be reclaimed by strict discipline," Baylor informed the owner, "then I shall certainly return them." Hirers could not afford to keep slaves who refused to respect their mastery, for such behavior was infectious. "I cannot keep, in my service," one hirer explained, "negros to be treated differently from my own & others in the same service. All my hired servants must be subjected to the same treatment & submit to the same discipline . . . I regret having to adopt this course but you will upon a moments reflection, see the impolicy of keeping amongst a gang of negroes a portion to be more favored than the rest. It would prevent all just and efficient discipline."[43]

As we have seen, Southern courts did recognize that hirers had a "qualified" right to punish slaves into obedience, but even so, hirers often felt compelled to give owners advance notice that their slaves were going to be disciplined. That they could not act without first laying out their intention to punish, as well as the reasons behind it, was the crux of the compromised position in which hirers found themselves. Thus Mrs. Harris informed Joseph Copes in 1853 that she was finding it "impossible to get along with the servant Cloe without her being punished." Similarly, a hirer wrote to William Richardson in 1855, "The leading men of your gang have shown recently a decided disposition to resist authority and I expect in a few days to have to flog at least two of them severely." And in 1853, William Anderson wrote to Georgia planter Farish Carter to inform him of the conduct of Cyrus, a slave Anderson had hired: "He has acted very triflin indeed," Anderson told Carter, "so much so that I cannot git along with him with out abusing him more perhaps than you would like." On receipt of Anderson's letter, Carter replied in a letter to concede that Cyrus's "conduct as you represent it has him such as to merit punishment." He suggested that Anderson have a marshal put Cyrus in jail, and that Ander-

son might then "punish him every Monday morning . . . or punish him until you are satisfied." Though Carter was liberal in granting Anderson the
right to punish Cyrus, the exchange of letters itself was evidence of the restricted position in which Anderson found himself. He could not punish
Cyrus on his own, without the sanction of the slave's owner, and indeed
Carter remained the ultimate arbiter of whether the slave deserved to be
punished or not.[44]

Because the legal standard held that hirers should treat rented slaves as a
"prudent" master would, hirers often recounted their actions in terms of
what owners would do if in their position. "Your boy Anderson has behaved well during his stay with me," William D. Cabell wrote to Iverson
Twyman in 1858, "has not been whipped at all, though has been continually reminded of the fact that he would *certainly get it* unless he walked
very straight. I have treated him in every respect as I would one of my own
negroes, and just as I would have you treat mine should I ever hire to you."
Like this one, the letters from hirers to owners that express an imminent
need to punish hired slaves were equally tentative and assertive in tone.
Perhaps nothing could better exemplify the bind in which hirers were
caught, or the inevitable ambivalence they felt about hiring the slaves of
other Southerners. In these letters, hirers insisted on their right to punish
the slaves in their control, but at the same time they were rationalizing
their actions and hoping to secure the sanction of owners. As much as the
hirers wanted to convey the impression of acting with absolute authority,
the letters themselves were evidence of the extent to which their mastery
had been reined in by custom and law. The restrictions on hirers' behavior
did not preclude the abuse of slaves; in fact, those restrictions may have
made many hirers more disposed to lose their tempers.[45]

Slaves used hirers' ambiguous situation, when they could, to avoid punishment. The above exchange of letters in 1853 between William Anderson and Farish Carter regarding the behavior of Cyrus was actually initiated by Cyrus's insistence that he would never allow Anderson to punish
him. "He sais his marster don't whip him," Anderson recounted to Carter,
"and he will be damned if any other man shall strike him." In 1853, Henry
Bruce was hired to "a poor white man" named David Hampton, who one
day ordered Bruce to remove his shirt to receive a beating (for slapping
Hampton's son). "Of course I refused to obey and told him so in language
which he understood . . . ," Bruce recounted in his narrative: "I would be
ashamed of myself, even now, had I allowed that poor white man to
whip me." But Hampton did not give up, and as Bruce wryly noted,
"the fun came later." While Bruce was seated at a table eating his dinner,
Hampton's wife came at him from behind with a hickory switch. By employing his wife to punish Bruce, Hampton had turned the dynamics of the

situation in his favor. As a hirer, he lacked some leverage over the slave. But as a black man, Bruce lacked any means to resist the assault of a white woman. Bruce knew that he "could not afford to resist her," and he could not get away "until she had given me several blows." Bruce had tried to use the dynamics of hiring to escape punishment, but Hampton successfully trumped him by using the dynamics of sex and race.[46]

Hirers desired, more than anything else, to be recognized—by owners, by their peers, but, most important, by slaves—as masters. They were much relieved when owners made it clear to their slaves that they would have to obey their hirers as if they were their only masters. For this reason, John E. Jones, a railroad superintendent, was willing to pay John Buxton Williams more for his slaves in 1855 than he would other owners because, as he wrote to Williams, "you make your negroes know their duty to yourself and us, thereby relieving us of much unpleasant management." In the absence of such assistance from owners, hirers were often forced to return slaves who refused to respect their position of mastery. "In regard to Absalom," W. Gill wrote to Iverson Twyman in 1859, "I have to say I shall not want him this year. He does not appear to like his place here, and good treatment does not seem to agree with him." With their hands tied by owners, by courts, and even by the slaves they hired, hirers had an especially difficult time with intractable slaves. All that hirers wanted was to be respected as the masters they considered themselves to be, but hired slaves had just enough leverage, given the presence of another master, to sidestep their temporary masters' earnest efforts.

Indeed, hirers often realized that the only way to be considered full masters was to purchase slaves and thus assume a less ambiguous position as owners. John Rutherfoord, who had been hiring Adeline from William B. Randolph to wait on his daughter, inquired in 1855 whether Randolph would consider selling the slave. "We think that she would be more valuable," Rutherfoord explained, "and more disposed to give satisfaction, if owned by and altogether dependent upon my daughter as her mistress, than if kept any longer as a hireling and liable to change her place at the end of each year. Adeline is capable, and could be made, I think, valuable to one whom she could recognize as her owner." In 1856, the trustees of a South Carolina school decided to purchase slaves, rather than continue renting them, because the trustees deemed hiring "an expensive and uncertain system attended with many disadvantages." First among those disadvantages was the compromised mastery that made slaves more difficult to manage. "Little reliance" could be placed in a hired slave, the trustees asserted, for "it is with much difficulty, trouble and loss of time he can be kept at home." "The best policy," the trustees insisted, "is to purchase."[47]

Hirers lived with inevitable insecurity over their mastery. Their self-doubt manifested itself most commonly in vehement insistence that the slaves they rented be considered fully theirs for the period covered by hiring contracts. Given the reluctance of both owners and Southern courts to recognize such absolute mastery, hirers were that much more concerned with what slaves were thinking. A sense of mastery rested largely on the willingness of slaves to acknowledge it, so hirers needed to probe the feelings and intentions of the slaves they rented. Thus, the primary question on hiring grounds was something akin to "Will you obey my orders?" Hirers wanted to be masters, enjoying the social and economic rewards that such a position entailed in the slave South, but they needed slaves to play along.

Consider, for instance, a telling episode that Peter Still recounted of an occasion when he was confronted by his hirer. The hirer, Mr. Norton, questioned Still about where he had been one afternoon, and Still responded that he had been "up home." The word "home" set Norton off. "Where is your *home,* you rascal," he demanded. When Still replied that he had returned to "Mars Nattie's" place, Norton exploded: "I'll let you know, nigger, that this is your home, and that I am your master!" Peter Still understood all too well the dynamics of this confrontation. His hirer's identity as a master had been subverted by Still's reference to his owner as his "master." "It always made him angry," Still recounts in his narrative, "for one of his *hired* servants to call his owner, '*Master;'—it was his law* that in his shop no one should receive that ennobling title except himself." With the hiring of slaves came the title of master, the greatest cultural distinction conferred in the slave South. When slaves refused to recognize the position, it was too much for many hirers to bear. Such resistance made confrontations between Southern whites over the proper bounds of mastery all the more likely and also increased the likelihood of abuse.[48]

Harriet Tubman also recounted an incident in her narrative that exemplified the difference between owning and hiring a slave. The incident involved a slave named Joe who had "become so absolutely necessary to the planter to whom he was hired" that the man decided to purchase Joe. The sale was carried out, and Joe became the property of his former hirer. That the hirer had never felt completely in command of Joe as a hired slave was evidenced by his behavior in the aftermath of the sale. He went immediately to Joe's cabin, and though he had "no complaint to make" about Joe or his work, he demanded that Joe submit to a whipping. "You're a good nigger, an' you've always worked well," the man began, "but you belong to *me* now; you're *my* nigger, and the first lesson my niggers have to learn is that I am master and they belong to me, and are never to resist anything I order them to do. So I always begin by giving them a good licking. Now strip and take it." Mastery was central to life in the South, but for a hirer it could never be complete. Once this hirer became an owner, he was determined to make his domination absolutely unmistakable to the slave.[49]

For those who had call for the labor of slaves, hiring was promising and exasperating at the same time. The practice had much to recommend it. Most important, it was cheaper than buying slaves. And for many white Southerners, hiring offered their first taste of mastery. But that taste was precisely what so many hirers found frustrating. Their mastery was kept in check from so many different quarters that trying to play the role of master before hired slaves seemed an exercise in futility. Thousands of hiring transactions were conducted each year, so the practice continued apace, but each one of those transactions was fraught with tension—tension generated by hirers who believed fervently that they had purchased the right of complete mastery, by owners and judges who deemed such a perspective impractical, and by slaves who lost no chance to exploit the compromised mastery of those who held them. White Southerners could never escape the situation they had created: by defining mastery as a form of property—that is, by trying to make slavery fit in with the reigning capitalist ideology—they made division of that mastery increasingly difficult and acrimonious.

Resistance and Abuse

It was a concerted plan with the negroes to tell the tales they had
to to prevent their being sent back.

Samuel Drewry to John Buford, 1855

THE SHARPEST disagreements between owners and hirers were occasioned by the punishment of the slaves they shared. Physical correction of slaves was a daily occurrence in the South, but within hiring arrangements the dynamics, and the implications, of such punishment was
entirely different. Hirers considered the right to punish the slaves they
rented to be fundamental to the short-term mastery they had purchased.
But owners cringed at the thought of other people whipping their slaves,
especially when those people had no incentive to stop whipping once they
got started.

When slaves were hired out, they engaged in the same types of daily resistance that they did when they were on their owners' farms and plantations. They stole food, feigned illness, talked back, and refused to work.
Hirers responded in the way most owners would, by bringing out the
whip. Sometimes the whippings were especially brutal, and when they
were, owners and hirers were drawn into bitter conflicts and viewed the
situation from antithetical standpoints. Owners, who already assumed
that no hirer could be trusted to act "prudently" when meting out punishments, looked on abusive hirers as a threat to their property rights in
slaves—slaves they hoped to hire or sell in the future. Hirers, however,
maintained that extreme punishments resulted when slaves were inordi-
nately recalcitrant, not when they themselves lost control, and that to
forego the prerogative of beating slaves into submission would imperil
their mastery. Eruptions over hirers' treatment of slaves further fractured
white solidarity on the way slavery should function. And these eruptions
were inevitable, given that hired slaves belonged to two white households
at once. Both owners and hirers considered their claims to material suc-

cess, patriarchal honor, and social independence to be predicated on their ability to protect, control, and supervise all the dependents—but especially the slaves—in their households.

The flare-ups between owners and hirers always required a spark. Between hirers' abuse of slaves and owners' outbursts lay a crucial intermediary stage: the decision by slaves to report such mistreatment. Owners could not know how hirers treated their slaves unless the slaves informed them. Most owners found that their slaves were their most trusted informants, the best witnesses to whether hirers were living up to contractual stipulations about food, clothing, shelter, and punishment. It was on the subject of physical treatment that owners were especially reliant on slaves to serve as their eyes and ears. And, indeed, it was a common occurrence for hired slaves to run away from hirers before their terms expired, in order to report abuse to their owners.

The manner in which such situations played out from beginning to end—from a slave's anxious decision to flee and through roadside confrontations between owners and hirers to the eventual courtroom showdown (in which the slave's actions played a crucial role)—provides several important insights. The concrete particulars reveal the leverage that slaves with two masters often had and the way they used it to bring white people into conflict. By offering a look at how slaves presented themselves to their owners—as abused chattel or assaulted dependents—such situations illuminate the ways that slave hiring influenced relations between masters and slaves. We also gain insight into the powerful influence that slave resistance, even if not collective or aimed at overthrowing the slave regime, could have on master-slave relationships, on the law of slavery, and on the social relations of white people. The actions of hired slaves who ran away to protest abuse cause us to rethink both the local and the systemic effects of individual acts of slave resistance. In running away, these slaves exposed the contradictions of divided mastery, making it impossible to ignore that the property claims of owners and hirers were diametrically opposed.

Conventional wisdom in the South held that hirers, lacking as they did a lifetime investment in the slaves they rented, were the least likely of all Southern masters to trouble about the health and welfare of slaves under their control. Whether hirers were in fact crueler than other masters is impossible to determine empirically. But there was no doubt a kernel of truth in the perceptions about hirers, for owners frequently expressed exasperation, if only to themselves in their private diaries, about the outrageous cruelty of hirers. The Virginian William F. G. Garrett removed his slave from Brackets Tavern in 1844 because the slave "was so inhumanly treated that I considered it advisable for him not to return." In 1848, Nich-

olas Massenburg grumbled in his plantation record book that he would
have to confront the hirer of Mariah because the man treated her "*so bad* I
have to take her away." And when Jesse Thornton learned that his slaves
had been forced to work while sick, that they had been refused permission
to nurse their infants, and that one had been threatened with hanging, he
brought the hirer to court on accusations of "cruelty" and "inhumanity."[1]
These examples are important not because they are evidence of hirers' cruelty, for Southern slave owners carried out equally brutal beatings, but
rather because in each situation owners and judges learned about instances
of abuse by hirers from the slaves themselves.

There was an elemental power in such reports of abuse. By appealing to
owners, slaves played a role in determining the appropriate boundaries of
treatment; at a minimum, they made those boundaries a subject for debate
among whites. Such an outcome was what Judge Ruffin had feared when,
in his famous decision in *State v. Mann,* he held that a hirer had not acted
illegally when he shot his hired slave in the back as she ran away after a
brutal beating. "The slave, to remain a slave, must be made sensible,"
Ruffin insisted in his ruling, "that there is no appeal from his master; that
his power is in no instance usurped; but is conferred by the laws of man at
least, if not by the law of God."[2] Ruffin's reasoning did not correspond to
the reality of Southern slavery, however. When slaves had two masters
rather than one, it was easier for them to make the sorts of appeals he deplored—to play one master off the other. Ruffin also missed the extent to
which, for Southern slaveholders, the defense of absolute property rights
increasingly rivaled in importance the defense of absolute domination over
slaves. Owners and hirers were so resolute in their defense of their respective property rights that both parties overlooked the root of their conflicts:
acts of slave resistance. Perhaps even more surprising, in these property
disputes slaves served as material witnesses. The slave's very decision to
flee was invoked in courtrooms as tacit evidence against hirers. In short, if
slaves had stories to tell about abuse at the hands of hirers, then owners
and judges found themselves compelled to listen, and sometimes even to
invest those reports with greater credibility than they did the denials of
white hirers.

Telling the Story in Full

When she was bid off to a "poor white" man at a Virginia hiring day in the
late 1850s, Nancy Williams was no more than thirteen or fourteen years
old. Like so many other young girls hired out by their owners, Nancy Williams served her new master's family as a domestic slave. She cooked,

cleaned, and minded the baby. While working one morning, Williams heard the baby crying, ran to see what was wrong, and found the baby choking, its skin darkening from lack of oxygen. The anxious parents also rushed in and, seeing the baby, berated Williams for her negligence. A tongue-lashing was not all she was in for, however. The husband dragged Williams outside the house, tied her hands one across the other, threw her on the ground, and whipped her with a leather paddle "until [she] couldn't holler." As soon as she could breathe again, though, Williams got up and ran toward her owner's home. She stayed away from the road, where the hirer had taken pursuit—he surely knew exactly where she was headed. Williams, with blood streaming down her legs and one remaining piece of clothing stuck around her waist, reached her owner's home just before the hirer did, and there she "fell on the door and almost busted it open."

The owner's surprise at finding Williams on his front porch quickly turned to shock at her battered appearance. Williams no doubt quickly tried to explain all that had passed, as her hirer appeared in the front yard. Her owner's immediate response succinctly captured the dynamics of the confrontation, for it combined an accusation of transgressed honor and authority and a reassertion of prevailing property rights: "What have you done to my nigger?" he yelled at the hirer. Reaching for the gun he kept just inside the front door, the owner started after the hirer: "I got great mind to kill you right where you is! Damn you! Get home to your lazy wife and nurse your own baby. You shan't have this nigger no more, neither the money for her." He chased the hirer from the yard "like he was hunting rabbits," Williams remembered later. Spared from serving the man any longer, Williams returned to the community of slaves from which she had been separated. "First thing they did," she recalled, "was grease me and get me well."[3]

Nancy Williams exploited the fact that she had another master. She knew that there was a very good chance that her owner would intercede on her behalf once she told him her story. Neither her story nor her course of action was unusual. Hired slaves across the South shared similar experiences of running to their owners to protest abuse they had endured while living with temporary masters. Many slaves confronted their hirers before their owners became involved, but when things got intolerable, they fled. The result was not always what they had hoped—some were sent back immediately to their hirers—but many slaves would have recognized their own experience in Nancy Williams'.

That experience had some notable incongruities. Williams apparently went unpunished for having run away; in fact, her transgression secured two significant advantages: she no longer had to work for the hirer, and she was able to return to a slave community prepared to "get [her] well." The second peculiarity in Williams' experience was that two white men nearly came to blows, nearly killed each other even, over the word of a slave. Racial solidarity in the slave South apparently had its limits when property rights were at stake.

The confrontation might not have occurred had Nancy Williams not decided to run away. In all likelihood, her owner would have been unaware of the assault had she not reported it to him. But such a decision to abscond was not easily made. The Georgia supreme court ruled, for example, that runaway hired slaves could be tracked with dogs, provided only that the pursuing dogs would not "materially injure the slave." (How that could be guaranteed, if indeed it could, the court did not spell out.) Backcountry roads were dangerous places for runaway slaves, whether they were running to freedom or away from abuse. Fifteen-year-old Mehala was found dead "on or near the way" leading from her hirer's place to her owner's; though the cause of death was unclear, her owner thought that she had been coming to report the "ill and inhumane treatment" of her hirer. Getting caught was a real possibility for runaways, and the result could often make a bad situation worse. When he ran away, William Wells Brown did not make it far before he was caught by the dogs that his hirer had set after him. He was taken back to his hirer's place, tied up in the smokehouse, and "severely whipped." Fearing such an outcome, many hired slaves put off the inevitable until it was absolutely necessary. For instance, after watching his friend Ike get whipped for supposed indolence, Henry Bruce was tempted to "break and run" to his master, but he decided not to take that fateful step until called to take his "share of this thrashing." Eventually, though, he opted to "take chances on being shot" because he "could not and would not stand such punishment as was given Ike." Bruce's fear of being shot was not unfounded. Recall that in *State v. Mann* Judge Ruffin vindicated a hirer who had shot a slave in the back as she ran away to protest a beating.[4]

Surrounding every slave's decision to flee was a swarm of unanswerable questions: Will I be able to make it all the way home without getting caught? If I do make it back, how will my owner respond? Should I present myself as an abused person or as abused chattel? What if he sends me back? Will I just be worse off then? Moreover, this mental reckoning regularly had to take into account another factor: a battered body. For most runaway hired slaves, an instance of serious abuse had been the catalyst that led them to decamp. Fleeing several miles was hard enough; fleeing with bruised muscles and bleeding wounds required a desperate energy difficult to summon. If slaves brought their white masters into conflict, it was only at great risk to themselves and in the face of dismaying uncertainty about how owners would respond. A slave's decision to flee was ultimately an act of self-reliance.

Frederick Douglass's experience with Edward Covey provides a good example of how hired slaves assessed the situation before making their escape to protest harsh treatment. Covey was an especially brutal hirer, but Thomas Auld, Douglass's owner, had chosen this famous "negro breaker" because Auld wanted Douglass stripped of his willfulness and impudence. It thus took an especially heinous beating to induce Douglass to consider an appeal to his owner. After claiming one hot day that a burning headache prevented him from working any further, Douglass incurred several wrathful kicks from Covey. When his head cleared, Douglass was left with a difficult choice: "Shall I return to my work, or shall I find my way to St. Michael's, and make Capt. Auld acquainted with the atrocious cruelty of his brother Covey, and beseech him to get me another master?" Douglass had to admit that given Auld's original objective in hiring him to Covey—having him broken—"there was little ground to hope for a favorable reception." But he decided to make a run for it anyway. The prospect was daunting. The direct route to his owner's home in St. Michael's was seven miles, and Covey was sure to follow. Douglass was exhausted from exertion and loss of blood, able to feel bruises appearing where Covey's boots had struck his head and torso: "I was, in every way, in an unfavorable plight for the journey."[5] As it did for Douglass, the decision to flee involved formidable issues for other hired slaves, not least of which was what stamina they could call forth in their sad condition for an arduous trek.

Douglass's next dilemma involved determining how to present himself to Auld once he arrived in St. Michael's. Any hired slave would have had doubts about how an owner would respond, but for Douglass the chance of asylum seemed especially dubious. He needed to pique the sentiments that would most likely rouse Auld to action in his defense. Should he appeal to his owner's "motives of humanity," or was it best to strike the chord of "selfish considerations"? Douglass ultimately appealed, as most hired slaves did, to both the "humanity" and the "interest" of his owner. Reasoning that Auld would not "allow his property to be thus bruised and battered, marred and defaced," Douglass resolved to tell him the "simple truth" of how he had been treated. He pleaded with Auld for "the interposition of his power and authority, to protect me from further abuse and violence." Significantly, Douglass demanded protection not because it was inherent in their personal relationship as master and slave, but rather because it was the prudent way to deal with valuable slave property.

Douglass insisted that Covey would "ruin [him] for future service," perhaps even kill him.[6]

Like all hired slaves who ran to their owners, Douglass painted a clear picture of egregious brutality, all in the hope that an ensuing battle over property rights would occasion his release from the abusive hirer. But Auld's response was the one that hired slaves dreaded. Auld launched into a "full justification" of Covey and a "passionate condemnation" of Douglass. In this case, Auld was probably adhering to his original intention to have Douglass "broken" by whatever means necessary. "You belong to Mr. Covey for one year," Auld made clear, "and you *must go back* to him, come what will." But Auld may also have been gambling Douglass's long-term resale value against his short-term capacity to serve as a source of quick cash. "Besides, if you should leave Covey now," Auld added, ". . . I should lose your wages for the entire year." Auld dispatched Douglass with a warning not to bother him any more with stories about Covey. (Several years later, when Douglass was beaten by white workers in a Baltimore shipyard, Auld's response was different, perhaps because Douglass was then paying over high wages as a self-hired slave. In that instance, Auld was deeply angered by the beating, and as Douglass discerned, the response "resulted from the thought that his rights of property, in my person, had not been respected, more than from any sense of the outrage committed on me *as a man*.")[7]

Douglass was not alone in such disappointment. Other hired slaves also encountered indifferent owners, and they found that having two masters, so far from offering a source of leverage, only made life doubly bad. When Ned and William ran away from their hirer in 1857, for example, their owner "whipped them severely and told them if they ran off again and were brought to me, or came to my house, I would give them a thousand." When owners sent slaves back to abusive hirers in this way, they usually did so because they were more interested in securing short-term cash returns than in safeguarding the long-term value of their slaves. Thus, when William Wells Brown complained to his owner about the violent fits of anger to which his hirer was prone, "it made no difference" because his owner "cared nothing about it so long as he received the money for my labor." In 1860, Cornelia complained to her owner, Dick Coleman, about her hirer, but Coleman simply whipped her and sent her back to the hirer. Coleman did send a letter to the hirer, though, to tell him that he would gladly take Cornelia back if the hirer so desired, for he had found someone who was willing to pay even more for her. Once these slaves were back with their hirers, their situations were even more dire than they had been previously because the hirers now knew that the slaves could have no recourse to owners in the event of future beatings. Aaron, given fifty lashes by his hirer for leaving a knife "not as clean as it might have been," ran away from the St. Louis hotel where he worked but was sent directly back by his owner. The hirer then "gave him a more severe whipping than before."[8]

Sometimes it took repeated appeals to get an owner to act. In 1853, Randall ran away and returned to his owner, who promptly "delivered him up" to the hirer, but Randall ran away again. This time, his owner offered to forego the $150 he would have received for Randall's hire, perhaps judging that it was more prudent to preserve Randall's future hiring value at the expense of one year's wages. Sometimes owners needed to see the behavior of hirers for themselves before they agreed to remove slaves from their employment. In 1810, William Flournoy hired out his slaves to work in Railey's coal pits in Virginia, but they ran away during that year and returned to Flournoy. Flournoy brought the slaves back to the coal pits "without delay," but when the owner of the pits prepared to "correct" them for having run away, Flournoy declared that the man "should have nothing to do" with the slaves. Flournoy had personally delivered up his slaves when he decided to give their hirer a second chance, but not all owners could do so. Sometimes, these owners relied on their slaves to serve as informants. In 1854, an owner in Arkansas sent his slaves back to their hirer when they ran to him, but he told them that they should "come home again" if the hirer "should hit them a lick." It was just the hook the slaves needed. Sure enough, they ran away again, and this time the owner "kept and harbored them, and . . . refused to deliver them up."[9]

Even if slaves were not sent back to their hirers immediately, some owners still wanted to impress on slaves that determining abusive behavior was a white prerogative, not a black one. These owners understood that the ramifications would be profound if slaves were led to believe that they could play a role in delineating the boundaries of "proper" slave mastery. Peter Still was whipped severely by his hirer and several of the hirer's friends, but with the "little remaining strength" left in his body he "crept" to his owner's home. His owner had not a "gentle word" for him, but Peter had "guessed rightly" that his owner, though himself also extremely cruel, would bridle at the sight of "his property thus damaged by others." The owner's reaction was a careful one, though. He privately sought out the hirer and "cursed him roundly" for the abuse inflicted on Peter, but he also refused to intimate in any way to Peter that "a white man could do him wrong." Nevertheless, Peter's life improved tangibly (and he clearly learned, in some way, of his owner's rebuke of the hirer). He was allowed to stay at home for a week before being sent back, and even then he never again received so much as an "unkind word" from the hirer. Another owner wrote to a hirer in 1852 that he was sending his slave back to work, conceding that the slave's conduct had been "almost unpardonable." He asked, however, that the hirer "pass it over in silence," claiming that he had taken the slave and "chastised him severely." But the slave's working conditions did improve: the owner also asked that the slave not be put back under the overseer against whom "his principle complaint seemed to be lodged." Neither this slave nor Peter Still probably took away the lesson his owner had hoped he would. Each surely discerned that to influence debates among white people over what constituted "proper" mastery, it was imperative to raise the specter of violated property rights.[10]

As mentioned, slaves and their hirers sometimes came into conflict even before the confrontations escalated to include owners as well. In these conflicts, hired slaves had more leverage than other slaves might have had because they could more easily cite their value as property to influence the behavior of hirers. John Thompson's battles with his hirer, Mr. Barber, offer a good illustration. On one occasion, Thompson actually seized a whip as he was being beaten by Barber and struck the hirer on the head with it. Barber called constables to pick up Thompson and threatened to have him punished by a magistrate. Thompson swore that if he suffered any whipping it would be "the last time" on Barber's farm. Asked what he planned to do, Thompson candidly and tersely replied, "Run away." He then spelled out the situation clearly for Barbour: "If you whip me so that I am unable to walk, I can do you no good; but if I can walk, I will take the balance of the year to myself, and go home to my mistress at Christmas." The laws in most Southern states required hirers to pay for any time lost by a slave's flight as well as any costs incurred in capturing the slave. The laws were intended to protect the property rights of owners, and they were interpreted by judges who worked under the assumption that slaves fled hirers in response to excessively harsh treatment. Thompson thus used the laws, and their underlying assumptions, to his advantage, for he understood that he was making a weighty threat when he promised to run away. Not at all pleased by the thought of paying for a missing hired slave, Barber told the magistrate he would "forgive" Thompson this time. Hirers like Barber had to monitor their actions not because owners were necessarily nearby, but rather because, first, they knew that slaves could (and would) run away and, second, hirers could not be sure that they would win my-word-against-his arguments before owners. Because owners' contractual stipulations and judges' views on "proper" slave mastery for hirers were difficult to enforce on a practical level, the surest check on hirers' behavior was often slaves themselves.[11]

On more than one occasion, John Thompson proved to be a savvy manipulator of the unique legal and political dynamics of hiring transactions. The next time a hirer (Mr. Hughes this time) caught him in a transgression (visiting women on a neighboring plantation), he was brought before a magistrate, tried, and given a public whipping. The hirer probably wanted to avoid any possible impressions of misconduct on his part, so he had the punishment carried out legally by the appropriate authorities. But when released, Thompson went straight to his mistress and "related to her the whole story." The mistress was outraged, and the reasons for her anger are significant. She felt that she had been "imposed upon" because she was a single woman—that the hirer and the magistrate had "grudged her her property." There may have been something to her complaint, but male owners would have responded in the same way.

In these clashes, the slave's flight dropped from view, as the two whites battled over whether the slave's beating should be read as a rightful assertion of mastery over a recalcitrant slave or as an unwarranted usurpation of mastery not transferred by the hiring contract. Slaves watched these battles and gleaned valuable insights into the feelings that animated the men and women who held them in bondage. John Thompson's mistress, for example, had him repeat his story to her brother Richard, whose response was extreme but not unusual. He first went to the hirer's home and (in front of Thompson) berated him for the severe beating. He then demanded the name of the magistrate and took Thompson with him. When the two of them entered the office, the magistrate, on recognizing Thompson, "suspected something was wrong, and commenced explaining before being asked." Richard berated the magistrate and then used a horsewhip on the constable who had actually carried out the beating. The experience was no doubt startling for Thompson. It was not every day that a slave witnessed the beating of a white man—a constable no less—because of a story that he had told of his mistreatment. The feeling was probably the same for Nancy Williams as she watched her owner chase her hirer "like he was hunting rabbits." Such situations were a clear reminder to slaves of the powerful role property rights played in the social relations of Southern whites, a reminder of the ways that they could use their own value to bring white people into conflict.[12]

Like John Thompson and Nancy Williams, other slaves also found that their masters responded in the ways that they had hoped. Harve remembered an overseer ordering that he be whipped after he had broken a hoe handle while working on his hirer's cotton crop. Harve "broke and ran" to his owner's place, where he "told the story in full." The overseer came after him, but Harve's owner refused to turn him over, preferring instead to void the hiring contract. Mary Carpenter's mother, rented to a neighboring planter toward the end of the Civil War, also defied her hirer's attempt to whip her: "My ma had never been whooped in her life," Mary remembered, "and wasn't going to allow no white man who didn't own her to touch her." When the hirer went off to get help in whipping her, Mary's mother sent a young slave to alert her owner. The hirer and two accomplices had just succeeded in tying her to a tree when her owner "loped up on his horse just in time." The owner warned off the hirer, cut Mary down from the tree, took her home on his horse, and kept all the money paid for her. Similarly, when Gabe ran from his hirer in Alabama, his owner ignored the hirer's demands that Gabe return immediately and "refused to let him go back again."[13] These slaves learned that they held some small power, even as they were claimed as property by two white men at once. They decided that particular beatings were outside proper bounds of mastery, and they saw those decisions ratified by their owners. It was not lost on these slaves that it was their value as property, not their status as dependents, that brought about their owners' intercession. That knowledge could be used again and again.

Making reports of abuse and exploiting the outrage of owners was much more difficult for slaves hired out at great distances. But not impossible. Twice in January 1852 Hetty went to the home of M. A. Franklin, who she knew was a friend of her owner, to make, according to Franklin, "desperate complaints of bad treatment by the people who have hired her this year." She "begs me to write to you on the subject," Franklin wrote to Farish Carter, Hetty's owner. Franklin professed not to know anything about Hetty's hirer but was inclined to think, "from her bruised appearance," that Hetty's protests were probably well founded. Similarly, Grandison ran away from his hirer in 1839 and appealed to a relative of his owner, asking the man to write a letter to his owner outlining his complaint. The relative subsequently made a "strict inquiry" into the "character" of the hirer, finding that he was indeed considered by many "a very drunken ill tempered man." Grandison did not have to return. If they could find no one locally in whom they could confide their difficulties with hirers, determined slaves set off on long trips to see their owners. In 1855, Simon was whipped by his hirer and ran away, making it to his owner's home a full two weeks later, at which time he still "bore on his back, arms and legs, the marks of a severe whipping." Hetty, Grandison, and Simon no doubt understood that to make their owners indignant over the abuse of their property, they had to be *seen* by their owners, or at least by one of their acquaintances. In 1846, when several of James McDowell's slaves reported their hirer's harsh treatment to their owner's agent, the agent informed McDowell that "the talk is not without color, for these boys and Henry look badly, having grown little or none and always dirty and badly clad."[14]

After running away, hired slaves often found that their lives improved in tangible ways. Most important, they extricated themselves from living situations in which they felt perpetually threatened with bodily harm. Many of them—Nancy Williams is an example—were able to return to communities from which they had been separated while hired out. But, equally significant, hired slaves achieved these changes through a daring act of assertiveness that most often went unpunished. It is easy to forget that by running away these slaves were violating the slave system's bedrock principle: the total subordination of slave to master. Horace Cowles Atwater, a traveler in the South, noted with surprise that hired slaves were not only "very apt to betake themselves to the woods" and return to their masters but also quite likely to "escape all punishment."[15] Owners wanted to protect their property rights in slaves who were hired out and relied on reports of abuse from those slaves at every step. Slaves who ran away to make such reports placed their owners in the unenviable position of having to overlook a serious transgression—a reaction that could haunt both individual masters and the system in the long run. By running away and telling their stories, slaves cultivated a self-reliance that forestalled psychological dependence on protective owners, even when they appealed to the intervention of those owners. Moreover, their actions exposed the fundamental brutality of Southern slavery, gave powerful witness to slaves' rejection of their enslavement, and, not insignificantly, limited the possibility of their being hired out to abusive men and women in the future. But more than anything else, slaves were confirmed in their suspicion that property rights —the slaves' own commodification—lay at the heart of white social relations. The political effects of their individual acts of resistance rippled beyond particular master-slave relationships, beyond individual farms, to Southern courtrooms and white social relations.

"Your Man Told You Lies"

One right that Southern courts deemed impossible to transfer from owners to hirers was "the duty of protection." Owners had the right to protect their slaves from abuse, even while the slaves were hired out and even if the abuse was inflicted by their slaves' temporary masters. In fact, some judges did more than grant owners the right to take slaves from abusive hirers; they instructed owners to do so. "Of course the master should protect his slave against the inhumanity of those to whom he may be hired," ruled a

Missouri judge in 1853: "For ill-treatment a master ought to interfere, and take his slave from the employment of those who are guilty of such conduct." Such situations were distinguished by a threshold of violence that judges and owners considered unacceptable. "The hirer by his contract, acquired the right of enforcing obedience by moderate correction," South Carolina's Judge O'Neall explained in 1831, but if he "transcended and abused his authority," then "the right of personal protection belongs to the master." The difficulty, of course, was to determine that threshold, the exact point at which a hirer "transcended and abused his authority." Where did a hirer's right to "moderate correction" end and an owner's right to "personal protection" begin? The question was especially difficult when hirers and slaves were the only witnesses to abuse. Even though slave testimony was forbidden in Southern courtrooms, judges routinely read the actions of slaves to determine the liability of hirers.[16]

In 1837, Judge O'Neall spelled out the reasons for which owners should retain the right of protection during terms of hiring. The rationale grew out of the awkward relation between slavery and capitalism. The right of protection derived, O'Neall maintained, from slaves' dual status as both property and dependents. "In the case of hiring a slave," O'Neall explained, "the hirer acquires a right to his services for a limited period, but the general interest and rights of property . . . remain in the owner." In order to protect the value of slaves, owners had to be allowed to step in and remove slaves from abusive hirers. "Slaves are our most valuable property," O'Neall pointed out: "for its preservation, too many guards cannot be interposed between it and violent unprincipled men." A hirer without self-interest in slaves was as much a threat, it would appear, as any abolitionist, if for different reasons. But the right of protection also had to be reserved for owners because of the dependent and unfree status in which slaves were kept in Southern society. "Slaves, although chattels personal, cannot in every respect be treated by the rules which apply to and govern personal estate," O'Neal noted: "They are human beings, with passions and feelings like our own, and . . . , if in a state of nature, would have the right of self-protection, which is given by the great Creator to every human being." In their transfer from a state of nature to a state of slavery, O'Neall maintained, slaves did not lose the right to self-protection; it was merely shifted from them to their owners. The two rationales outlined by Judge O'Neall were interconnected: owners provided the protection that slaves, as human beings, deserved only because those slaves were also valuable property in which the owners had invested. The same could not hold true for hirers, who merely rented slave property. The significance of this logic for slaves was that when they appealed to owners they had to emphasize their status as valuable property, even if they also presented themselves as abused dependents.[17]

The "duty of protection" reserved by owners during hiring transactions, according to Judge O'Neall, suggests a paternalist conception of master-slave relationships grounded in an organic sense of reciprocal obligations. In this view of master-slave relationships, slaveholders provided protection and the necessities of life in return for the labor performed by their slaves. "Under such a state of things," opined a contributor to *DeBow's Review* in 1855, "the master knows the man; the man, his master. The master feels confident that the man is attached to him, and will consult his interest. The man feels confident that the master will only require what is right of him, and will abundantly provide for all his wants and that of his family." When owners assumed such a view of their position, slaves found in paternalism itself as a weapon of resistance, for it gave them occasion to demand certain rights or privileges from their owners. But such a strategy had its costs, for in asking for rights from their owners, slaves implicitly conceded that those rights did indeed flow from their captors. Paternalist relationships drew slaves into a dialectic of accommodation and resistance to slavery: as they made demands of their owners as paternal protectors, they gained some rights and privileges, but they simultaneously reinforced the paternalism that legitimized slavery in the eyes of their masters. At its theoretical best, paternalism circumscribed the political power of all slave resistance that fell short of outright revolt, by containing it within the unbroken circle of a single slave and single master.[18]

At first glance, the paternalist conception of master-slave relationships seems readily to explain the actions of hired slaves who ran to their owners to protest harsh treatment. To be sure, these slaves were resisting the inherent cruelty of their enslavement, but they were also appealing to their owners for protection, an act that, while successfully achieving certain aims, implicitly legitimized slaveholders' interpretation of slavery as an exchange of paternal protection for bonded labor. By running to their owners, hired slaves could be seen as having accommodated to the very system they were resisting. According to such a view, their actions were not ultimately threatening to master-slave relationships overall.[19]

But on closer look, the actions of abused hired slaves suggest the need to rethink slaves' relation to the paternalist world of their masters. The evidence of how hired slaves pitched their appeals for protection—that is, what exactly they said to their owners—is unsurprisingly scant, but the hints that do survive in the record are telling. Evidence from slave narratives suggests that hired slaves demanded that their owners fulfill their roles as protectors on the basis of the slaves' status as property, not because they felt it was due to them as part of a reciprocal relationship. Recall Frederick Douglass's thoughts regarding his owner as he fled from Edward Covey: "'He cannot,' thought I, 'allow his property to be thus bruised and battered, marred and defaced.'" Or Peter Still's surmise, when beaten by his hirer, that his owner "would not like to see his property thus damaged by others." These slaves were requesting protection, and they were demanding that their owners fulfill certain duties, but they were not necessarily falling into a paternalist trap. They approached their owners in the guise of property rather than as dependents.[20]

For most slaves, the paramount oppression of slavery was being owned by another human being. Insecurity of family life, lack of rights, deprivation, cruelty—all of these stemmed from the unavoidable fact that slaves were property. Former slave James Pennington wrote that "the very being of slavery, its soul and body, lives and moves in the chattel principle, the property principle, the bill of sale principle; the cart-whip, starvation, and nakedness, are its consequences to a greater or lesser extent, warring with the dispositions of men." Such a view explains why most slaves found even the most paternal master ultimately insufferable. But the very enormity of slavery in slaves' eyes was also their most potent weapon. Slaves had a value—in the fields, at hiring day, on the auction block—that their masters were interested in safeguarding. Slaves demanded rights and privileges, but they understood those rights to emerge not so much out of an organic relationship between master and dependent as out of a deeply "interested" relation between an owner and his property. There are suggestions that owners felt the same way. "Of all the motives which influence the intercourse between men," noted a writer in *DeBow's Review* in 1855, "*interest* is certainly the strongest." From this fact flowed "the motive of the master in taking good care of the slave, and thus extending the time of his usefulness." Furthermore, as South Carolina's Judge O'Neall maintained in 1837, owners retained the "right of protection" because they, and not hirers, had a property stake in hired slaves. It is important to recognize that when slaves appealed as property to their owners—a status slaves never internalized—they did not implicitly legitimize their positions as slaves. And as long as slaves prevented the conflation of property and self—as they succeeded in doing through day-to-day resistance, the culture of the quarters, and religion—they were resisting the system, forcing it to sustain itself through a violence that was ultimately antithetical to slaveholders' property interest.[21]

Even those slaves who may have approached their owners as dependents, as no doubt many did, should not necessarily be seen as reinforcing the hegemony of their masters. If slaves thought that their particular owners would be likely to respond to appeals made to their paternalism, they probably did so. In these instances, slaves had an important stake in maintaining the appearance of the masters' domination. But the apparent accommodation on the part of these slaves was in itself an act of resistance.[22] By placing their owners in the position of "protector," these slaves asserted themselves as the arbiters of mastery, of "good masters" and "bad masters." Of course, admitting that there was such a category as "good masters" could come close to legitimizing the power of such owners, but such an admission was a gambit that left slaves in a favorable position. They liberated themselves from the harsh control of their hirers and precluded the possibility of being hired to such men in the future. As all these slaves attested through the act of running away, they were capable of rebellion; when circumstances allowed, they acted in ways that denied the legitimacy of their enslavement. In this sense, what they did was more important than what they said.

Indeed, owners were regularly struck by their slaves' evident self-reliance in extricating themselves from abusive situations, rather than any apparent dependence on paternalist protection. Moving about from master to master, year after year, hired slaves were forced to rely on their own resourcefulness to shape their circumstances. That same self-confidence and independence helped them deal with brutal hirers, and owners sometimes recognized the subversive potential of their slaves' mettle. Robert Allen's slave Harrison twice bolted from the railroad contractor to whom he had been hired, and Allen was disquieted by the hardiness and conviction that such action was cultivating in his slave. "As Harrison has run away twice and has acquired some knowledge of the intervening country," Allen wrote to the hirer in 1857, "the next run may be to a nonslaveholding state and I lose him entirely." "Under these circumstances," Allen concluded, "as he has already been severely punished for his running away and it has had no good effect on him, I think I had best compromise matters . . . and keep him at home." Similarly, in 1853, William Fitzhugh wrote to a hiring agent for his aunt to explain a situation involving one of his aunt's slaves who defiantly refused to return to a hirer. Fitzhugh's aunt had hired Peter to the Richmond & Petersburg Railroad, but he had fled when the contractor "beat him with a stick." The aunt happened, by chance, to encounter Peter in her neighborhood, and she "endeavored to persuade him to return which he positively refuses to do." "The negro seems determined," Fitzhugh explained to the hiring agent, "to be sold before he will consent to return, . . . and in another effort to escape he would probably not stop in this neighborhood. My aunt is fearful of losing him entirely." From the perspectives of many owners, when slaves ran away from hirers, it was their independence and self-reliance, not their dependence, that shone through.[23]

When slaves actually made the agonizing decision to run away, they could be sure of one thing: their hirers (or their hirers' dogs) would be following at their heels. It is ironic, though not surprising, that confrontations between owners and hirers over these slaves with two masters often unfolded on the roads that connected their two households. One thing stands out in contemporary accounts of these confrontations: owners often made clear to hirers that the stories slaves told carried more weight than the demands hirers made for the slaves' return. When Fanny ran away from her hirer, Mr. Wier, she went straight to her owner, Eleanor Williams. Wier went to Williams' home and demanded that Fanny be turned over to him. Williams insisted in response that she was keeping Fanny because the contract had stipulated that he not treat her "cruelly." George Law also refused to turn over a slave, even though the hirer showed up at his home and promised that the slave "should not be treated harshly." Law insisted that he "had reason to believe that the slave had been treated with inhumanity." L. D. Phillips was confronted by a hirer "on the street before [his] house" by a hirer who had used dogs to trail a slave fleeing to secure Phillips' intervention. Phillips, "after some conversation" with the hirer, "refused to deliver the slave." In each of these confrontations, the owner heard about the cruelty and inhumanity of the hirer from a slave, and in each case the owner placed the slave's word before the demands of a fellow master. Owners listened to their slaves as they recounted episodes of abuse, and these stories served as reliable proof that the owners' property rights had been violated.[24]

Both white and black people in the antebellum South knew that taking the word of a slave over that of a white person was likely to provoke anger. Many Southern whites assumed that slaves lied by nature, that their mendacity was a genetic trait.[25] Peter Randolph noted that although he and his fellow slaves knew that their overseer was stealing from their master, informing the master "would have done no good, for he could not believe a slave."[26] Lying was one of the many criteria that whites used to set slaves apart in Southern society. As Kenneth Greenberg points out, "masters and potential masters distinguished themselves from slaves in many ways, but one of the most important distinctions involved the issue of lying." While the words of a white man "had to be accorded respect and accepted as true," Greenberg explains, the words of a slave "could never become objects of honor."[27] For this reason, Nathaniel Hart challenged Joel Twiman to a duel in Kentucky in 1827, claiming that Twiman had relied "upon information derived from a negro" in support of a charge made against Hart and that "such conduct [was] proof that the negro, instead of a gentleman, was the companion of Twiman."[28] By taking the word of a slave over that of a hirer, owners contravened a deep-seated convention in the antebellum South, a convention intended to honor white people and demean slaves.[29]

Because it was bound up with whiteness, masculinity, honor, and prosperity, mastery was a touchy subject in the South, so confrontations over it could easily escalate into violence. For owners, mastery meant protecting a lifelong investment, and abuse of their slaves consequently sent them to the courtroom. But it sometimes first sent them into fits of rage. Recall that Nancy Williams' master chased her hirer with a gun—"like he was hunting rabbits"—threatening to shoot him for the way Williams had been treated. Recall as well that John Thompson was able to watch as his owner's brother not only dressed down his hirer but then horsewhipped the constable who had beaten Thompson. For hirers, mastery meant absolute power over a slave, including the right to force a slave into obedience, a power they felt was compromised by meddlesome owners. They, too, responded with violence. When a hirer in Missouri went to Alvira West's home looking for a woman he had hired from West's husband, he found her, as he had suspected, in West's front yard. He "ordered" the slave to return with him, but she refused, and he "commenced whipping her with a cowhide." West then came out of the house and the slave ran and caught her around the waist. At this point, the hirer "did not stop his blows," some of which landed on West. In the antebellum South, striking a white woman who was not one's dependent was no small matter, but the hirer was enraged by the slave's refusal to obey him and West's subversion of his attempts to make the slave comply. The depths of resentment that both owners and hirers felt in conflicts over the treatment of hired slaves often found expression in violent outbursts. Social relations among whites were not immune to divisiveness emerging from the actions of resisting slaves.[30]

Fits of rage characterized the initial confrontations between owners and hirers, but eventually, after tempers had somewhat cooled, the conflicts reached Southern courts. Once there, owners carefully crafted their arguments around the property value that had been undermined by the actions of hirers. One North Carolina owner, for instance, argued in 1811 that the hirer of his slave had "beaten him with such severity as to occasion the rupture and consequent diminution of value" of the slave. Some owners were much more precise about the losses incurred at the hands of irresponsible hirers. Even though his slave's "capacity for labor was only imperiled for a month or two" as a result of a beating by a hirer, Dixon Hall still sued the hirer because "the market value of the slave was permanently injured, from \$100 to \$300, by reason of the scars left on his body." Similarly,

David Pierce argued that "while she was hired out," his slave "was so cru-elly and inhumanly treated as to greatly injure her value as a slave, thus di-minishing the value of her services." The hirer had not only rendered her "incapable of doing work which she was before able to do," but also prob-ably threatened her ability to reproduce, by which Pierce would have been able to increase his slave capital. Owners worried less about transgressions of paternal authority, at least in court, than they did about violations of property and profit.[31]

When confrontations developed into lawsuits, the slave's act of running away became central to the legal wrangling. Southern courts did grant hir-ers a sizable measure of physical power over the slaves they had rented—enough, the courts reasoned, to ensure the submission of slaves. Hirers, like owners, were thus legally sanctioned in the use of force to deal with recalcitrant slaves, although hirers always had to meet the standard of "moderation," as owners did not.[32] Thus, when questions of abuse came before them, judges followed the legal standard established by most South-ern courts that "the hirer must take the same care of a hired slave that a prudent and humane master is bound to take of his own."[33] Hirers were li-able, then, only in those instances in which they inflicted "inhuman treat-ment in the form of immoderate chastisement."[34] So when hired slaves ran away, the question raised in court was very simple: Did the slaves run away because of bad treatment or simply of their own will and volition (or, as one judge put it, "by reason of their contumacious perversity")?[35] Hir-ers therefore dragged witnesses into court to testify that they were "good masters." They were forced implicitly to debunk the claims hired slaves had made to their owners.[36]

Although slave testimony was not admissible in Southern courts, judges found that when making their decisions they had to rely in part on the re-ports they heard of slaves' behavior. Not a few judges complained that the question before them—"What is reasonable punishment, and when it can be affirmed that correction has gone beyond this boundary?"—was one that "admits of no certain and uniform solution." The primary difficulty was that witnesses to such punishment included only the hirer and slave in question. To judges, it was not patently clear which of the two was more reliable. Slave testimony could not be taken as evidence, but hirers, as so many judges ruled, had stronger tendency than most masters toward bru-tality because they lacked the check of self-interest. In these cases, there-fore, judges looked to what slaves had *done,* rather than what they might say in court, to help them determine liability. When slaves ran away, for in-stance, they did not always run to their masters. Some headed to the North, to Canada, or to Mexico and were gone forever. In such cases, hirers were rarely forced to compensate the owner for the price of the slave. If the slave was gone, it was very difficult to prove, as the courts required, "that the negro was induced to run away, by the cruelty or ill treatment" of the hirer.[37] In short, the slave could have been escaping slavery rather than a brutal hirer.

If slaves ran to owners, however, matters were different. Judges often assumed that this action indicated a strong likelihood that hirers had behaved abusively. Judge Holmes, ruling in a case before the Missouri high court, put great stock in the fact that, as he put it, "the slave found refuge with his master." According to the court record reflecting his decision, an owner could recover damages from a hirer "for an injury done to the slave by an inhuman and cruel beating, in consequence of which the slave returned to his master before the time for which he had been hired had expired." A Mississippi judge likewise ruled that an owner "would be justifiable in refusing to surrender the slave to the hirer" if "the slave be driven, by his cruel treatment, to seek the protection of the master."[38] To slaveholders who thought carefully about these decisions, they must have seemed troubling legal formulations. The rulings came very close to making hired slaves themselves the arbiters of what the court euphemism called immoderate chastisement and what the slaves themselves would have called abuse. It was when the slave ran to an owner that it seemed obvious to observers that a hirer had exceeded the bounds of "proper" mastery. If that knowledge spread to slave quarters, then slaves' appeals for "protection" from their owners were based on a shrewdness that threatened paternalism.

For several reasons, then, runaway hired slaves presented serious problems for hirers. Beyond losing the labor hired slaves would have provided, and beyond losing any money paid under contract, when hired slaves ran away hirers could also incur disrepute that might make other owners reluctant to hire slaves to them in the future. Those who relied heavily on hired slaves—small farmers, steamboat operators, owners of gold mines, producers of naval stores—could ill afford to be vilified by the slaves they rented. They knew that owners listened carefully to the allegations made by their slaves, allegations that shaped future hiring decisions. "Hands came Home from Mines several days ago," James Hervey Greenlee recorded in his diary—"said they were mistreated." That he heeded their tales is evidenced by the following day's entry: "Declined sending the boys back to the mines."[39] Francis T. Anderson, an ironmaster in Virginia, received a disturbing letter in November 1849 from the distressed owner of a slave he had hired. "My boy Edmond . . . got here the eighth of this month," the owner wrote; "he says that your overseer is so cruel that he could not stand him." Edmond's past hirer had been "very much pleased with him," according to the owner, and Edmond always worked well un-

less his master was "barbourse." Anderson could not stay in business long
if his furnace earned a reputation for barbarity, so he had his manager
draft a response. The manager wrote to the owner that Edmond had "behaved very badly," and, more important, "told you lies." "You will please
inquire of the negroes which came from the same neighbourhood," the letter concluded, "namely—Ben Swan, Randle Swan, Fister, Burbage, and
Beverly Beasly all of them will prove the correctness of my statement."[40]
That the manager's rejoinder invoked the testimony of other slaves under-
scores that the stories hired slaves told about their treatment carried great
weight in the slave South.

Many owners made it a regular practice to collect reports on hirers from
their slaves at year's end, before they determined whether to send their
slaves to the same places for another year. Joseph Watkins, for example,
noted to a friend in December 1835 that "it is the time for hiring my negroes and a host of them are now belaboring me with their complaints of
their bad treatment of the last year."[41] Despite his tone of exasperation,
Watkins probably relied heavily on these complaints to determine where to
send his slaves. Consider also the Cocke family's "List of Servants to be
Hired," especially the evidence it contains of the significance owners accorded to their slaves' testimony about hirers:

Cynthia—hired to Mr. George Seay—has all her things except her hat & is
well satisfied with her place

Katy—has all her things—but complains of hard treatment . . .

Beckey—hired again to the same—has all her things—but is not to be hired to
Mr. Guerrant again

Julianna—hired to Mrs. Stone—has all her things except head kerchief or hat.
Complains of hard treatment & begs not to be hired to her again

Mirna—hired to Robt. Richardson—has all her clothes except head handkerchief or hat—has no objection to returning to Mr. Richardson

Charlotte—hired to Mr. Cary Jones. Has had no blanket, no shoes, no hat or
handkerchief. Wants to be hired to someone else.

Harriet—Hired to Mr. John Key—has had no hat or handkerchief. Does not
like her place

Violet—Hired to Mr. Wm. Clements. Has all her things except head handker-
chiefs & likes her place. Less wages might be taken from Mr. C. than another.

Evelina—hired on the line last year. Well furnished—but not to be hired to
any contractor again.[42]

The list reveals the extent to which owners relied on slaves to report hirers' failure to meet stipulations made in contracts—stipulations about everything from food and clothing to treatment. In these reports, slaves also let their own wishes be known, thus shaping, to varying degrees, the course their work and family lives would take during their absence. In the everyday operation of hiring, and especially in the event of property disputes with hirers, the "dependence" often manifested was that of owners on their slaves.

The stories slaves told were not necessarily always true. Slaves understood well enough the dynamics of Southern society and of their owners' dependence on them to know that the mere accusation of abuse was enough to influence situations in their favor. Samuel Drewry, who hired slaves for railroad contractor John Buford, reported in December 1854 that a Mr. Wrenn had refused to send his slaves back to Buford's line because "the negroes request he will sell them sooner than return them" and because one of the slaves appeared "almost worthless from hard driving or bad treatment." The slaves told Wrenn that "they have to wash their clothes on the Sabbath," that "they do not have a sufficiency of food," and that "more labor was required than they could well do." The complaints were well crafted, designed to make Wrenn think that his slave capital was not being appropriately cared for on the railroad. Furthermore, the complaints were substantiated by the battered appearance of Charles, whom Wrenn now looked on "as being almost worthless." Drewry, baffled by the complaints, told Wrenn the slaves were lying. Wrenn, though, cautious about his slave property, refused to hire the slaves out again. Three weeks later, Drewry ran into Wrenn and learned that the slaves had subsequently been hired out to another person. Drewry inquired why the situation had changed. "He laughed," Drewry reported to Buford, "and remarked it turned out as I said to him a few days before. It was a concerted plan with the negroes to tell the tales they had to to prevent their being sent back." Wrenn admitted that the slaves "had lied" and that "Charles had much deceived him." To Drewry the lesson seemed patently clear: "There is too much attention paid, as I think, to gratifying servants in choosing their homes." He could "see this plainly" from the mere fact that "hands returning dissatisfied" was now enough to dissuade an owner from hiring out. When valuable property was at stake, the presumption of truth, from owners' perspectives, had to rest with slaves. Owners would sooner affront hirers than ignore their slaves. While Wrenn "laughed" at the whole affair, Drewry stewed.[43]

Because stories give shape and meaning to experience, telling them was a well guarded prerogative in the antebellum South. Slaves had precious few

opportunities to define the world they shared with whites, for giving words
to experience provided occasion to pass judgment, and whites reserved the
right to say what was just in Southern society. It was for this reason that
black people were forbidden from testifying against whites in Southern
courtrooms, the place where stories were granted not only wider audiences
but also greater legitimacy. But owners who worried about how their hired
slaves were being treated by strangers—strangers thought to be ungov-
erned by duty or restraint—found themselves trusting their slaves as informants and witnesses. Slaves fully exploited these moments when white
people took their complaints seriously.

The stories hired slaves told had effects that were both local and far-
reaching. Slaves who had been beaten or who hoped to forestall abuse
learned that they could use the triangular relation of owner, hirer, and
slave to their advantage. By blowing the whistle on their hirers, they invoked the protection of one master to preempt abuse by another. But the
effect of their tales of abuse went beyond improving their immediate living
situation. Slaves watched as white people entered into heated confrontations, both on the street and in the courtroom, that had often originated in
declarations that those slaves themselves had made. Owners defending
their long-term investments in slaves clashed with hirers asserting their
prerogative of coercion. In the process, slaves escaped punishment for the
serious transgression of having run away. In fact, those acts of running
away to seek asylum could in many instances be the linchpin in suits
brought against abusive hirers. Owners were outraged by the stories their
slaves told them; hirers were outraged by the owners' willingness even to
listen to their slaves in the first place. But owners did listen. In a remarkable distortion of the Southern racial hierarchy, owners often took the
word of a slave over that of a white person. As they tried to repossess their
slaves, owners battled with hirers over who had the stronger property
claim to mastery over the slaves in question. Such conflicts could have serious repercussions. Political support for slavery was sustained through a
usually tacit, network of compromises and concessions among the different classes of Southern whites, but that network had its weak points—
weak points that could be probed by the resistance of individual slaves,
whether those slaves intended that result or not. A woman complained to
Frederick Law Olmsted as he traveled through Texas that she did not like
to hire slaves, because "very often" owners "take them away" on the "pretext" of mistreatment.[44] In a small but important exercise of power, a slave
usually supplied that pretext.

Working Alone

There is no middle ground between slavery and freedom; no such thing as qualified freedom, or qualified slavery.

Thomas R. R. Cobb, *The Law of Negro Slavery in the United States* (1858)

SOME slaves who were hired out in the South decided on their own where to work, how long to stay with their hirers, and even what prices to charge. The practice occurred all over the South but predominated in cities and towns, where slaves were sent out to live on their own and to roam the streets looking for work. Self-hired slaves paid over a stipulated sum to their owners by the week or month (one contemporary observer referred to these payments as "body rent"), and sometimes they kept any money they earned beyond their set hire.[1]

The practice of self-hire, which occupied shaky legal ground in the South, was pursued as inconspicuously as possible by owners, hirers, and slaves alike. There were at least two major legal hurdles to slaves' hiring themselves out on their own time. That slaves were not recognized as persons before the law presented a sizable hindrance, for slaves could not legally make binding contracts, whether marriage contracts or work contracts. Self-hire arrangements thus rested on a tacit agreement, among the white Southerners involved, to wink at the intrinsic illegality of slaves' carrying out transactions on their own. A second and even more germane obstacle to self-hire was that legislatures across the South specifically forbade the practice of slaves' renting their own time. These proscriptions came largely in response to petitions from white workers, who felt that their dignity and their pocketbooks suffered from the competition with slaves who leased their own time. Despite its illegality, however, self-hire thrived in the cities of the South. For owners, self-hire represented a financial boon, so they were eager to turn a blind eye to both customs and laws that militated against giving slaves what appeared—at least to many white Southerners —to be a form of independence. Hirers, too, were inclined to overlook regulations against self-hire, especially in urban areas, because the short-term, cheap labor that self-hired slaves offered was a practical necessity.

What self-hire meant for slaves is a trickier question. At first glance, self-hire would appear to have been a blessing for any slave, since it seemingly offered an opportunity for nearly full autonomy. But the story is more complicated. Consider, for example, the general outlines of a self-hire arrangement as they were described by Frederick Douglass, who for a period hired his own time as a caulker in the shipyards of Baltimore. "I was to be allowed all my time," Douglass explained of the arrangement he made with his owner, Thomas Auld, "to make all bargains for work; to find my own employment, and to collect my own wages; and, in return for this liberty, I was required, or obliged, to pay him three dollars at the end of each week, and to board and clothe myself, and buy my own calking tools. A failure in any of these particulars would put an end to my privilege. This was a hard bargain." This short explanation brings to light some of the difficulties involved in the practice of self-hire from the perspective of slaves themselves. Douglass described his experience as at once a "liberty," a "privilege," and a "hard bargain." A question inevitably arises: Could self-hire, however hard the life it entailed, make a slave feel freer?[2]

Historians have turned their attention to self-hire more frequently than to any other aspect of slave hiring, primarily because it appears a tantalizing aberration in a slave society. By and large, they latch onto such notions as liberty and privilege, often with explicit reference to Frederick Douglass, when explaining the significance of hiring slaves out to themselves. Of self-hire, Frederic Bancroft maintained that "to the slaves it seemed like attaining semi-freedom, and was accordingly much sought after." Robert Starobin argued that those slaves granted the "privilege" of leasing their own time "were probably in a 'twilight zone' between bondage and freedom." In a similar vein, other historians have resorted to the notion of "quasi freedom" to explain the position of self-hired slaves. Here, a different story emerges, a story predicated on the assumption that reference to "privileged"—and especially "quasi-free"—slaves is fraught with peril. The most obvious danger lies in using words uttered by white Southerners to shed light on slaves' perceptions of the practice. By avoiding the assumption that self-hired slaves must have been "privileged," it is easier to approach whole categories of questions that might otherwise be obscured, including how these slaves lived every day, how their existence affected the slave regime, and, most important, what it meant for them to be *slaves,* regardless of the modifier that preceded the word.[3]

Much of the existing scholarship on self-hire ignores the evidence left

behind by self-hired slaves themselves. Yet the letters, interviews, and narratives of slaves allow us to look at the experience of self-hire from the perspective of the those who lived through it. A surprising number of extant
slave letters in the manuscript collections of Southern slaveholders are
from slaves who had been hired out to themselves, and these letters provide the opportunity to go beyond complacent notions of privilege to understand what life as a hired slave was like in the South. There is no doubt
that self-hire had its perquisites; indeed, the number of extant letters itself
indicates that self-hired slaves had more opportunities to achieve literacy,
for example, than did other slaves. But the experience was, as the words of
self-hired slaves themselves will attest, slavery nonetheless. There is abundant evidence, for example, that Frederick Douglass did not mean, in reference to hiring his own time, for the word "liberty" to be taken literally.
Self-hire, in his mind, was not a lesser form of enslavement; on the contrary, Douglass asserted that paying over his wages every week to his
owner "kept the nature and character of slavery constantly before me."
Slavery and freedom did not fade, by shades or degrees, the one into the
other. Rather than opposing ends of a spectrum, slavery and freedom were
opposing poles, holding each other in orbit, at once attracting and repel-
ling each other because the twain could never meet. Self-hired slaves knew
that "quasi freedom" was a specious concept.[4]

At the same time that self-hire extended and sustained the slave regime,
it further disturbed the social relations of white Southerners. While the
practice allowed for "flexibility" in ever-changing urban economies, it was
also a cause of deep strife among white Southerners. White workers were
outraged when they were forced to compete with slaves who hired their
own time, and they appealed repeatedly to state legislatures across the
South for stricter enforcement of existing laws against self-hire. These laborers' livelihood and their sense of whiteness were both under assault
when they were undercut by lower-bidding slave workers. Whether the
white workers were day laborers or skilled craftsmen, they felt that allowing self-hired slaves to make their own contracts brought down wages, diminished the quality of the work, and elevated slaves to the status of
whites. Like the friction between owners and hirers, the animosity between
white workers and slaveholders over the practice of self-hire undermined
the strength of the system, because it exposed to public view the extent of
the discord over how the system of slavery should operate in practice.
Frederick Douglass, for one, was sure that the competition between self-
hired slaves and white mechanics was "a phase of slavery destined to become an important element in the overthrow of the slave system."[5]

Hired to Themselves

The exact number of slaves who leased their own time in the South is virtually impossible to determine. Because the practice was illegal, records of such illicit employment were probably discouraged by anxious owners and hirers alike. In addition, the work was usually of such short duration—carrying luggage from a train station to a hotel, sweeping dirt from a storefront, hawking fruit or fish, washing a load of laundry—that hirers simply made oral agreements with the slaves offering their labor. Since records of the number of individual self-hire transactions do not exist, estimates must remain speculative. Estimates can be based on subjective impressions from references to self-hired slaves in slaveholders' letters, in newspapers, and in court cases. In this connection, historian Loren Schweninger conjectures that there were 2,500 self-hired slaves in Virginia in 1860—that is, roughly 1 percent of all enslaved Virginians (246,981), and 10 percent of hired slaves (about 25,000). Schweninger insists, though, that his estimate, however rough, is a conservative one. The number of self-hired slaves was probably even larger.[6]

Every day in the colonial and antebellum South, these slaves went out, at the direction of their owners, to find their own work, but they always did so under a cloud of illegality. Legislation proscribing self-hire varied throughout the Southern colonies and then the Southern states, but the practice was prohibited altogether at one time or another in all parts of the South. These legislative injunctions stemmed for the most part from protests by whites that self-hired slaves were impudent, disorderly, and, worst of all, unfairly competitive with white workers. The earliest such protests appeared in Charleston at the beginning of the eighteenth century. An act promulgated there in 1712 attested that many of the city's slave owners were allowing their slaves "to do what and go whither they will and work where they please, upon condition that their said slaves do bring their aforesaid masters so much money as between the said master and slave is agreed upon." These slaves, the act further noted, had been found "looking for opportunities to steal, in order to raise money to pay their masters, as well as to maintain themselves, and other slaves their companions, in drunkenness and other evil courses." Despite its earnest language, however, the act would languish in legislative limbo well into the future, for its enforcement could never be more than sporadic at best. Charleston petitioners, like those in other regions of the South, would complain again and again, even up to the outbreak of the Civil War, that the "evil" of self-hire had scarcely been alleviated.[7]

Though enforcement was lax, Southern legislatures did write and rewrite their laws against self-hire under pressure from opponents of the practice, particularly white workers. Virginia, for example, forbade the practice in 1782, and then again in 1819, when the state made it legal for any white person to apprehend slaves hiring their own time and then receive a portion of any resulting fines. Maryland and North Carolina followed suit in 1787 and 1794, respectively, although Maryland allowed a ten-day exception during the all-important, labor-intensive wheat harvest. In 1798, Kentucky outlawed the practice and made the penalty for violation of the law nothing less than forfeiture of the slave involved. Four years later, Kentucky made the law less severe, by requiring offending slave owners merely to pay a fine. Similar laws were passed in Georgia in 1803, Louisiana in 1806, Tennessee in 1813, Mississippi in 1822, Florida in 1822, Missouri in 1841, Texas in 1846, and Alabama in 1848. Some of these states allowed owners to send their slaves out to hire themselves by day, so long as the slaves returned to their owners' places each night.[8]

Seldom, however, were these laws against self-hire assiduously enforced. In 1793, a group of Charleston's white master coopers complained that "the very great and growing evil" of slaves' hiring their own time went unabated as a result of "inattention" to laws passed by South Carolina's General Assembly in 1740 and 1783, not to mention the original act of 1712. In 1802, eight years after North Carolina had codified its law against self-hire, a petition from Wilmington mechanics claimed that very little had changed, that slaves continued to hire their own time, "notwithstanding the Acts of the Assembly." Petitions streamed into state legislatures across the South, railing against the "inefficiency" of the laws against self-hire, especially the limp penalties and lax enforcement that so enervated the laws. In Charleston such laws had been on the books since 1712, but even as late as 1858 they were, according to a petition by the city's workingmen, "as yet a dead letter." To opponents of self-hire, the laws seemed barely to exist, so completely were they flouted across the South. "Despite the laws of the land forbidding under penalty the hiring of their time by slaves," an editorial in South Carolina's Columbia *Bulletin* lamented in 1859, "it is much regretted that the pernicious practice still exists."[9]

Some opponents of self-hire questioned whether lawmakers ever intended the laws to be enforced in the first place. Their petitions to Southern legislatures, while appropriately formal and decorous, thinly masked disgust at the manner in which the laws against self-hire were executed. In some cases, the petitioners observed, lawmakers had failed to designate a specific legal authority to be responsible for prosecuting violations. In 1802, workingmen in Wilmington, North Carolina, pointed out that execution and enforcement were not "the particular province of any person," and that the laws therefore lay "neglected, and of no avail." Likewise, Charleston mechanics asserted in 1828 that the "salutary law" against self-hire "fell dead" because no process had been outlined by which the law was to be "carried into execution." Thirty years later, in 1858, petitioners in Marion District, South Carolina, noted that their state's law was "altogether ineffectual in remedying the evil" of self-hire because, first, the assessed fines were "trifling," and second, no one had been granted the authority to indict offenders. Though the South Carolina law fell under the jurisdiction of the state's Court of Sessions, "no Courts are held," the petitioners claimed, and "no Judge rides the Circuit." For white workers in particular, the perfunctory enforcement of laws against self-hire was just a further slight to their pride and their livelihood, a slight that would elicit from them vociferous opposition to some of the ways that slaves were used in the South.[10]

Though the opponents of self-hire were exasperated by lax enforcement, they surely understood all too well why their protests went unheeded. There were at least two significant factors explaining why the laws against self-hire languished as dead letters on the statute books of the South. First, employers in urban economies required that slaves be able to contract for short-term work on their own. Slaves had to be able to act independently if they were going to work as porters, hucksters, laundresses, and draymen, or if they were going to meet the demand for skilled labor by working as coopers, cobblers, or blacksmiths. Whites who needed such labor did not wish to be bothered with seeking out a slave's owner before contracting for the slave's services.

Second, and perhaps more compellingly, self-hire was an extremely lucrative practice for slave owners. Frederick Douglass was not surprised that his owner agreed to let him hire his own time as a ship caulker in Maryland, for the arrangement "was decidedly in his favor": "It relieved him of all anxiety concerning me. His money was sure." Similarly, Hamilton Brown's agent in Macon, Georgia, allowed Brown's slave Larkin to hire his own time in 1836, "because if he will do as he can do he will make double the amount of what he would hire for." This would be true even if Larkin were picked up by the police during the year and Brown fined for allowing his slave to lease his own time. The agent assured Brown that Larkin "will make money enough this year to clear all charges," adding, "so I have just turned him out to do the best he can." Opponents of self-hire knew that the ease and profit owners realized through hiring their slaves out to themselves made any conformity to existing laws against the practice highly unlikely. "Such is the indolence of Mankind," a group of Charleston mechanics pointed out in 1828, referring to the proceeds made through self-hire, "that there are but few owners who do not prefer turning loose their slaves upon the Community." In the face of protests, self-hire would always have convenience and profit to recommend it.[11]

Those slaves who wanted to hire their own time understood this logic and made their case to their owners with enticing promises of increased wealth. Hamilton Brown received a letter in 1832 from a blacksmith he hired out by the year, and in asking to hire his own time, the slave professed to be "satisfied that I can do well and that my profits will amount to a great deal more than any one would be willing to pay for my hire." Similarly, when Alfred Steele wrote to his owner in 1835 to ask that he be given the opportunity to rent his own time in Raleigh, North Carolina, where his wife lived, he assured him: "[I] will give you as mutch or more than any body els[e]." He promised, in addition, to "pay you in eny way that you want me to pay you if it is by the month or by the year." In 1847, Ephraim, a Virginia slave, proposed to his owner through an acquaintance that he be allowed to hire himself out to a railroad being built through Roanoke, and he asserted that "he could make the money to pay his hire long before Christmas." Sometimes, though, such claims could come back to haunt slaves. Five years later, in 1852, Ephraim again asked that he be able to hire himself out, but the man he chose turned out to be delinquent in his payments at the end of the year, and Ephraim's owner was forced to sue. His owner ultimately decided that Ephraim "ought to pay the lawyer his fee out of his part." The bind in which Ephraim found himself was one that all self-hired slaves encountered in one manner or another. Their owners were most concerned about their money, and the slaves had to be ready to do anything in order to supply it.[12]

Accordingly, the work that slaves did while hiring themselves out was diverse. The nature of the work was determined to a large degree, though, by the slave's gender. For the same reason that it is difficult to estimate the number of self-hired slaves as a whole, it is hard to assign a definite figure to the men and women who leased their own time. For certain, though, slave men had the most opportunities to hire themselves out as skilled artisans. They could find their own work as blacksmiths, coopers, carpenters, and builders, whereas women were restricted to such tasks as marketing, peddling, and washing. Both men and women, though, cobbled together a variety of tasks to keep up their payments to owners. Reuben Madison paid his owner ten dollars per month in the 1820s by "trafficking in rags." To meet his twelve-dollar monthly payments, Lewis Clarke "split rails, burned coal, peddled grass seed, and took hold of whatever else I could find to do." James Maguire met his owner's demand for twenty dollars per month in the 1840s through "hair dressing and waiting on parties." In Vir-

ginia, Mary Ann Wyatt would get oysters every day from the Rappahannock River and tote them sixteen miles to sell in town, where she eventually became known as the Oyster Maid. Other women took in work as
seamstresses or hawked fruit and vegetables, and many earned their hire
by washing dirty clothes. Old Sarah, for example, lived in a cabin "in the
suburbs of Macon," where in 1835, according to her owner's hiring agent,
"she takes in washing and can make her $8 per month very easy." The
agent's assurance that it would be "very easy" for the elderly Sarah to earn
her hire obscured the hardscrabble effort it took this woman, and other
self-hired slaves, to keep ahead of an owner's demands for money.[13]

Because their work was often temporary and intermittent, self-hired
slaves did not live with those who hired them. Rather, they lived on their
own in rooms or houses rented by the week or month. "Living out," as the
practice was called, was most frequent in cities, but it occurred in rural
areas as well. As early as 1772, a Charleston contributor to the *South
Carolina Gazette* regretted "that *many rooms, kitchens,* &c. are hired to
or for the use of *slaves* in *this town;* and by such slaves, let to others, in
subdivisions." As with laws against self-hire, laws against living out were
on the books, as well. South Carolina's law dated from 1740, but complaints of nonenforcement continued through the antebellum era. Historian Claudia Dale Goldin estimates, for example, that 15 percent of
Charleston's slaves were living out on their own in 1861. In Richmond,
where tobacco factories brought into the city large numbers of hired slaves
from the surrounding countryside, factory managers gave slaves a dollar
per week to find their own room and board. The practice saved factory
owners the huge expense of erecting dormitories on-site for their workers,
but the tolerance of authorities was always precarious. Living-out arrangements disquieted not a few white townspeople, who feared that such "autonomy" bred more opportunities for vice among slave populations. But
rather than enforce laws against self-hire and living out, many city councils
opted for regulation and taxation over outright prohibition. By the antebellum era, local authorities in many Southern cities required slaves living
and working on their own to purchase, and wear, badges that identified
them as hired slaves.[14]

Given the vehement opposition to self-hire, owners often found it prudent to ask friends or associates to stand in as "protectors" for slaves hired
out to themselves. A Virginian, James D. Watts, wrote to his friend Iverson
Twyman in 1852 to inform him that his slave Edmund, employed as a
shoemaker, was going to "occupy a house in the vicinity of your residence," and to ask Twyman to look out for Edmund's welfare, "as you
are living close by his situation." "As he will be some distance from

home," Watts explained, "he will stand in need of a Protector and advisor." Keeping an eye on the slaves, protectors would make sure that they worked consistently, that they did not spend too much time in local grog shops, and that they did not unduly arouse the suspicions of local police. In fact, owners were especially concerned that one of their self-hired slaves might be arrested without their knowledge; slaves who sat in jail for long enough might be hired out or even sold to pay for their upkeep. Owners also wanted to make sure that their slaves were at least partially protected from the potential depredations of white workers and others angered by the idea that the slaves were working on their own and arranging their own contracts. Thus, in 1836, Hamilton Brown's slaves Larkin and Sarah, who leased their own time in Macon, Georgia, were placed in the charge of a Methodist preacher in the city who would "protect them and see they are not abused." Protectors were, in short, a safeguard put in place by owners to protect their interests.[15]

Though protectors acted to safeguard the interests of owners, self-hired slaves often recognized the merits of having such a person to watch over them. Leasing out one's own time was a precarious occupation, and these slaves knew that it could be valuable to have a white person to vouch for them in the event of trouble with authorities or to support them in wage disputes with employers. "It will be necessary that you authorize some one to act as my master in this country," Charles White, Hamilton Brown's self-hired blacksmith, wrote in 1832, "to prevent difficulties arising from the strictness of the laws." With his own blacksmith shop, White knew he stood to gain money for himself, and he proposed to pay out of his own pocket for such a legal guardian: "If you will empower them," he told his owner, "I can compensate them for their trouble." Protectors could give local authorities the impression of being a master, thus limiting chances of slaves' arrest, but also stood behind slaves when employers were dilatory in their payments. "Dear Master you will be so good as to write word to Mr. Souter or some other gentleman to be my protector," Jack Lewis wrote to his owner, Christopher Tompkins, in 1832, "so that I can get my money to pay my Board, and that he can give me a pass for fear that I may be taken up." Protectors may have stood in for owners, but they could play a positive role for slaves, as well.[16]

Moving from job to job was at once the blessing and the bane of existence as a hired slave. Consider, for example, the experience of Anderson Henderson. Henderson belonged to Archibald and Mary Henderson, a North Carolina planter family, and from 1849 through the end of the Civil War he hired his own time in the town of Wilmington. Some of the letters that Henderson wrote to his owners during those years still exist, and they give an illuminating glimpse into the life of one hired slave. When Henderson arrived in Wilmington in 1849, his owners' agent informed him that he could decide whether he wanted to hire himself out by the month or by the year. Henderson chose to hire himself out by the month, for twelve dollars, at one of the city's many hotels. Explaining his decision to hire by the month in a letter to his owners, Henderson noted, "Then if I do not like one house I could go to another for ther[e] is a good many Hotels here that I could get in if I did not like this." The ability to move from employer to employer, or from task to task, was one of the options that made self-hire attractive to many slaves, including Henderson.[17]

But it took the smallest change in circumstances, even a sprained ankle, to turn the search for work and the effort to make one's monthly hire into torment. In 1857, Anderson Henderson was still living in Wilmington, and again he took "pen in hand" to inform his owners of "how I am getting along." Among the perils lying in wait for all self-hired slaves was a long bout of illness or a serious injury, either of which could prevent them from meeting their owners' demands for money and their own needs for food and shelter. Henderson mentioned to his owners that he was well, "except my ankle that I sprained last summer and is not well yet." He could not move on the ankle unless he used a walking stick, a situation that hampered him in his usual employment, which was "walking or toating trunks up and down stair cases in a Hotel." To overcome the obstacle his ankle presented to paying his monthly hire, Henderson began to "haul baggage with a one horse wagon about Town." But it appears that such work was not so remunerative as Henderson had hoped, for he noted that "produce and every thing is very high at this time," a fact that "keeps me busy to make my alls & ends meet." Henderson had a strong personal reason to keep up his payments and remain working on his own in Wilmington—his family. With pragmatic servility, Henderson reminded his owners that he had, "by hard pushing," met his hire consistently to this point, "and I will always try and get your money as long as you and Mistress have been so good as to let me living with my family." All day long on his swollen ankle, Anderson Henderson carted the baggage of itinerant white Southerners through Wilmington, until he managed to make enough money to pay his owners what they demanded, and he did so with the integrity of his family life always on his mind.[18]

In living with his wife and children, Anderson Henderson was fortunate, for his experience of family life was different from that of most self-hired slaves. More commonly, family cohesion was maintained by women living on their own and leasing their own time, providing the wherewithal not only for their hire but also for the support of their children. Bethany

Veney, for example, worked on her own in Luray, Virginia, and she earned enough to pay her owner her hire and to keep herself and her son fixed for food, clothing, and shelter. Such maintenance was not easy, and it became all the more difficult as children grew older and owners began to require hire from them as well. Mary Ann Wyatt, the "Oyster Maid" of the Rappahannock, paid her owner for her own time, but also a supplemental amount for the time of her children, based on their ages. Her owner demanded five dollars per year for the youngest children and up to forty-five dollars for the oldest, yet through her sales of oysters, along with fruits from her garden and "truck patch," Wyatt kept her family "from the hammer of the auctioneer." Charlotte, a slave interviewed by the American Freedman's Inquiry Commission (AFIC) in 1863, had been renting out her own time for fifteen years, paying a dollar a week to her owner for her own time and two dollars per week for each of her two children. The boys, aged thirteen and seventeen, worked in tobacconists shops and lived with their mother in one room, for which they paid three dollars per month. The conditions were cramped, but they were at least together ("You couldn't pay me to live at home," Charlotte insisted, referring to her owner's place.) Of course, living with loved ones, including children, was never guaranteed for any slaves, no matter how hard they worked or how much money they turned over to their owners. "I pay them $73 a year for myself, and clothe myself, and pay my house rent and doctor's bill," Lavina Bell pointed out to her interviewers from the AFIC in 1863, "and as soon as my children grow up, they take them." An owner's chance decision was all that separated a self-hired slave from the deepest bitterness the slave system could occasion.[19]

Beyond negotiations over family life, another important issue for self-hired slaves was haggling with owners over the rate of hire they would turn over. Slaves of course tried to keep the price as low as possible, not just because they wished to work as little as possible or because they wished to save money for themselves, but because they knew how difficult it often could be to find work. Anderson Henderson's sprained ankle was just one of any number of afflictions that could hamper a slave's efforts to meet their expected "body rent." Trying to meet their owners' exorbitant demands usually meant scrounging for money at the end of the month, trying to find anything that would provide a little extra cash. James E. Cooke, for example, allowed his slave Fanny to lease her own time in Virginia in the early 1850s, and he set the price at fifteen dollars. Cooke's agent reported to him in 1851 that Fanny had been to see him, protesting that the price was "too much" and pleading that Cooke not "deal so hard with her." "She says she paid last year all that you demanded," the agent added, noting as well that Fanny considered this "more than sufficient." Apparently, Cooke did not relent, because the agent reported to him again at the beginning of 1852 that, though "Fanny had put in my hands funds to pay her hire," she turned out to be "a little short." She had earned twelve dollars by selling "a little corn, fodder hay, &c.," and the agent thought that the "little parcel of Tobacco" she also had to sell would make up the three-dollar shortfall, but it turned out to be worth far less. "She has in fact been able to pay only $13," the agent reported to Cooke. The two dollars was not forgiven: Cooke added it to the price due for the following year.[20]

When they could not meet demands for money, slaves made themselves scarce, and not infrequently owners or their agents found themselves pursuing self-hired slaves who were delinquent in their payments. Henry Laurens expended considerable effort in chasing after Ishmael and George, who had been allowed to hire themselves out in revolutionary Charleston, and in trying to get them "to account for their time," but they were exasperatingly adept at staying just out of his reach. Even when Laurens found them, they always insisted that "they were in search for Masters & employment." Hiring agent Elijah Fuller complained in 1845 to the owner of Toby that the slave "is a cunning, shrewd fellow and it is hard work to get much money out of him unless he is closely watched." Falling behind in payments to owners was a risky business for self-hired slaves. As slaves, they were still subject to the worst punishments the system could inflict. Hiring agent D. R. Carroll informed several self-hired slaves in New Orleans in 1845 that they had to make up for missing payments as soon as possible and that "unless they did so, they should be whipped." "I am in hopes the *threat* will be sufficient," Carroll wrote to the owner of the slaves, but the agent was more than ready to carry out the threat. Though not under the daily watch of an overseer, self-hired slaves could never completely escape the lash. In that sense, they were no more "free" than any other slaves in the South.[21]

Though to romanticize the "autonomy" of self-hired slaves is to overlook the harsh reality of their lives as slaves, it is at the same time important to recognize that these slaves had opportunities not open to others. First among these opportunities was the chance to make some money for themselves. "Once master of my own time," Frederick Douglass wrote in his narrative, "I felt sure that I could make, over and above, my obligation to him [his owner, Thomas Auld], a dollar or two every week." Similarly, Susan Boggs told an interviewer in 1863 in Canada that "I paid my mistress a quarter of a dollar a day for my time, but I got more than that, and had the rest to myself." A. C. Pruitt remembered that his grandmother was able to go anywhere to get jobs, doing whatever she pleased, as long as she turned in half of what she made to her owner. The extra money that self-hired slaves earned was useful in any number of ways. They could use it to rent better accommodations, improve their diet, buy alcohol, or purchase gifts for family. Asked by an interviewer in 1880 what he had done with the money he earned while hiring his own time, Parke Johnston insisted that "he always spent it as fast as he made it." Slaves could never rest easy with money, for it legally belonged to their owners, so Johnston unloaded what he earned as quickly as he could on "many little comforts for himself and his family," including "dainties for the Sunday dinner," which he delivered after traveling every Saturday evening to see his wife and children.[22]

For slaves who had a secure way to save their money as well as owners who were open to the proposition, the greatest purchase such money could underwrite was freedom. Interviews with former slaves as well as slave narratives recount instances of self-hired slaves' making enough money to purchase themselves from their owners. Ann Garrison, a former slave interviewed in 1841, recounted that her son Robert had "contracted for his freedom for a certain sum of money" and then earned it "by his services." Betsy Crissman hired her own time for fifteen dollars per month and "by hard work saved enough to purchase my freedom" for three hundred dollars, a low price for a slave who paid nearly two hundred dollars per year in hire, but Crissman was getting old, and fortuitously, her owner needed the money to fund a move away from an outbreak of smallpox. William Jackson, when a slave in Louisiana and Kentucky, saved fifty dollars per year for twenty years from his earnings as a self-hired slave; he eventually presented his owner with $1005 for his freedom, which did not include the "almost $6000" he had paid as hire over the years. Moses Grandy's daughter worked as a stewardess on a Mississippi steamboat, and she earned enough through her wages and her sales of apples and oranges on board to pay her owner thirty dollars for her hire and thirty dollars towards her freedom. She continued in this way until she had paid twelve hundred dollars and secured her freedom. Although in some instances slaves were able to use self-hire as a stepping stone to freedom, it is important to see that they attained that freedom only in a final leap, not by degrees. Until the final payment, they were as unfree as the next slave.[23]

Nothing could bring this brutal fact more clearly to light for self-hired slaves than when owners cheated them out of their payments toward freedom. At one point in his life, Moses Grandy saved up and paid over to his owner six hundred dollars toward his freedom, receiving a receipt from his owner after each payment. When he reached the agreed sum, however, the owner tore up the receipts and sold Grandy. Dimmock Charlton had a similar experience: he worked as a stevedore in Savannah and eventually saved eight hundred dollars to purchase himself from his owner, William Robinson. Robinson, however, "had no sooner received the money than he sent [Charlton] to jail, and kept him there on sale till a new buyer was found for him." Dispiriting swindles such as these occurred with great regularity—the evidence suggests with a regularity equal to or greater than successful self-purchases—and slaves were justifiably wary when they tendered their money. George Williams saved up the amount he needed to purchase his freedom, but when he "found they were going to cheat me out of it," he decided to make his flight to Canada, with his money. Though self-hired slaves had opportunities open to them that many other slaves might have envied—from living and working on their own to saving money against self-purchase—self-hire was never in itself an escape from slavery. Slaves who had been cheated out of their freedom money could attest that a slave was always a slave, that self-hire could never alter the essence of slavery, the denial of personal freedom.[24]

"All the Evils of Being a Slave"

Many white Southerners nevertheless construed self-hire as an aberrant example of freedom in a slave society. To them, the sight of slaves renting out their own time conjured up images of unruliness and dissolution. A slave not under the physical control of a master, so their reasoning went, was no longer a slave. In 1859, a New Orleans resident griped in the pages of the *Picayune* that "a species of *quasi* freedom has been granted by many masters to their slaves." These slaves, the writer pointed out, "have been permitted to hire their own time, and with nominal protection of their masters, though with none of their oversight, to engage in business on their own account, to live according to their own fancy, to be idle or industrious . . . provided only the monthly wages are regularly gained." As this gloss on self-hire suggests, many white Southerners thought that slaves who hired their own time, found their own work, and lived on their own, were, by virtue of these activities, at least halfway to a condition of freedom. The readers of *DeBow's Review* would not have been surprised, therefore, that a contributor to the periodical in 1851 considered slaves who were "permitted to hire their own time" to be "half free slaves." They also would not have been surprised by the contributor's fervent claim that these "half free" slaves, ostensibly wallowing in all manner of degeneracy, were largely responsible for high disease and mortality rates in New Orleans. To many white Southerners, self-hired slaves, being "quasi-free," were a scourge in more ways than one.[25]

White Southerners' claims that self-hired slaves were somehow less enslaved than others in the South have tended to be taken at face value. In 1954, Richard B. Morris wrote that, living in "quasi freedom," self-hired slaves "dwelt in a shadowland enjoying a status neither fully slave nor entirely free." In 1960, Clement Eaton summed up slave hiring in the upper South as "a step toward freedom" for those slaves who found their own work. In 1964, Richard Wade argued that self-hire "created a new dimension of independence for the Negroes" and that the practice did nothing less than bring a slave "into a new relationship with his owner, more like that of tenant and landlord than bondage in the usual sense." In 1991, Loren Schweninger, echoing Morris and Eaton, reiterated the position that self-hired slaves were "quasi-free" and that they themselves "viewed self-hire as 'a step toward freedom.'"[26] The phrase "a step toward freedom" has achieved heightened historiographic currency because it is borrowed from Frederick Douglass, who used a variant of it to describe his own experience as a self-hired slave. To be sure, Douglass did write in his narrative that self-hire was "a valuable privilege—another step in my career toward freedom." To understand what Douglass meant, however, requires placing these words in the context of Douglass's life and the remainder of his narrative. Douglass did not mean that *as* a hired slave, he became freer. In fact, in the sentence preceding this one Douglass insists that, even while hiring his own time, he "endured all the evils of being a slave."[27] True, Douglass and other slaves like him did ask for the opportunity to hire their own time. But to Douglass there was nothing inherently "freer" about being a self-hired slave, even though it did provide a chance for crossing to freedom in a way that working under close white supervision did not.

Rather than being "allowed" to, most slaves were ordered to hire their own time by owners looking to increase earnings on their slave capital. Self-hire could in fact be more a burden than a privilege to some slaves. Eliza Smith, for example, was sent out by her mistress to find work by the day, and if she ever returned in the evening without money to pay over, she was "turned out of the kitchen to seek food and shelter where she could find it." Similarly, Matthew Watts was left behind to hire himself out in Virginia in the 1830s when his owner's family moved to Kentucky. Watts was instructed to send eleven dollars per month in hire to Kentucky, and while he was at times able to meet the demand, he often found that making enough to cover his hire as well as his food and shelter was an insuperable challenge. He complained to his owner at the end of 1837 that his hire was "rather more than I can make and clothe myself." During that year, Watts explained, "times were hard and money Scarce and I could not make it so easy." In fact, Watts had already gone without new summer clothes to meet his hire once that year and, at the time he wrote the letter to his owner, was deferring the purchase of winter clothes as well, hoping that his plea might result in some abatement of the hire his owner expected him to send to Kentucky.[28]

Letters back to owners, from the slaves themselves or from agents to whom the slaves reported periodically, often make note of the difficulties that slaves encountered in finding work. In 1842, George Davis, a Missouri resident, had at least two slaves who hired their own time in New Orleans and periodically reported to his agent, John B. Murison. Murison informed Davis that year that Isaac, trained as a barber, had not yet "succeeded in obtaining of steady employment," and that "he says times are very hard with the barber fraternity." Isaac reported, though, that he was "acting in the capacity of a quack doctor with some degree of success." Communication between owners and slaves was often—from both quarters—a morass of prevarication and evasion, so the complaints made by self-hired slaves about the difficulties of finding work are difficult to penetrate. It could have been true, for example, that Isaac encountered limited demand for barbers, but it could equally have been the case that Isaac preferred to work as "a quack doctor," a position which would have given him more contact with other slaves and free black people. It is unlikely that whites made up much of his medical practice, whereas they might have made up the majority of his customers when he worked as a barber.[29]

The letters from many self-hired slaves express a distress that was unmistakably genuine, distress that was a consistent part of their lives. It took a great deal of effort for self-hired slaves to stay ahead of the demands of owners, not to mention the costs of food, clothing, and shelter, and all their best efforts could be invalidated by a single bout of illness or by a debilitating injury. George Renkins, for instance, a slave who hired his time in Richmond, had to write to his owner, William B. Randolph, for some coal when he suddenly fell very ill. "I am more unwell to day than I have been for several days," Renkins wrote. "Dear Master I am the best part of my time unable to go from & to my bed . . . I am oblige[d] to keep fires up all night & brown coles are going vary fast I would be vary thankful to you if you will please give me some cole for that purpose." Another slave hired out by Randolph wrote in an even more dire situation in December 1857. "Dear Master William," Isaac Ballandine began, "I write these few lines to you to inform you of my situation." Ballandine then informed his owner that he was "out of work out of money and almost out of doores," and that the money he had earned so far that year was "all exausted." Particularly burdensome had been paying the five-dollar tax that the state of Virginia levied on slaves of his assessed value and that Randolph had already instructed him to pay out of his own earnings. Having paid the tax, Isaac found that there was "very often not enough to eat." Furthermore, now that winter had arrived, "I have no money to buy neither fuel nor provissions with," Ballandine admitted, telling his owner that he would "feel humbly greatful if you will help me." Ballandine wanted only "a little wood or any thing else" and insisted that "I do make this request of you because I am in nead." George Renkins and Isaac Ballandine were not alone in being left by their owners to fend completely for themselves. As Charlotte, a slave interviewed by the AFIC, stated in 1863, "My master doesn't supply me with anything—not even a little medicine—no more than if I didn't belong to him."[30]

Having been through equally distressing experiences, authors of slave narratives were especially insistent that their condition as self-hired slaves should not be misconstrued as a lesser form of slavery. Thomas H. Jones, who hired his time out on the docks of Wilmington, North Carolina, and lived in a rented house with his wife and children, was "comparatively happy." But he could never escape "the agony of the terrible thought, 'I am a slave, my wife is a slave, my precious children are slaves"—a thought that "grew bitter and insupportable" even as he enjoyed the "distinct and abounding" joy of family life. Jones eventually fell under the curse to which every self-hired slave was vulnerable precisely by reason of being a slave: his family was "carried off into returnless exile." Left a "heart broken, lonely man" after being separated from his family, Jones found that the ostensible privileges of self-hire no longer seemed so bright. He "continued to toil on, but not as I had done before"; "my home," he lamented, "was darker than the hold of ships in which I worked."[31]

Peter Randolph brought the perspective of self-hired slaves even more directly to the fore. He admonished the "casual observer" of city slaves, who might presume that their lot was "not . . . so hard as one would imagine," to look more closely. "You may think you see bright spots," he wrote, "but look at the surroundings of those spots and you will see nothing but gloom and darkness." A self-hired urban slave might live in "comparative comfort and happiness," but this could all change when he "suddenly finds himself on the auction block, knocked down to the highest bidder, and carried far and forever from those dearer to him than life." From the point of view of the self-hired slave, Randolph made clear, finding one's own work could neither preclude suffering nor hide the unavoidable fact that self-hired slaves were still slaves; as unfree people, they would always be vulnerable to the caprice of their owners, not to mention that of the owners of family members. With eloquent lucidity, Randolph concluded that "Slavery is *Slavery,* wherever it is found. Dress it up as you may, in the city or on the plantation, the human being must feel that which binds him to another's will. Be the fetters of silk, or hemp, or iron, all alike warp the mind and goad the soul." As the words of self-hired slaves make clear, we need to talk about the benefits these slaves enjoyed—benefits many slaves would have gladly assumed—without implying that these slaves were any less enslaved, or any freer, than their friends and family who worked out their days under whip-yielding overseers.[32]

Perhaps the best evidence that self-hired slaves did not consider themselves quasi-free is that two of the largest slave revolts in American history—those led by Gabriel Prosser in 1800 and Denmark Vesey in 1822—were made up primarily of self-hired slaves. The fact that self-hired slaves led these revolts can of course be read in two ways. First, these slaves enjoyed some freedom of movement that allowed them to organize their revolts, so it is an indication of the "privileged" position that they enjoyed. But before we read too much into that privileged position, we have to remember that the slaves were in fact leading a *revolt.* They were trying to gain their freedom, and not simply that last little bit that had been denied to them. They wanted a wholesale liberation from the bonds of slavery for themselves and for as many others as they could recruit to their cause. Self-hired slaves were more loosely supervised by whites than were other slaves, and this fact put them in a better position to lead a revolt, but it did not make them any less enslaved. There is no better evidence for this fact than the revolts themselves. The self-hired rebels surely would have found a common faith in Frederick Douglass's credo: "It was *slavery*—not its mere *incidents*—that I hated."[33]

As the letters, interviews, and narratives of self-hired slaves attest, their lives were anything but easy, and certainly not infused with healthy doses of freedom. Self-hired slaves always made a very clear distinction between slavery and freedom, between the perquisites sometimes open to them and the perpetual denial of their personal liberty. Thomas Likers, who had hired his own time as a waiter in Maryland, believed that self-hire had indeed insulated him from many of the "sufferings" that other slaves endured. But he did not consider himself quasi-free. "No matter what privileges I had," he told an interviewer in Canada in 1863, "I felt that I had not my rights as long as I was deprived of liberty." His view, however, contrasted sharply with that of the white majority. White Southerners, especially white workers, saw self-hired slaves as virtually free. With no mind to the contradiction, Southern whites denounced self-hired slaves as, by turns, insufferably indolent and unduly competitive.[34]

"Competition Too Powerful to Resist"

The contrast between what slaves and whites felt about self-hire could not have been starker. While self-hired slaves struggled daily with all the evils of being slaves, trying desperately to make enough money to pay their owners as well as to keep themselves fed, clothed, and sheltered, many white Southerners perceived the lives these slaves led as carefree, even dissolute. In particular, white Southerners who were opposed to self-hire condemned the unbearable insolence they associated with slaves who hired their own time. Slaves allowed even the remotest sense of independence, they argued, were a walking threat to master-slave relationships everywhere. And they were an especial threat to the livelihood of white workers, who allegedly could not compete, even through the strictest economy, with perpetually underbidding self-hired slaves. Owners determined not to be told how to use their slave property faced off against white workers determined to protect their right to a decent livelihood from the predation of greedy planters.

The opponents of self-hire continually insisted that slaves sent out to find their own work were insidious anomalies with no proper place in a slave society. To place a slave at some remove from the control of a master was to flirt with danger, they argued, for not only did such separation breed inappropriate notions of freedom and autonomy in the slave, but those notions were notoriously contagious and could easily infect other slaves as well. Eliza Smith, a former slave from Virginia, remembered that she had been prohibited from hiring her own time when her owner decided that the practice "gave niggers such stuck up notions of freedom." In the same way, Parke Johnston, who hired his own time in eastern Virginia as a carpenter, shoemaker, and general "jobber," remembered being thrown into jail from time to time by angry whites who found his "independent life" to be an "example injurious to their slaves." Politicians, too, picked up on the theme of self-hire as a threat to the proper subordination of slaves. In 1860, Robert C. Wickliffe, the governor of Louisiana, inveighed against the "pernicious" practice of self-hire, insisting that it gave slaves "liberties and privileges totally inconsistent with their proper condition and good government."[35]

Beyond the folly of giving slaves an inappropriate taste of freedom, opponents observed, self-hire also allowed slaves to indulge in their allegedly natural propensity toward laziness, thievery, and drunkenness. Assumed to have a great deal of time and money of their own, self-hired slaves were deemed a community hazard. Petitioners from the Richland District of

South Carolina complained to the legislature in 1819 that the money self-hired slaves earned for themselves was "spent in the indulgence of vicious habits." Charleston workers declared in 1793 that self-hire did nothing more than "encourage Negroes in Stealing" and declared in 1828 that it made slaves "more Licentious than if they were Free." In 1858, inhabitants of Marion County, South Carolina, observed that permitting self-hired slaves to "rent houses separate to themselves" was especially ill-advised, for such houses inevitably served as "a depot for stolen goods." Such was the "lazy, indolent life" led by self-hired slaves, the petitioners added, that it made them "discontented with their condition." The particulars of what made self-hire objectionable to white Southerners varied according to their perspective, for the observations of indolence contradicted simultaneous complaints, especially by white workers, that self-hired slaves were overly competitive for jobs.[36]

In the aftermath of Denmark Vesey's rebellion in Charleston, petitions to the South Carolina legislature drew special attention to the time that self-hired slaves had to themselves, time, white people feared, that could be used to hatch conspiracy and rebellion. A petition in 1822 noted that "the late intended Insurrection" undeniably proved that self-hired slaves were all potential rebels, "for with a very few exceptions, the negroes involved in that conspiracy were mechanics or persons working out." Self-hired slaves were a danger to society, the petition claimed, because they had been "released from the controul of their masters." As a consequence, the petition declared, self-hired slaves "assemble together whenever they wish," during which times they "can originate, prepare and mature their plans for insurrection." By contrast, slaves kept "in the yards of their masters" were more easily frustrated in attempts to meet regularly with fellow slaves, and thus less able to "act in concert." The obvious course of action, according to the petitioners, was to limit the availability of employment as craftsmen to white workers, for the result would be the recall of self-hired slaves to their owners' plantations. Subsequently, their places could be "supplied by white laborers from Europe and the Northern States."[37]

For most white workers, the alleged insolence, dissolution, and insurgency of self-hired slaves were secondary concerns, for the whites were primarily interested in eliminating the competition that these slaves presented in Southern cities. Such competition had been a cause of tension since the colonial period. As early as 1734, South Carolina's General Assembly noted with dismay, in a remonstrance sent to Britain, that "many Negroes are now train'd up to be Handicraft Tradesmen, to the great discouragement of Your Majestys White Subjects." The tension only increased in the revolutionary and antebellum eras. Charleston's house carpenters and bricklayers complained to their General Assembly in 1783 that, since the outbreak of the Revolutionary War, they had "scarce had sufficient Employment to support their families, owing, . . . in great Measure, to a number of Jobbing Negro Tradesmen." In 1828, a contributor to Georgia's *Augusta Chronicle* offered an answer to why "every poor mechanic" in the city—by which he meant poor, *white* mechanics—faced terrible difficulty in providing "a daily support for himself and his family." The difficulty resulted, he claimed, from the fact that "so many slaves in the city" were allowed to "hire their own time from their owners." He went on to deplore that these slaves did nothing but "reduce the price of jobs so low that it is almost impossible for an honest mechanic to gain a sufficiency to subsist on." By the time of the Civil War, when hiring was at its peak, most white Southerners would have agreed that the market in hired slaves, and self-hired slaves in particular, did in fact drive down the wages that white workers could command, if it did not eliminate them from competition altogether. In an 1862 letter to his brother, the North Carolina minister John S. Grasty maintained that "for the sake of the poor, no man ought to hire a negro low next year." "It should be the aim of every good man," Grasty continued, "to raise the price of every laboring man."[38]

White workers contended to all who would listen that competition with slaves was unfair because slaves could (allegedly) work for less than whites could. South Carolina petitioners claimed in 1819, for example, that "the Slave who hires his time, is from the greater cheapness in his living, & from other accidental occurrences able to work for cheaper & still make his wages than it is possible for white Journeymen to do." The "accidental occurrences" alluded to included the presumed presence of a provisioning master, the presumed absence of a family to support, and even a presumed unscrupulousness. On this last point, Charleston's house carpenters and bricklayers had pointed out in 1783 that slaves were taking jobs for "very little more than the Materials would cost," which they adduced as evidence that "the Stuff they work with cannot be honestly acquired." "For obvious reasons," a group of Charleston mechanics concluded in an 1828 petition, "the competition of Negro and Colored Workmen, whether Bond or Free, . . . is too powerful to resist." Slaves, they claimed, could "live on a great deal less" because they did not have to worry about doctors' bills, hungry children, and other "harassing cares and fearful anticipations that accompany the Poor Man's reflections upon the future." To make matters worse, the mechanics observed, many of the wealthiest inhabitants of Charleston, rather than decide the particulars of household repairs themselves, would "leave it to their Domestics to employ what workmen they please." These domestic slaves, the mechanics asserted, of course "prefer

Men of their own Color and condition," a propensity that exacerbated an already dire situation and left self-hired slaves with "as complete a monopoly as if it were secured to them by Law." Though their sentiments are not evident in the historical record of protests against self-hire, poor white women, especially those who worked as washerwomen or as domestic servants, no doubt deplored the competition of slave workers as much as white men did.[39]

The often conflicting sentiments of free black people, who made their living in the same jobs for which slaves were hired, are equally unclear in the historical record. Many free black people surely competed with self-hired slaves, in the same way that white workers did, for the temporary labor available in Southern cities. But free black people also had friendship and family ties with slaves that white workers rarely, if ever, had. Free black people made a concerted effort to buy enslaved family members whenever possible, and self-hired slaves who earned extra money could contribute to those purchases. Adding to the complexity of free black people's relation to the practice of self-hire is the fact that they sometimes owned slaves themselves, whom they often allowed to hire their own time. This was especially true in cities like Charleston and New Orleans, where an "elite" caste of free black people earned enough money to become slaveholders. Free black women in these cities, for example, may have relied on the income of self-hired slaves in the same way that white women did. Census returns and tax lists for Charleston reveal that Elsey Lee, Hannah Humphrey, Ann Walker, Jennette Bonneau, and other free black women lived on income derived from hired slaves from the 1830s through the 1850s.[40]

If free black people ever opposed the practice of self-hire, their opposition grew exclusively out of the material issues of earning a decent livelihood. That was not true for white workers, who worried as much about threats to whiteness and social status as about threats to economic survival. A petition signed by Mississippi workers in 1847 stated that a slave who worked on his own, charging less than a white worker ostensibly could, was placed "above the white mechanic." This invocation of social status signaled the intersection of concerns over whiteness—that is, the social and psychic rewards of being white in a society based on racial slavery—with concerns over livelihood. These Mississippi mechanics had already succeeded in convincing their legislature to end the practice of putting white convicts to work as craftsmen and laborers. But the mechanics wanted lawmakers to take the next step and prohibit self-hired slaves from the work as well, for to them competition with black, enslaved workers was as much socially demeaning as it was economically injurious. Their 1847 protest observed that they could find "but little choice between the white villain and the black slave, if we have to compete with either." But if compelled to make a choice, the mechanics averred, "we should rather choose him who is of our own country, color, and blood." Whiteness was a form of property in the South, to be defended as vehemently as one's right to make a decent livelihood, if not more so.[41]

White workers in other states also made a connection between economics and whiteness. Mechanics in Wilmington, North Carolina, complained in an 1802 petition that self-hired slaves in their city were able to take on jobs for less than half the rate that "a regular bred white Mechanic could afford to do it." As elsewhere in the South, the issue at stake here was not so much unfair competition as it was black competition. Like the workers in Mississippi, white laborers across the South voiced their ire at being degraded by having to work alongside self-hired slaves. Frederick Douglass observed that white apprentices in the Maryland shipyards where he worked "began to feel it to be degrading to work with me," that they would "talk contemptuously and maliciously of *'the niggers.'"* Workers in Arkansas in 1858 were especially explicit about how mortifying it was for them to work alongside black slaves in their chosen professions:

> What is still worse—we find ourselves *morally* degraded by seeing ourselves yoked with hired slave mechanics in the public streets and thoroughfares in the towns of our state, or being confined in the same rooms (shops) with a lot of sweating and puffing hired black slave buck mechanics . . . How humiliating for us to be yoked with hired slave mechanics . . . in towns and crowded cities, in full view of all passers-by. How painful must it be to a noble wife, a loving mother, an adoring daughter or a tender-hearted sister to see the well-cultivated, high-minded husband, the devoted father, the noble son, the kind brother, yoked with hired slave mechanics, on *"the corners of the streets,* and in the market-places."

To white workers, self-hired slaves represented a challenge to their livelihood as family providers, but also to their dignity as white men. Whiteness presumably entailed some prerogatives in the slave South—including a sense of independence and distinction—but these were undercut, white workers argued, when slave owners followed their pocketbooks and allowed self-hire to flourish illicitly at the expense of white laborers. "Stop negroes from trafficking about the streets, hiring their own time," one Southerner opined in the pages of the *Southern Cultivator* in 1860, "because it gives the negro facility to idle, trade and all concomitants—*interfering with the white man's rights."* Not surprisingly, the clamor raised by this issue convinced Frederick Douglass that the competition of self-hired slaves with whites for jobs would someday be "an important element in the overthrow of the slave system."[42]

White workers and other opponents of self-hire carefully crafted their petitions, however, to voice specific opposition to self-hire, not to slavery in general. Charleston's workers, who made a long career of petitioning the South Carolina legislature for more rigid enforcement of existing laws, always made a point of indicating the threat that self-hire posed to the interests of all slaveholders, not just those of white workers. As the city's master coopers asserted in 1793, slaves hiring their own time would "destroy that Subordination which the Situation of this State requires from the Slave toward his master." Likewise, Charleston workers warned in 1828 that their city would "in a very short time, be in the condition of a West India Town," if self-hire were allowed to continue, and that the city would then "be impossible to defend without a Regular Military Force." In 1858, they argued that the practice was "affecting not only the interests of the mechanic and workingman, but also of the owner of the slaves, as well as the property itself." Charleston workers noted that the reforms they called for would, to be sure, make it easier for them to earn a living, but they would also be "eminently conducive to the best interests and prosperity of the State, her institutions and her citizens, and to the well-being and usefulness of the slave himself." But to owners who considerably increased their profits through self-hire, many of whom were conceivably members of the legislature, such arguments fell rather flat.[43]

Some Southern leaders were aware nonetheless that the sentiments expressed in these petitions, despite their adamant disavowals of antislavery intent, were potentially dangerous. Opinions about how to react to workers' complaints could be quite mixed, though. On the one hand, those who relied heavily on hired slaves were sufficiently alarmed to ascribe antislavery consequences, if not intentions, to the workers' campaigns. When white workers went on strike at Joseph Anderson's Tredegar Iron Works in Richmond in 1847 because they opposed the use of hired slave laborers, for example, Anderson dismissed the recalcitrant whites and rationalized his action by pointing out the implicit threat such protests presented to the slave system. The *Richmond Enquirer* agreed with Anderson, noting that such actions on the part of white workers would "render slave property utterly valueless." At the same time, other Southern leaders, while they too recognized the implicit threat posed by workers' complaints and petitions, were more sympathetic than Joseph Anderson and the *Richmond Enquirer* had been. Some Southern politicians knew that if white workingmen continued to feel disgraced by their competition with slave laborers, they might readily transfer the focus of their opposition from the operation of the slave system to its very existence, and that that opposition might be difficult to contain. A Mississippi delegate to a Southern Convention in

1859 advocated that the Convention resolve to "condemn the practice of making [slaves] competing public mechanics," a practice that had already succeeded, he claimed, in "creating a degree of opposition in our very midst to the institution of slavery." A contributor to *DeBow's Review* suggested in 1858 that it might be time for the South to fashion a labor system that would allow for an equilibrium between slave and free labor, an equilibrium obtained by "confining the negro to domestic and field service," while leaving "the mechanical pursuits to the exclusive occupation of the whites."[44]

White workers were not the only Southerners opposed to self-hire. Many residents of the countryside thought that the practice was a bad idea in general, and some claimed specific hardship occasioned by owners' allowing their slaves to hire their own time. A 1782 petition from rural Henrico County, Virginia, pointed out, for example, that self-hired slaves were "Idle and disorderly," and that they stole from surrounding farms. Petitioners from Colleton District, South Carolina, urged their legislature in 1820 to restrict self-hire to "Incorporated Towns and Cities" after they noticed that neighboring slaveholders had given some of their slaves passes, lasting a month or longer, that allowed them to work out on their own. The slaves, the petitioners complained, "of course are not subject to the Patrol Laws, as they have no fixed residence or place to work," and their presence—since many had "horses and can go when and where they please"—was "the means of much Injury to the Slaves in general." Similarly, petitioners from Craven County, North Carolina, claimed in 1831 to have been "much injured and interrupted" in "the management of their farms and negroes" by the presence of slaves allowed by owners to come up the Neuse River from Newbern "to sell, buy, traffick, and fish in the neighborhood." These slaves "trade with, and corrupt the slaves" in the area, the petitioners asserted, often inducing them to run away or to pilfer from nearby farms. An 1831 petition from Lenoir County, North Carolina, also complained about self-hired slaves from Newbern, slaves whose owners sent them out to "retail cakes, tobacco, & spiritous liquors." These petitioners were equally concerned that the slaves might steal from them, but they were more worried about "a far more serious & incalculable injury" caused by "the dissemination of seditious writings & notions" by these itinerant peddlers. The slaves, "enjoying the privilege of travelling in their little Carts from one County [or] town to another," the petitioners claimed, had it "in their power" to spread furtively—"in every nook" of the country—"the murderous plans of a Nat Turner." White workers were not alone in their ardent opposition to self-hire, but even the petitions of slaveholders themselves did little to turn the situation in their favor.[45]

Indeed, the incessant flow of petitions from opponents of self-hire went largely unheeded. In 1859, for example, the South Carolina legislature agreed that the complaints made in the petitions of white workers were well founded. "We agree fully with the memorialists, who complain of this evil," read the report issued by the legislature's Committee on Negro Population. But the committee was more concerned with "general" consequences of self-hire than with the "specific one"—competition between free and slave labor for the same jobs—complained of in the workingmen's petitions. To the committee members' way of thinking, "the evil lies in the breaking down the relation between master and slave—the removal of the slave from the master's discipline and control, and the assumption of freedom and independence on the part of the slave." Such independent behavior, the report added, simply offered more opportunity for disorder and crime, which in turn required the "trouble and expense" of "additional police regulations." This was not what white workers wanted to hear. They cared less about the breakdown of master-slave relationships, although they frequently invoked that specter to support their claims, than they did about the degrading necessity of competing with enslaved black men for jobs.

The committee was not unaware of the sentiment behind the petitions, or of the "specific" complaint that self-hire brought white and slave labor into competition. But the committee could see no way to remedy the situation, and its sympathy extended only so far. The report tersely reminded the petitioners that Southerners "are, as a slaveholding people, habituated to slave labor." The fundamental issue, the committee noted, was that "we have towns and villages . . . where ordinary labor is to be performed which can be done by either whites or negroes." White workers wanted, ideally, to have all such work reserved for them, or at least to require that those employing slave labor make contracts with the owners of the slaves, and not with the slaves themselves. The committee deemed such demands a practical impossibility. "It would be impossible to have this sort of slave labor," the report observed, "if there must be a contract with the owner for every specific job." There was simply too much short-term work that needed to be done in Southern cities—"for instance, the transportation of a load in a wagon or dray, the carrying of a passenger's trunk to or from a railroad, &c."—for the law to require a separate contract for each task. It was much easier to allow slaves to find such work on their own and turn over the money they earned to their owners. Any law that tried to eliminate such slave labor would ultimately fail because people had become so habituated to its availability. "Until you can change the direction of the public prejudice, prepossession and habit," the committee's report flatly concluded, "you can never enforce a law which conflicts with them." The practice of self-hire was simply too convenient and too profitable to be done away with, in spite of the straitened conditions in which it might place white workers.[46]

Despite their relatively small numbers, self-hired slaves had a significant impact on their contemporaries. To the owners who sent out slaves to find their own work and lodgings, self-hire was another means to augment financial return on slave capital. To those who employed the labor of self-hired slaves, the practice was a necessity, a way to get laundry washed, fences painted, and warehouses unloaded. But to the opponents of self-hire, the profit and convenience that self-hire had to recommend it were nothing more than the delusions of wayward white Southerners. When they passed self-hired slaves on the streets of Southern towns and cities, these white Southerners saw slaves they presumed to be at least half free. They saw slaves cut loose from the direct supervision of a master, leading idyllic lives, working when they pleased. Moreover, when they did work, opponents pointed out, self-hired slaves were a source of unfair and inappropriate competition for white workers. Indeed, the anger and resentment aroused in white workers over the issue of self-hire was no small matter. For these men, the sight of slaves working and living by their own lights called up fears and anxieties about competition with slaves, competition not simply for livelihood but also, more important, for social acceptance, a sense of personal independence, and an acknowledgement of the perquisites of whiteness. The animosity that simmered behind workers' incessant, and futile, petitions against self-hire never exploded into full-scale opposition to the use of slaves in cities, but that animosity was always inches below the surface of everyday life. The debates about self-hire were one more example of the ways that slavery, and hiring in particular, could be a source of dissension—rather than the much extolled concord—in the social relations of Southern whites. Self-hire was but another of the myriad ways that hired slaves were able to use that discord as a source of leverage in widening control over their lives and in taking advantage of the chinks in the slaveholding armor, thereby preventing the system of slavery from ever taking its ease.

But even as hired slaves used their white captors' concerns over personal and social independence to their advantage, they themselves always remained enslaved, stripped of personal liberty. There were no "privileges" that self-hired slaves, or any hired slaves, could secure for themselves that could make them "quasi-free." The concept of quasi freedom, which began with the gripes of white opponents of self-hire, was never mirrored in the words of slaves themselves. Slave hire—in whatever shape or form—was not "a step toward freedom," but merely another form of slavery.

Epilogue

FREDERICK Douglass's life as a slave was shaped in no small measure by the practice of slave hiring. To begin with, like so many other children in slavery, Douglass scarcely knew his own mother—and slave hiring was to blame. Douglass's mother was rented out by their owner to neighboring farmers every year, and though she made surreptitious nighttime visits when she could, Douglass rarely saw her. Later in his life, he decried the way that hiring separated mothers from children as "a marked feature of the cruelty and barbarity of the slave system."[1] When Douglass reached his teenage years, he too was hired out by his owner. As a child he had always worked as a house servant, but now he labored in the fields for the first time. Under the watchful eyes of such tenant farmers as Edward Covey and William Freeland, he was first "broken" of his "impudence" and then trained as a prime field hand. Douglass's owner had more remunerative ambitions for his slave than fieldwork, however; when Douglass was in his twenties, he was hired out to Baltimore shipyards to learn the caulking trade. Douglass would eventually go on to hire his own time in Baltimore, making his own contracts and sending several dollars per week to his owner. Like many other self-hired slaves, Douglass was deeply resented by the white apprentices with whom he competed for jobs. Indeed, he suffered at least one severe beating at their hands while working in the city. Though in all other respects extraordinary, Frederick Douglass had experiences with hiring that typified those of many other slaves.

Slave hiring figured so centrally in Douglass's life, as it did in the lives of most slaves, because the practice pervaded Southern slavery. Every new year began, in cities and towns across the region, with the much anticipated "hiring day." Slaves, auctioned off to the highest bidders, were sent away with temporary masters to work in the farms, factories, shops, and homes of the South. By no means confined to New Year's Day, hiring transactions continued apace throughout the year. The back pages of Southern newspapers were crowded with advertisements placed by people looking to rent slaves for all sorts of work. And owners routinely fielded hiring requests from neighbors and acquaintances who needed slave labor but could not afford the prohibitive prices of the slave pens. As a result, hired slaves were everywhere in the South. They picked cotton, rolled tobacco, built barns, drove wagons, fashioned horseshoes, laid rails, nursed babies, dusted, washed, and served. If there was work to be done, a slave could be hired to perform it.

So widespread was the practice of renting slaves that it developed its own rules and regulations, its own patterns of contract, its own class of brokers, and its own set of customs. Slave hiring was anomalous. It was in a category apart, both in theory and in practice, because of its atypical dynamics. Creating slaves with two masters, hiring transactions deviated, in their triangularity, from the customary polarity of master-slave relationships.

As we have seen, that triangular nature of the transaction had significant repercussions not only for the relations between masters and slaves, but also for the relations among Southern whites themselves. Ordinarily, slaveholders took for granted the insularity of the relation between a master and his slaves, presuming always that outsiders could not and should not interfere with the total subordination of slave to master. As Frederick Douglass put it, slaveholders stoutly held that there "must be no force between the slave and the slave-holder, to restrain the power of the one, and protect the weakness of the other."[2] In this sense, slaveholders considered their relationships with slaves to be similar to those with other dependents in their households. As masters, slaveholders considered themselves entitled to demand labor and obedience from the subordinate members of their households—women, children, and slaves alike—in return for their own promises to provide sustenance, supervision, and protection. As the masters governed relations with their dependents, they expected only minimal intrusions, if any, from neighbors and state authorities. When managing their slaves, masters assumed the power to issue orders, punish infractions, disburse rewards, and meet needs as they saw fit, their sway mediated by nothing more than their own self-interest in the smooth functioning of their farms and households. The force of law, and the voice of the community, dissipated as soon as one entered the enclosure of the Southern household.

Hiring transactions necessarily forced a departure from this way of thinking about master-slave relationships. The fact that hired slaves had two masters both destroyed the customary insularity of master-slave relations and guaranteed constant disputes over the precise boundaries of the mastery that owners transferred to hirers. These disputes, which routinely ended up in Southern courtrooms, centered on the right of property. "The contract of hiring," one Tennessee judge explained in 1855, "does not, as is sometimes loosely expressed, transfer the right of property in the slave to the bailee for the term." Rather, the owner "parts with the use, possession and control of the property for the time agreed upon, and nothing more passes to the hirer." Specifically, the title to the slave was not in any way affected: "The labor of the slave is sold for a time, but not the slave himself." Owners and hirers returned again and again to Southern courtrooms to argue over the "use, possession, and control" that hirers enjoyed, and the law thereby acquired a presence in hiring transactions that was far more prominent than in ordinary master-slave relations. That presence inevitably shaped how the whites involved characterized their rights: both owners and hirers contended that their respective property rights should prevail. It was one of the many ways that slave hiring reinforced for white Southerners that slaves were property and capital first, persons and dependents second.

Conflict between owners and hirers was nearly inevitable. To protect valuable slaves, owners did whatever they could to limit the power that hirers exercised. But at the same time, hirers insisted that they had purchased the right to exert unmitigated control over the slaves they worked. Southern judges for the most part shared the owners' view that hirers lacked the "prudence" that would lead them to treat slaves humanely, work them moderately, and call doctors when necessary. The same Tennessee judge quoted above observed that many hirers came into court with "false conclusions" about the "rights and powers" they could exercise over the slaves they rented. They failed to recognize that they were "bound by law . . . to provide for the comfort and safety of a slave, in sickness and in health"—that their treatment of hired slaves must be "such as ordinary masters bestow on their slaves." The judge discerned that hiring transactions, in reorienting the customary polarity of master-slave relationships, removed the presumed basis for every "prudent" master's decisions about slave treatment: self-interest. "It is unfortunate," the judge continued, "that it is the interest of the hirer to get all the labor he can out of the hired slave, without regard to his comfort, or the effect upon his permanent health and value." Legal rules were required "to guard against the influence of this selfish feeling," and thus to provide for "the protection of the owner and his property."[3] Hirers, of course, resented any attempts, by owners or by judges, to restrict the mastery they felt to be rightfully theirs. They agreed that title to slaves did not pass to them through hiring contracts, but they did insist that slave labor was worthless to those who could not exercise complete domination. They understood all too well that "everything must be absolute here," as Frederick Douglass observed of power in master-slave relationships.[4]

In these ways, slave hiring exemplified the crucial difference that liberal capitalism made for Southern slavery. Both the owner and the hirer claimed a property interest in the same slave—the former a long-term interest in the title to a slave, the latter a short-term interest in the slave's labor. Both these rights were property rights, and in a liberal capitalist world, property rights are absolute; they cannot be divided without being violated. Ordinarily, the rights to title and to mastery would have redounded to a single person, but when they were divided by the temporal boundaries delineated in hiring contracts, conflict was almost inevitable. By defining mastery as a form of property, slaveholders made the division of that mastery an increasingly difficult endeavor. But at the same time, slaveholders wanted to meet the demands of world markets as efficiently as possible—and that virtually required a rental market in slave labor. Slaveholders were caught in a bind: they wanted profits and efficient market production, but the labor system they relied upon to achieve those aims was inherently rigid, and it did not accommodate flexibility easily. Indeed, the liberal capitalist values on which slaveholders relied to shield themselves from the onslaught of abolitionists worked simultaneously to subvert slavery from the inside and made the system's evolution toward increased flexibility more difficult.

In fact, when injected with more flexibility, the system did what it wasn't supposed to do: it brought white people into conflict and it conferred some additional room to maneuver on slaves. All slaves were experienced at finding loopholes in the system to which they were subject, and hired slaves were especially adept at exploiting the compromised authority of their temporary masters. They knew how to use their owners' unremitting property interests to their own advantage. When they could, they refused to do certain kinds of work, they demanded the opportunity to visit family members, they resisted punishment, or they ran away. In the face of such resistance, hirers were, not surprisingly, often ambivalent about the desirability of renting slave labor. To be sure, slave hiring was a significantly cheaper route to slaveholding than was purchasing at a slave auction. But when slaves could play their two masters off each other, many hirers concluded that trying to assume the role of master before hired slaves was an exercise in futility.

The influence that this ubiquitous practice had on the lives of both black and white Southerners was unmistakable. By allowing slaveholders to pursue production or speculation with their slaves—to exploit them as either labor or capital—slave hiring influenced the way that slaveholders viewed their slaves. Surveying the operations on his various plantations in 1786, Thomas Jefferson concluded that "after stating the amount of the crop, and deducting Overseer's and steward's parts, transportation, negroes clothes, tools, medicine, and taxes, the profits of the whole estate would be no more than the hire of the few negroes hired out would amount to." With hiring as a possibility, slaveowners like Jefferson could look at the slaves they possessed and see individual units of investment return rather than a bloc that could be thinned or expanded only through sale. Jefferson was not alone in asking, once he could see that his slaves would be more profitable rented out to others than laboring on his own plantations, whether "it be better to hire more where good masters could be got."[5] This line of thinking made slaveholders both managers of capital and managers of slaves. Their slaves in many ways became a cash crop in themselves, for hiring offered returns on slaveholders' investment that could rival what they earned by selling cotton or tobacco. More than a few white Southerners lived comfortably off the annuities provided by the slaves they rented out.

Of course, slave hiring also affected the way that slaves viewed their owners. Hired slaves could see that they were sources of revenue, not dependents who provided labor in exchange for promises of protection and material support. Isaac Mason, hired out to cover his owner's twenty-five-dollar doctor's bill, put it simply: "I was only the property of another, working to pay the debt of another."[6] When Frederick Douglass reported to his owner that he had been beaten by white workers in Baltimore while on hire, he knew that his owner's anger sprang from the realization that Douglass, one of his prime assets, had lost value. "His indignation was really strong and healthy," Douglass observed, "but, unfortunately, it resulted from the thought that his rights of property, in my person, had not been respected, more than from any sense of the outrage committed on me *as a man*."[7] In these ways, slaves and owners saw that it was the chattel principle—the fact that slaves were valuable property—rather than the mutual obligations of paternalism that mediated the relations between them. When slaves moved from master to master every year—or when the possibility of such movement hovered in the wings—it was difficult for slaves to form paternal relations with owners they often barely even knew.

Indeed, when owners could turn to rental markets to earn a profit on their slaves, no one in the slave quarters could dismiss the possibility of being sent, on any given day, to work for some other white Southerner. Most slaves could expect to be hired out at least once in their lives, and many, like Frederick Douglass, were hired out repeatedly, to different masters. In fact, at the stage in their lives when they were least likely to be sold—when they were very old or very young—slaves were prime candidates for hiring. On the outskirts of the Southern plantations subsisted innumerable poor farmers for whom entry into the master classes entailed taking in children to sweep and dust, cook and mind babies—and the helpers were slaves so small that their owners requested nothing more in return than the children's "victuals and clothing." Because even the youngest and oldest slaves were vulnerable, hiring was an inescapable part of slave life, and slaves were forced to accommodate it in their strategies for survival.

But some slaves were actually successful in using their value as property to their advantage. Recall that this was the primary reason that Frank Ruffin denounced slave hiring as an "evil" in the pages of the *Southern Planter.* The property interests of owners and hirers were diametrically opposed, and slaves knew it. Many hired slaves, for instance, gained some small measure of control from their ability to report instances of abuse by hirers to their owners. They knew that there was a good likelihood that their owners would believe their reports, whether true or not, because their owners had an incentive to safeguard the remuneration slaves might reap in the future. In the process of playing their masters off against each other, hired slaves learned to rely on themselves rather than the unpredictable solicitude of their owners, and to use their value however they could to shape their own lives. By bringing the white Southerners who enslaved them into conflict, they succeeded in disrupting a system grounded in racial solidarity among free persons.

If slave hiring was so contentious and destabilizing, why did white Southerners continue the practice year after year? The simple answer is that slave hiring, despite the acrimony it often caused, made good economic sense. Renting out slaves provided a flexibility that was crucial to the survival of slavery as a labor system. White Southerners could calibrate their labor needs more easily when sale was not the only way to shed or acquire slaves. Owners did not have to worry about losing their title to slaves they might need in the future, and hirers did not have to raise the requisite sums of cash to purchase slaves. Hiring was, in short, a way to separate the market in slave labor from the market in slaves.

It is no surprise that slave hiring emerged from the South's experience with the market revolution. Throughout the colonial and antebellum periods, change in the South was driven by slaveholders' unstinting efforts to meet international demand for cotton, wheat, tobacco, and other staples. Production for the market dominated every aspect of life, affecting Southerners' decisions about the periodicals to which they should subscribe, the candidates for whom they should vote, and the places to which they might move. As slaveholders streamlined their operations, and as a nascent industrial economy emerged in the South's major cities, the flexibility of a rental market in slaves became increasingly attractive. In the eighteenth century, slave hiring was fundamental to the burgeoning and diverse urban economy of Charleston. It facilitated the transition from tobacco to wheat cultivation in the Revolutionary Chesapeake. And it was indispensable in the effort to spread the system of slavery to the Southwest, to the untried lands that would eventually generate the Kingdom of Cotton.

Hiring was thus indispensable to the diversification and expansion that white Southerners pursued in their persistent efforts to meet the demands of local and world markets. Farms were more efficient and more productive when worked by rented slave labor. Edmund Ruffin, a tireless agricultural reformer, observed in 1859 that "a young negro man may now be hired for a year at $130 and his maintenance; and his labor, applied to all the other capital of a farm that needed his labor, would probably add not less than $300 to the net sales of products of the farm."[8] But the economic benefits of hiring spread beyond agriculture. An expanding economy also required transportation networks, and the roads, canals, and railroads of the South were largely constructed by slaves. Their hirers were public contractors who, as their projects moved from one county to the next, sought out labor from neighboring slaveholders. Hiring markets also facilitated efforts to diversify the Southern economy. Grain mills, lumber and turpentine operations, ironworks, and coal pits would have been impracticable had their managers been forced to purchase all the labor their enterprises required. Southern cities never approximated the thriving urban economies of the North, but they would have been significantly less bustling than they were had slaves not been authorized by their owners to negotiate wages for themselves for individual jobs. Perhaps more important than the energizing of regional economies and local enterprises was the critical role slave hiring played in the geographical expansion of slavery as a labor system. The migrants who left seaboard states throughout the early nineteenth century to re-create a slaveholding world farther to the west would have been hamstrung, perhaps irreversibly, had a thriving rental market in slaves not made it possible to earn cash by hiring out slaves who would otherwise have been idle. In rewarding slaveholders both individually and collectively, slave hiring was critical to the continued viability of slavery as a labor system in the colonial and antebellum periods.

Slave hiring continued year after year because it increased production, facilitated the spread of slavery into the western territories, and gave increasing numbers of white Southerners a taste of mastery that they might not otherwise have won. But hiring offered flexibility to slaves as well as masters, unwonted encouragement in their efforts to shape their own lives, and that leeway helped destabilize a system predicated on white solidarity.

Abbreviations

DU   Rare Book, Manuscript, and Special Collections Library, William
         Perkins Library, Duke University, Durham, North Carolina

HL   The Huntington Library, San Marino, California

LC   The Library of Congress, Manuscript Room, Washington, D.C.

LSU   Louisiana and Lower Mississippi Valley Collections, Hill Memorial
         Library, Louisiana State University, Baton Rouge, Louisiana

MDAH   Mississippi Department of Archives and History, Jackson, Mississippi

NA   National Archives, Washington, D.C.

SHC   Southern Historical Collection, Wilson Library, University of North
         Carolina at Chapel Hill, Chapel Hill, North Carolina

TU   Howard-Tilton Memorial Library, Tulane University, New Orleans,
         Louisiana

UVA   Alderman Library, University of Virginia, Charlottesville, Virginia

VHS   Virginia Historical Society, Richmond, Virginia

WM   Earl Gregg Swem Library, College of William and Mary,
         Williamsburg, Virginia

Notes

Introduction: Slaves with Two Masters

1. Interview with Sister Harrison, in Charles L. Perdue, Jr., Thomas E. Barden, and Robert K. Phillips, eds., *Weevils in the Wheat: Interviews with Virginia Ex-Slaves* (Charlottesville: University Press of Virginia, 1976), 135.

2. John W. Nash to Joseph Hobson, 30 November 1822, Nash Family Papers, section 2, VHS.

3. *Southern Planter* 12 (December 1852): 376–379.

4. Edward B. Bryan, *The Rightful Remedy: Addressed to the Slaveholders of the South* (Charleston: Press of Walker & James, 1850), 10–12. Emphasis in original.

5. Frances Anne Kemble, *Journal of a Residence on a Georgian Plantation in 1838–1839,* John A. Scott, ed. (1863; New York: Knopf, 1961), 104–105.

6. Ann Kussmaul, *Servants in Husbandry in Early Modern England* (New York: Cambridge University Press, 1981), 31–59; Edmund S. Morgan, "The First American Boom: Virginia, 1618 to 1630," *William and Mary Quarterly* 28 (April 1971): 176, 187, 197.

7. Edmund S. Morgan, *American Slavery, American Freedom: The Ordeal of Colonial Virginia* (New York: W. W. Norton, 1975), 296; Richard B. Morris, *Government and Labor in Early America* (1946; New York: Harper & Row, 1965), 402–411.

8. On the limitations of the 1860 census, see Clement Eaton, "Slave-Hiring in the Upper South," *Mississippi Valley Historical Review* 46 (March 1960): 673–675. Claudia Dale Goldin used the 1860 census figures for several cities to show the numbers of male and female hired slaves as percentages of the population as a whole, but she cautioned that the numbers should "be taken as lower bounds because many slaves who were hired were probably not listed as such." Claudia Dale Goldin, *Urban Slavery in the American South, 1820–1860: A Quantitative History* (Chicago: University of Chicago Press, 1976), 36.

9. Barbara Jeanne Fields, *Slavery and Freedom on the Middle Ground: Maryland during the Nineteenth Century* (New Haven: Yale University Press, 1985), 27; Frederic Bancroft, *Slave Trading in the Old South* (1931; New York: Frederick Ungar Publishing Co., 1959), 147; Eugene D. Genovese, *Roll, Jordan, Roll: The World the Slaves Made* (New York: Vintage, 1974), 390; Robert William Fogel and Stanley L. Engerman, *Time on the Cross: The Economics of American Negro Slavery* (1974; New York: W. W. Norton & Company, 1989), 56. See also Thomas D. Morris, *Southern Slavery and the Law, 1619–1860* (Chapel Hill: University of North Carolina Press, 1996), 132.

10. Fogel and Engerman, *Time on the Cross,* 53 (1.92 percent chance of sale); Herbert Gutman and Richard Sutch, "The Slave Family: Protected Agent of Capitalist Masters or Victim of the Slave Trade," in Paul A. David, Herbert G. Gutman, Richard Sutch, Peter Temin, and Gavin Wright, *Reckoning with Slavery: A Critical Study in the Quantitative History of American Negro Slavery* (New York: Oxford University Press, 1976), 110–111 (3.46 percent chance of sale); Sarah S. Hughes, "Slaves for Hire: The Allocation of Black Labor in Elizabeth City County, Virginia, 1782 to 1810," *William and Mary Quarterly* 35 (April 1978): 260; Brenda E. Stevenson, *Life in Black and White: Family and Community in the Slave South* (New York: Oxford University Press, 1996), 184.

11. The historiography of slave hiring is broader than it is deep. As a start, see the chapter devoted to the subject in Bancroft, *Slave Trading in the Old South,* 145–164. The state-focused studies of slavery published through the late 1950s often contain a chapter on the practice of hiring, but these works tend to be more descriptive than analytical. See, for example, Charles S. Sydnor, *Slavery in Mississippi* (Baton Rouge: Louisiana State University Press, 1933), 172–180; Ralph Betts Flanders, *Plantation Slavery in Georgia* (Chapel Hill: University of North Carolina Press, 1933), 194–208; J. Winston Coleman, Jr., *Slavery Times in Kentucky* (Chapel Hill: University of North Carolina Press, 1940), 123–127; James Benson Sellers, *Slavery in Alabama* (University: University of Alabama Press, 1950), 195–214; Chase C. Mooney, *Slavery in Tennessee* (Bloomington: Indiana University Press, 1957), 29–34; and Orville W. Taylor, *Negro Slavery in Arkansas* (Durham, N.C.: Duke University Press, 1958), 82–91. A few articles have described the hiring out of specific slaves, usually self-hirings. See, for example, William A. Byrne, "The Hiring of Woodson, Slave Carpenter of Savannah," *Georgia Historical Quarterly* 77 (Summer 1993): 245–263; Juliet E. K. Walker, "Pioneer Slave Entrepreneurship—Patterns, Processes, and Perspectives: The Case of the Slave Free Frank on the Kentucky Pennyroyal, 1795–1819," *Journal of Negro History* 68 (Summer 1983): 289–308; and John Hebron Moore, "Simon Gray, Riverman: A Slave Who Was Almost Free," *Mississippi Valley Historical Review* 49 (December 1962): 472–484. An excellent article for data on slave hirers in rural Texas is Randolph B. Campbell, "Research Note: Slave Hiring in Texas," *American Historical Review* 93 (February 1988): 107–114. Articles that probe the implications of a rental market in slaves include Richard B. Morris, "The Measure of Bondage in the Slave States," *Mississippi Valley Historical Review* 41 (1954): 219–240; Clement Eaton, "Slave Hiring in the Upper South," *Mississippi Valley Historical Review* 46 (1960): 663–678; Hughes, "Slaves for

Hire"; and Keith C. Barton, "'Good Cooks and Washers': Slave Hiring, Domestic Labor, and the Market in Bourbon County, Kentucky," *Journal of American History* 84 (September 1997): 436–460. For an in-depth look at slave hiring in Virginia, see John Joseph Zaborney, "Slaves for Rent: Slave Hiring in Virginia," Ph.D. diss., University of Maine, 1997. For discussions of hiring in the law of slavery, see Morris, *Southern Slavery and the Law,* 132–158; Jenny Bourne Wahl, *The Bondsman's Burden: An Economic Analysis of the Common Law of Southern Slavery* (New York: Cambridge University Press, 1998), 49–77; and Mark V. Tushnet, *The American Law of Slavery, 1810–1860: Considerations of Humanity and Interest* (Princeton, N.J.: Princeton University Press, 1981), 170–188. For discussions of hiring of urban and industrial slaves, see S. Sydney Bradford, "The Negro Ironworker in Ante Bellum Virginia," *Journal of Southern History* 25 (May 1959): 194–206; Robert S. Starobin, *Industrial Slavery in the Old South* (New York: Oxford University Press, 1970), esp. 128–137; Charles B. Dew, *Bond of Iron: Master and Slave at Buffalo Forge* (New York: W. W. Norton, 1994); Goldin, *Urban Slavery;* Richard C. Wade, *Slavery in the Cities: The South, 1820–1860* (New York: Oxford University Press, 1964); and Midori Takagi, *"Rearing Wolves to Our Own Destruction": Slavery in Richmond, Virginia, 1782–1865* (Charlottesville: University Press of Virginia, 1999).

12. Randall M. Miller and John David Smith, eds., *Dictionary of Afro-American Slavery* (New York: Greenwood Press, 1988), 321.

13. Many scholars have questioned the reliability of evidence culled from the 1930s WPA interviews, calling attention to the influence of white interviewers' prejudices on answers and the length of time that had elapsed between the interviews and the experiences the subjects describe. The typicality of the evidence has also come under scrutiny, for the majority of the interviewees were children (under the age of fifteen) when they were enslaved. Important cautions must certainly be heeded when analyzing this material, but I believe that ex-slaves' interviews (as well as slave narratives) present no greater challenges to reliable interpretation than do other historical sources. They are invaluable for understanding the perspective of the enslaved. Throughout, I have modified the spelling of the dialect speech recorded by the interviewers and transcribers of the Federal Writers Project. I have done this for the sake of readability; but there is no reason to believe, moreover, that the transcribed dialect even accurately reflected the way these people spoke. I see no difference, for example, between "whut" and "what" or "wuz" and "was."

14. James Oakes, "Slaves without Contexts," *Journal of the Early Republic* 19 (Spring 1999), 106; James Oakes, *Slavery and Freedom: An Interpretation of the Old South* (New York: Vintage Books, 1990), 79.

15. *Southern Planter* 13 (January 1853): 23.

1. Slave Hiring in the Evolution of Slavery

1. On the South's transition from "a society with slaves" to "a slave society," see Ira Berlin, *Many Thousands Gone: The First Two Centuries of Slavery in North America* (Cambridge: Harvard University Press, 1998).

2. Quoted in James Oakes, *The Ruling Race: A History of American Slaveholders* (New York: Vintage Books, 1982), 73.

3. The two best overviews of these changes in the market culture of the slave South are Kenneth M. Stampp, *The Peculiar Institution: Slavery in the Antebellum South* (New York: Vintage Books, 1956) and Oakes, *The Ruling Race.* For the place of agricultural innovation and the world market in those changes see Lewis Cecil Gray, *History of Agriculture in the Southern United States to 1860,* 2 vols. (New York: Peter Smith, 1941), and John Solomon Otto, *The Southern Frontiers, 1607–1860: The Agricultural Evolution of the Colonial and Antebellum South* (Westport, Conn.: Greenwood Press, 1989). On the slave trade, see Michael Tadman, *Speculators and Slaves: Masters, Traders, and Slaves in the Old South* (Madison: University of Wisconsin Press, 1996), and Walter Johnson, *Soul By Soul: Life inside the Antebellum Slave Market* (Cambridge: Harvard University Press, 1999). On urban and industrial slavery, see Claudia Dale Goldin, *Urban Slavery in the American South, 1820–1860* (Chicago: University of Chicago Press, 1976); Robert S. Starobin, *Industrial Slavery in the Old South* (New York: Oxford University Press, 1970); and Charles B. Dew, *Bond of Iron: Master and Slave at Buffalo Forge* (New York: W. W. Norton, 1994). For a concise description of the growing influence of liberalism in the South, see James Oakes, "From Republicanism to Liberalism: Ideological Change and the Crisis of the Old South," *American Quarterly* 37 (Fall 1985): 551–571.

4. Eugene D. Genovese, *The Political Economy of Slavery: Studies in the Economy & Society of the Slave South,* 2nd ed. (Middletown, Conn.: Wesleyan University Press, 1989), 49. See also Ralph V. Anderson and Robert E. Gallman, "Slaves as Fixed Capital: Slave Labor and Southern Economic Development," *Journal of American History* 64 (June 1977): 24–46.

5. Thomas Jefferson to Nicholas Lewis, 29 July 1787, *The Papers of Thomas Jefferson,* Julian P. Boyd, ed. (Princeton, N.J.: Princeton University Press, 1950–), vol. 11, 640–641.

6. Quoted in Ulrich Bonnell Phillips, "The Slave Labor Problem in the Charleston District," in *Plantation, Town, and County: Essays in the Local History of American Slave Society,* Elinor Miller and Eugene D. Genovese, eds. (Urbana: University of Illinois Press, 1974), 13.

7. Philip D. Morgan, "Black Life in Eighteenth-Century Charleston," *Perspectives in American History,* n.s., vol. 1 (New York: Cambridge University Press, 1984), 188, 194–201; George C. Rogers, Jr., *Charleston in the Age of the Pinckneys* (Norman: University of Oklahoma Press, 1969), 7–8, 15–16; Robert Olwell, "'Loose, Idle and Disorderly': Slave Women in the Eighteenth Century Charleston Marketplace," in *More Than Chattel: Black Women and Slavery in the Americas,* David Barry Gaspar and Darlene Clark Hine, eds. (Bloomington: Indiana University Press, 1996), 97–110.

8. *South Carolina Gazette,* 20 January 1733 and 10 March 1733, both reprinted in *The Black Worker: A Documentary History from Colonial Times to the Present,* vol. 1: *The Black Worker to 1869,* Philip S. Foner and Ronald L. Lewis, eds. (Philadelphia: Temple University Press, 1978), 8.

9. On the wider availability of black craftsmen in the Carolinas, see Philip D. Morgan, *Slave Counterpoint: Black Culture in the Eighteenth-Century Chesapeake & Lowcountry* (Chapel Hill: University of North Carolina Press, 1998), 226–227.

10. Quoted in Joyce E. Chaplin, *The Anxious Pursuit: Agricultural Innovation and Modernity in the Lower South, 1730–1815* (Chapel Hill: University of North Carolina Press, 1993), 86.

11. *South Carolina Gazette,* 25 December 1740 and 17 October 1741, both reprinted in *The Black Worker,* 9.

12. Henry Laurens to James Laurens, 2 July 1775, in *The Papers of Henry Laurens,* Philip M. Hamer, ed. (Columbia: University of South Carolina Press, 1968–), vol. 10, 203.

13. Henry Laurens to James Laurens, 28 March 1777, in ibid., vol. 11, 323; Henry Laurens to James Laurens, 2 July 1775 and 20 August 1775, in ibid., vol. 10, 201–203, 317; Henry Laurens to James Laurens, 20 August 1775 and 22 September 1775, in ibid., vol. 10, 317, 414; Henry Laurens to James Laurens, 7 June 1777, in ibid., vol. 11, 346.

14. Noble Wimberly Jones to "Dear Sir," 13 February 1780, Noble Wimberly Jones Papers, DU.

15. *The Journal of Peter Gordon, 1732–1735,* E. Merton Coulter, ed. (Athens: University of Georgia Press, 1963), 43.

16. *Colonial Records of the State of Georgia,* Allen D. Candler and Lucian Lamar Knight, eds. (Atlanta: C. P. Byrd, 1904–1916), vol. 18, 277, 280, and vol. 19, pt. 2, pp. 2, 23–30.

17. Ibid., vol. 18, pp. 125, 135.

18. Betty C. Wood, *Slavery in Colonial Georgia, 1730–1775* (Athens: University of Georgia Press, 1984), 142.

19. Berlin, "Time, Space," 61–63.

20. Johann David Schoepf, *Travels in the Confederation, 1783–1784,* ed. and trans. Alfred J. Morison (Philadelphia, 1911), vol. 2, 147–148, 201–202.

21. John Brodnax Petition to the General Assembly, 1718, Virginia House of Burgesses Papers, VHS; *Virginia Gazette,* 15 April 1737, p. 4; Joan Rezner Gundersen, "The Double Bonds of Race and Sex: Black and White Women in a Colonial Virginia Parish," *Journal of Southern History* 52 (August 1986): 368–369; John Edmund Stealey III, "The Responsibilities and Liabilities of the Bailee of Slave Labor in Virginia," *American Journal of Legal History* 12 (1968): 337; Calvin B. Coulter, Jr., "The Import Trade of Colonial Virginia," *William and Mary Quarterly* 2 (1945): 310.

22. On tobacco's resonance in the Chesapeake, see T. H. Breen, *Tobacco Culture: The Mentality of the Great Tidewater Planters on the Eve of Revolution* (Princeton: Princeton University Press, 1985), and Ira Berlin, *Many Thousands Gone.* On the small size of towns in the region, see John C. Rainbolt, "The Absence of Towns in Seventeenth-Century Virginia," *Journal of Southern History* 35 (1969): 343–360, and John J. McCusker and Russell R. Menard, *The Economy of British North America, 1607–1789* (Chapel Hill: University of North Carolina Press, 1991), 131–133. On the resulting prominence of Lon-

don and Glasgow merchants in the Chesapeake, see Gray, *History of Agriculture,* vol. 1, 417–428; Jacob M. Price, "The Rise of Glasgow in the Chesapeake Tobacco Trade, 1707–1775," *William and Mary Quarterly* 11 (1954): 179–199; and T. M. Devine, "A Glasgow Merchant during the American War of Independence: Alexander Speirs of Elderslie, 1775–1781," *William and Mary Quarterly* 33 (1976): 501–513.

23. Gerald W. Mullin, "Rethinking American Negro Slavery from the Vantage Point of the Colonial Era," *Louisiana Studies* 12 (1973): 398–422; Gerald W. Mullin, *Flight and Rebellion: Slave Resistance in Eighteenth-Century Virginia* (New York: Oxford University Press, 1972), 19–33; Coulter, "Import Trade of Colonial Virginia," 310.

24. David Klingaman, "The Significance of Grain in the Development of the Tobacco Colonies," *Journal of Economic History* 29 (1969): 268, 274; McCusker and Menard, *Economy of British North America,* 129; Joyce Appleby, "Commercial Farming and the 'Agrarian Myth' in the Early Republic," *Journal of American History* 68 (March 1982): 833–849; Berlin, *Many Thousands Gone,* 264.

25. John T. Schlotterbeck, "The 'Social Economy' of an Upper South Community: Orange and Greene Counties, Virginia, 1815–1860," in *Class, Community, and Conflict: Antebellum Southern Community Studies,* Orville Vernon Burton and Robert C. McMath, Jr., eds. (Westport, Conn.: Greenwood Press, 1982), 5; Morgan, *Slave Counterpoint,* 171; Harold B. Gill, Jr., "Wheat Culture in Colonial Virginia," *Agricultural History* 52 (1978): 387–388; Jack P. Greene, ed., *The Diary of Colonel Landon Carter of Sabine Hall, 1752–1778,* vol. 2 (Charlottesville: University Press of Virginia, 1965), 1107; Richard Jones, Affidavit, 6 March 1815, Robins Family Papers, VHS; Edwin Morris Betts, ed., *Thomas Jefferson's Farm Book, with Commentary and Relevant Extracts from Other Writings* (Princeton: Princeton University Press, 1953), 58, 149. Jefferson's 1795 and 1796 slave lists show that he hired only men. See ibid., 49, 52.

26. Entries for 21 September 1791 and 4 May 1799, Common Memorandum Book, 1780–1804, pp. 17, 9, William Massie Papers, DU.

27. Ira Berlin, *Slaves without Masters: The Free Negro in the Antebellum South* (New York: New Press, 1974), chap. 1; Allan Kulikoff, *The Agrarian Origins of American Capitalism* (Charlottesville: University Press of Virginia, 1992), 231–245; Sarah S. Hughes, "Slaves for Hire: The Allocation of Black Labor in Elizabeth City County, Virginia, 1782 to 1810," *William and Mary Quarterly* 35 (1978): 264, 271; Thomas Jones Record Books, vol. 1, 1779, MS. 517, Maryland Historical Society, RASP, series D, reel 9. See also Lorena S. Walsh, "Rural African Americans in the Constitutional Era in Maryland, 1776–1810," *Maryland Historical Magazine* 84 (Winter 1989): 330–331.

28. Kulikoff, *Agrarian Origins of American Capitalism,* 105–106.

29. James Dick to Thomas Worthington, 15 January 1780, 18 January 1780, and 29 December 1780, Dick, James, & Stewart Company, Letter Book, 1773–1781, DU; Mullin, *Flight and Rebellion,* 87–88; *Virginia Gazette,* 16 October 1777, quoted in *The Black Worker,* Foner and Lewis, 14; Sylvia R. Frey, *Water*

from the Rock: Black Resistance in a Revolutionary Age (Princeton: Princeton University Press, 1991), 85–86; Peter Way, *Common Labor: Workers and the Digging of North American Canals, 1780–1860* (New York: Cambridge University Press, 1993), 25–26, 33.

30. Morgan, *Slave Counterpoint*, 230; T. Stephen Whitman, *The Price of Freedom: Slavery and Manumission in Baltimore and Early National Maryland* (Lexington: University Press of Kentucky, 1997), 14; Tina H. Sheller, "Freemen, Servants, and Slaves: Artisans and the Craft Structure of Revolutionary Baltimore Town," in *American Artisans: Crafting a Social Identity, 1750–1850*, Howard B. Rock, Paul A. Gilje, and Robert Asher, eds., (Baltimore: Johns Hopkins University Press, 1995), 18; *Virginia Gazette,* Purdie, 12 December 1777, p. 2.

31. Berlin, *Many Thousands Gone,* 275; Robert Evans, Jr., "The Economics of American Negro Slavery, 1830–1860," in *Aspects of Labor Economics: A Conference of the Universities' National Bureau Committee for Economic Research* (Princeton, N.J.: Princeton University Press, 1962).

32. For an example, see "Notes on Virginia Lands," enclosure in Thomas Jefferson to George Washington, 3 August 1791, *The Papers of Thomas Jefferson,* vol. 20, pp. 716–717.

33. Hughes, "Slaves for Hire," 268, 275.

34. Entries for 29 and 30 September 1845, James D. Trezevant Plantation Diary, South Caroliniana Library, University of South Carolina, *Records of Antebellum Southern Plantations,* series A, pt. 2, reel 3; *The WPA Oklahoma Slave Narratives,* T. Lindsay Baker and Julie P. Bakers, eds. (Norman: University of Oklahoma Press, 1996), 82.

35. Ellen Eslinger, "The Shape of Slavery on Virginia's Kentucky Frontier," in *Diversity and Accommodation: Essays on the Cultural Composition of the Virginia Frontier,* Michael J. Puglisi, ed., (Knoxville: The University of Tennessee Press, 1997), 173; Robert Terry to Joseph Terry, 6 January 1808, Joseph Terry Papers, DU; Samuel W. Womack to William Hatchett, 8 February 1830, Hatchett Family Papers, DU.

36. Samuel Meredith to John Breckinridge, 17 May 1792, William Russell to John Breckinridge, 19 May 1792, and John Breckinridge to "Dear Sir," 23 July 1793, Breckinridge Family Papers, LC.

37. Kulikoff, *Agrarian Origins of American Capitalism,* 236–241.

38. Joan E. Cashin, *A Family Venture: Men and Women on the Southern Frontier* (New York: Oxford University Press, 1991), 57.

39. See, for example, Thomas Harrison to James T. Harrison, 4 January 1836, James Thomas Harrison Papers, #2441, folder 4, SHC.

40. For Gustavus Pope, see Gustavus A. Pope to Ann Pope, 1 December 1833; William R. Pope to Gustavus A. Pope, 9 December 1833; Gustavus A. Pope to William R. Pope, 17 December 1833; and Gustavus A. Pope to Ann Pope, 31 December 1833, Pope-Carter Papers, DU. For Thomas Williams, see Robert J. Williams to Thomas C. Williams, 21 March 1829, Burwell Family Papers, #112, folder 8, SHC. For Albert Charlton, see Thomas Fox to William Massie, 29 October 1845, William Massie Papers, Barker Texas History Center, Uni-

versity of Texas at Austin, *Records of Ante-bellum Southern Plantations,* series G, pt. 2, reel 18.

41. Philip Pitts, draft of letter, 21 March 1839, Philip H. Pitts Papers, #602, folder 1, SHC.

42. John Townes Leigh to John Young Mason, 16 September 1846, Mason Family Papers, VHS.

43. Thomas Harrison to James T. Harrison, 4 January 1836, and Thomas Harrison to James T. Harrison, 6 January 1836, James Thomas Harrison Papers, #2441, Folder 4, SHC; P. Ricks to Hilliard Fort, 21 March 1822, Matthew Cary Whitaker Papers, #768, Folder 3, SHC.

44. P. Ricks to Hilliard Fort, 21 March 1822, Matthew Cary Whitaker Papers, #768, Folder 3, SHC; Charles M. Norton to John Baylor, 23 July 1810, Baylor Family Papers, VHS; John H. Norton to "Dear Cousin," 28 November 1816, Baylor Family Papers, #2257, UVA.

45. W. Felton to Hilliard Fort, 29 April 1822, Matthew Cary Whitaker Papers, #768, folder 3, SHC.

46. John Tutt to Richard Tutt, 15 June 1836, James A. Tutt Papers, DU; Eli H. Lide to Caleb Coher, 24 March 1836, in Fletcher M. Green, ed., *The Lides Go South . . . And West: The Record of a Planter Migration* (Columbia: University of South Carolina Press, 1952), 17; John Preston to John Preston, 11 November 1836, Preston Family Papers, VHS.

47. Thomas Harrison to James T. Harrison, 4 January 1836, James Thomas Harrison Papers, #2441, Folder 4, SHC.

48. H. C. Bruce, *The New Man: Twenty-Nine Years a Slave, Twenty-Nine Years a Free Man* (York, Penna.: P. Anstadt, 1895; reprint, Lincoln: University of Nebraska Press, 1996), 15, 17, 20–21, 34, 67.

2. A Blessing and a Curse

1. Edward B. Bryan, *The Rightful Remedy: Addressed to the Slaveholders of the South* (Charleston: Press of Walker & James, 1850), 10.

2. Solomon Northup, *Twelve Years a Slave,* Sue Eakin and Joseph Logsdon, eds. (Baton Rouge: Louisiana State University Press, 1968), 92.

3. Frederick Douglass, *My Bondage and My Freedom,* William L. Andrews, ed. (Urbana: University of Illinois Press, 1987), 110; Harriet A. Jacobs, *Incidents in the Life of a Slave Girl, Written by Herself,* Jean Fagan Yellin, ed. (1861; Cambridge: Harvard University Press, 1987), 15, 118.

4. Quoted in Brenda E. Stevenson, *Life in Black and White: Family and Community in the Slave South* (New York: Oxford University Press, 1996), 179.

5. Historians who interpret the structure of slave families in different ways largely agree that those families were generally stable. See, for example, Eugene D. Genovese, *Roll, Jordan, Roll: The World the Slaves Made* (New York: Vintage Books, 1974); Herbert G. Gutman, *The Black Family in Slavery and Freedom, 1750–1925* (New York: Pantheon, 1976); Deborah Gray White, *Ar'n't I A Woman? Female Slaves in the Plantation South* (New York: W. W. Norton, 1985); Ann Patton Malone, *Sweet Chariot: Slave Family and Household Structure in Nineteenth-Century Louisiana* (Chapel Hill: University of

North Carolina Press, 1992); and Stevenson, *Life in Black and White,* 160–161, 206–257.

6. Gutman, *Black Family in Slavery and Freedom,* 599 n. 35; Benjamin Drew, ed., *The Refugee: A North-Side View of Slavery* (1855; Reading, Mass.: Addison-Wesley, 1969), 264.

7. John W. Blassingame, ed., *Slave Testimony: Two Centuries of Letters, Speeches, Interviews, and Autobiographies* (Baton Rouge: Louisiana State University Press, 1977), 535; George P. Rawick, ed., *The American Slave: A Composite Autobiography* (Westport, Conn.: Greenwood Press, 1972), vol. 16, pt. 6, Tennessee Narratives, 31 (Measy Hudson); H. R. Helper, *The Impending Crisis: How to Meet It* (New York: A. B. Burdick, 1860), 147; T. Lindsay Baker and Julie P. Bakers, eds., *The WPA Oklahoma Slave Narratives* (Norman, Okla.: University of Oklahoma Press, 1996), 189 (Plomer Harshaw); Charles L. Perdue, Jr., Thomas E. Barden, and Robert K. Phillips, eds., *Weevils in the Wheat: Interviews with Virginia Ex-Slaves* (Charlottesville: University Press of Virginia, 1976), 135 (Sister Harrison); Jacobs, *Incidents in the Life of a Slave Girl,* 15. For white sociability at hiring day, see entries for 29 December 1857, 1 January 1858, and 1 January 1862, William C. Adams Diary, DU.

8. J. Milton Emerson Journal, entry for 28 December 1841, DU; Nan Netherton, Donald Sweig, Janice Artemel, Patricia Hickin, and Patrick Reed, *Fairfax County, Virginia: A History* (Fairfax, Va.: Fairfax County Board of Supervisors, 1978), 274; Blassingame, *Slave Testimony,* 535.

9. Jacobs, *Incidents in the Life of a Slave Girl,* 15; Perdue, Barden, and Phillips, *Weevils in the Wheat,* 318 (Nancy Williams); John E. Jones to John Buxton Williams, 8 January 1855, John Buxton Williams Papers, DU.

10. Frederick Law Olmsted, *A Journey in the Seaboard Slave States, with Remarks on Their Economy* (1856; New York: Negro Universities Press, 1968), 30–31; "Hiring-Out Negroes," business circular, 1860, Beale Family Papers, section 4, VHS.

11. George H. Young to James McDowell, 20 September 1843, James McDowell Papers, DU; R. H. Adams to Mary E. C. Gilliam, 26 November 1855 and 29 January 1855, Gilliam Family Papers, UVA; John E. Jones to John Buxton Williams, 8 January 1855, John Buxton Williams Papers, DU; Thomas D. Russell, "Articles Sell Best Singly: The Disruption of Slave Families at Court Sales," *Utah Law Review* 1996 (1996), 1194.

12. Joseph B. Anderson to Richard T. Archer, 24 May 1853, quoted in John Hope Franklin and Loren Schweninger, *Runaway Slaves: Rebels on the Plantation* (New York: Oxford University Press, 1999), 136–137; Anthony Trollope, *North America* (Philadelphia: Lippincott, 1863), 87; Joseph Jackson Halsey to Andrew Glasswell Grinnan, 22 December 1854, Grinnan Family Papers, VHS; A. Bethune to A. Henderson, 2 July 1850, John Steele Henderson Papers, #327, folder 18, SHC; Iverson L. Twyman to John Austin, 31 December 1849, Austin-Twyman Papers, WM; Hez Ford to James E. Cooke, 6 April 1853, Barker-Cooke Papers, WM.

13. George H. Young to James McDowell, 8 April 1842, 22 May 1844, and 10 December 1845, James McDowell Papers, DU.

14. Edgar B. Montague to Elizabeth B. Chowning, 1 March 1862, Harrison Fam-

ily Papers, VHS; Hiring Bond, C. J. Faulkner to Mary Timberlake, 14 December 183-, Faulkner Family Papers, VHS; A. P. Gray to Joseph S. Copes, 21 June 1853, Joseph S. Copes Papers, TU; *Myers v. Slack,* 5 Louisiana 53 (1833); George H. Young to James McDowell, 10 December 1845, James McDowell Papers, DU.

15. Hiring agreement between Andrew Johnson and Mary Peck, 21 September 1852, Henry Watson, Jr. Papers, DU; Iverson L. Twyman to John Austin, 2 January 1851, Austin-Twyman Papers, WM; J. P. Aylett to Lewis Hill, 31 December 1853, Lewis Hill Papers, HL.

16. H. C. Bruce, *The New Man: Twenty-Nine Years a Slave, Twenty-Nine Years a Free Man* (York, Penna.: P. Anstadt, 1895; reprinted Lincoln: University of Nebraska Press, 1996), 13; C. J. McDonald to Farish Carter, 23 December 1854, Farish Carter Papers, #2230, folder 56, SHC.

17. Osborne Copes to Joseph S. Copes, 9 December 1851, Bolivar Brick Works, Joseph S. Copes Papers, TU; Giney to "My dear Sons and daughters," [1850], Julien Sidney Devereux Papers, Barker Texas History Center, University of Texas at Austin, in Kenneth M. Stampp, ed., *Records of Ante-bellum Southern Plantations,* microfilm, series G, pt. 1 (emphasis in original); William Henry to "My Dear Miss," 3 October 1862, DeRosset Family Papers, #214, folder 55, SHC; Anderson F. Henderson to "Master & Mistress," 14 June 1857, John Steele Henderson Papers, #327, folder 23, SHC; Bella DeRosset to "My Dear Affectionate Mistress," 3 October 1862, Wilmington, N.C., DeRosset Family Papers, #214, folder 55, SHC.

18. Iverson L. Twyman to John Austin, 31 December 1849, Austin-Twyman Papers, WM; H. S. Clark to Daniel Jordan, 14 January 1856, Daniel W. Jordan Papers, DU (Austin); Elijah Fuller to Alexander McDowell, 29 March 1845, Thomas David Smith McDowell Papers, #460, folder 60, SHC (Toby); Alexander McDowell to David D. Allan, 5 January 1838, Thomas David Smith McDowell Papers, #460, folder 51, SHC; Alexander McDowell to Charles Mallett, 16 January 1838, Thomas David Smith McDowell Papers, #460, folder 51, SHC; M. W. Ransom to Daniel W. Jordan, 13 January 1856, Daniel W. Jordan Papers, DU.

19. William R. Arick to Joseph S. Copes, 8 June 1849, Joseph S. Copes Papers, TU; George G. Lyon to Alfred D. Kerr, 20 June 1851, Rufus Reid Papers, #2712, folder 13, SHC.

20. R. H. Adams to Mary E. C. Gilliam, 29 January 1855, Gilliam Family Papers, UVA (Katy); Frederick Kimball to "D[ea]r Nephew and Niece," 2 June 1808, 7 November 1808, Frederick Kimball Letters, LSU (Harriet); J. H. Cocke to John Winn, 18 December 1826, Cocke Family Papers, box 49, UVA. On slave women's use of reproduction in acts of resistance, see Darlene Hine and Kate Wittenstein, "Female Slave Resistance: The Economics of Sex," in *The Black Woman Cross-Culturally,* Filomina Chioma Steady, ed. (Cambridge, Mass.: Schenkman, 1981), 289–299.

21. Mrs. Emma L. C. Beard to Joseph S. Copes, 23 June 1855, Joseph S. Copes Papers, TU; John Walker Tomlin to Benjamin Brand, 6 January 1809, Benjamin Brand Papers, VHS; Walter S. Dunn to Iverson L. Twyman, 28 March 1855,

Austin-Twyman Papers, WM; C. E. Dexter to Farish Carter, 3 March 1852, Farish Carter Papers, #2230, folder 47, SHC; William T. Parham to James Grist, 1 May 1854, James Redding Grist Papers, DU.

22. John G. Gamble to J. H. Cocke, 5 January 1825, Cocke Family Papers, UVA.

23. Rawick, *American Slave*, series 1, vol. 2, pt. 4, p. 196.

24. R. H. Adams to Mary E. C. Gilliam, 26 November 1855, Gilliam Family Papers, UVA; John E. Jones to John Buxton Williams, 8 January 1855, John Buxton Williams Papers, DU.

25. Moses Grandy, *Narrative of the Life of Moses Grandy; Late a Slave in the United States of America* (London: C. Gilpin, 1843), 53; For examples of "low bids," see Account Book, vol. 2, p. 225, McElwee Family Papers, #2692-Z, folder 4, SHC; John W. Perrin to Thomas Crew, 27 December 1803, William K. Perrin Papers, WM; William Campbell to Caroline Foscue, 23 October 1860, folder 19, Foscue Family Papers, #4643, folder 19, SHC; *Cooper v. Purvis*, 48 N.C. 141 (1853).

26. *Smithwick v. Biggs et al.*, 23 N.C. 281. On laws prohibiting the separation through sale of children under ten from their mothers, see Russell, "Articles Sell Best Singly," 1171–1176; Genovese, *Roll, Jordan, Roll*, 455; and Judith Kelleher Schafer, "New Orleans Slavery in 1850 as Seen in Advertisements," *Journal of Southern History* 47 (1981): 37.

27. Juria B. Fariss to J. H. Cocke, 22 March 1831; Martin B. Shepherd to J. H. Cocke, 4 January 1837; Jesse Bowles to J. H. Cocke, Cocke Family Papers, #640, UVA.

28. "The condition of the hire of the Negroes belonging to the children of Benj. & Molsey Rivel," 1846–1849, and "The condition of the hire of the Negroes belonging to the minor heirs of Joshua Craddock," 1842–1849, John L. Clifton Papers, DU.

29. Testimony of Lavina Bell, American Freedmen's Inquiry Commission, file 7, p. 89, Letters Received by the Adjutant General's Office, 1861–1870, M-619, RG-94, reel 200, NA; Brenda E. Stevenson, "Gender Convention, Ideals, and Identity among Antebellum Virginia Slave Women," in David Barry Gaspar and Darlene Clark Hine, eds., *More Than Chattel: Black Women and Slavery in the Americas* (Bloomington: Indiana University Press, 1996), 170.

30. Henry Clay Bruce, *The New Man: Twenty-Nine Years a Slave, Twenty-Nine Years a Free Man* (1895; Lincoln: University of Nebraska Press, 1996), 21; for Farish Carter, see King, *Stolen Childhood*, 31; Gilley M. Lewis to J. H. Cocke, 7 December 1840, Cocke Family Papers, #640, Box 100, UVA; G. W. Mussfield to Bowker Preston, 23 December 1835, John Hook Papers, #247, UVA (hiring of plough boy); Drew, *The Refugee*, 209 (Isaac Riley); James W. C. Pennington, *The Fugitive Blacksmith; or, Events in the History of James W. C. Pennington* (1850; Westport, Conn.: Negro Universities Press, 1971), 4; Rawick, *American Slave*, supplement, series 2, Texas Narratives, vol. 6, pt. 5, 1995 (Harry Johnson).

31. Bethany Veney, *The Narrative of Bethany Veney, A Slave Woman* (Worcester, Mass., 1889), 10; Rawick, *American Slave*, vol. 16, pt. 6, Tennessee, 67 (Millie Simpkins); ibid., supplement, series 1, vol. 2, pt. 4, Missouri Narratives, 164

(Margaret Davis); ibid., supplement, series 2, Texas Narratives, vol. 4, pt. 3, 1282 (Mary Edwards).

32. F. Nims to Horace Nims, 24 April 1851, Nims and Rankin Family Papers, #4255, folder 3, SHC; R. H. Adams to Mary E. C. Gilliam, 29 January 1855, Gilliam Family Papers, UVA; "Dear Sir", 1 October 1857, Papers of William B. Randolph, LC; Hiring Contract, Peter Nevins to James McDowell, 12 July 1838, James McDowell Papers, DU.

33. Sarah H. Bradford, *Harriet: The Moses of Her People* (New York: Geo. R. Lockwood, 1886), 17–21.

34. Douglass, *My Bondage and My Freedom,* 29; Pennington, *The Fugitive Blacksmith,* 4.

35. Stillman & Ashlin to J. H. Cocke, 10 December 1836, Cocke Family Papers, UVA; Clem Hudgins to J. H. Cocke, 15 February 1844, Cocke Family Papers, UVA; George H. Young to James McDowell, 7 January 1842, James McDowell Papers, DU; "A List of Hirelings to be sent to Capt. Winns," 1 January 1828, Cocke Family Papers, UVA.

36. Rawick, *American Slave,* vol. 1, pt. 10, Nebraska Narratives, 319; Henry Bibb, "Narrative of the Life and Adventures of Henry Bibb, An American Slave," in *Puttin' on Ole Massa,* Gilbert Osofsky, ed. (New York: Harper & Row, 1969), 65.

37. W. W. Baldwin to Farish Carter, 1 December 1854, Farish Carter Papers, #2230, folder 56, SHC (Cyrus); J. N. Fry to J. H. Cocke, 31 October 1835, Cocke Family Papers, #640, box 82, UVA (Nelson); Tutwiler & Hart to J. H. Cocke, 26 December 1835, Cocke Family Papers, #640, box 82, UVA (Aron); Richard W. Cowherd to J. H. Cocke, 31 December 1843, Cocke Family Papers, #640, box 109, UVA (Hannah); M. M. Hastook to Elijah Fletcher, 15 December 1857, Indiana (Fletcher) Williams Papers, DU (Preston).

38. Gerald W. Mullin, *Flight and Rebellion: Slave Resistance in Eighteenth-Century Virginia* (New York: Oxford University Press, 1972), 180 n. 109; Walter Paine to Farish Carter, 8 May 1856, Farish Carter Papers, #2230, folder 58, SHC; J. G. Plant to Farish Carter, 8 January 1850, Farish Carter Papers, #2230, folder 38, SHC; R. H. Adams to Mary Gilliam, 28 July 1856, Gilliam Family Papers, UVA.

39. John Faggart to A. Henderson, 16 September 1853, John Steele Henderson Papers, #327, folder 19, SHC; Jane H. Criswell to Joseph S. Copes, 14 December 1857, Joseph S. Copes Papers, TU; Wilson J. Cary to Mrs. Virginia Cary, 16 January 1822, Richmond, Carr-Cary Papers, UVA; Lannell Wimbish & Miller to Elisha Barksdale, 30 November 1847, Peter Barksdale Papers, DU.

40. Edmund to Joseph S. Copes, 23 September 1849, Baton Rouge, Joseph S. Copes Papers, TU; Gran B. Davis to Joseph S. Copes, 5 December 1849, Joseph S. Copes Papers, TU.

41. Hez Ford to James E. Cooke, 18 March 1851, Barker-Cooke Papers, WM; Lewis to Lucy A. Goulden, 28 October 1860, Plain View, Palmore Family Papers, UVA; Alfred Steele to Mary Steele, 15 November 1835, John Steele Papers, #689, folder 71, SHC.

42. John W. Nash to Joseph Hobson, 30 November 1822, Nash Family Papers,

Section 2. VHS; Barbara Jeanne Fields, *Slavery and Freedom on the Middle Ground: Maryland during the Nineteenth Century* (New Haven: Yale University Press, 1985), 27.

43. D. D. Allan to Alexander McDowell, 8 January 1838, Thomas David Smith McDowell Papers, DU; Alexander McDowell to Charles Mallet, 16 January 1838, Thomas David Smith McDowell Papers, DU; G. S. Gillespie to T. D. McDowell, 23 February 1848, Thomas David Smith McDowell Papers, DU; William Staples to William Weaver, 4 January 1830, Weaver-Brady Papers, UVA.

44. Bryan, *The Rightful Remedy,* 10; William A. Drennan Diary, vol. 1, entry for 3 January 1862, William A. Drennan Papers, MDAH; Iverson L. Twyman to John Austin, 31 December 1849, Austin-Twyman Papers, WM; Iverson L. Twyman to John Austin, 2 January 1851, Austin-Twyman Papers, WM; Rebecca B. Yongue to William H. Gilliland, 10 January 1858, William H. Gilliland Papers, DU (Yongue reported that the slave "got a very wealthy man who lives adjoining us by the name of J. H. Atwood to buy him").

3. Risks and Returns

1. *State v. Levi, a Slave,* 44 N.C. 6, 6–8 (1852).

2. George H. Young to James McDowell, 7 December 1844, James McDowell Papers, DU.

3. Edmund Taylor to Lewis Hill, 4 January 1852, Lewis Hill Papers, Brock Collection, HL; Solomon Northup, *Twelve Years a Slave,* Sue Eakin and Joseph Logsdon, eds. (Baton Rouge: Louisiana State University, 1968), 145–147.

4. Robert William Fogel and Stanley L. Engerman, *Time on the Cross: The Economics of Negro Slavery* (New York: W. W. Norton & Co., 1974), 151; "Hires & cost of negroes belonging to Emma, Susan, St. George, & Simon B. Mason, minor children of J. Y. Mason, deceased," 1860, Mason Family Papers, VHS; George W. Johnson to William Johnson, 10 November 1836, William Johnson Papers, #380, Folder 6, SHC.

5. Robert Taylor Scott to Fanny Scott, 3 January 1861, Keith Family Papers, VHS; Daniel B. Pinson to Elizabeth A. Pinson, 10 March 1849, Nancy Pinson Papers, #828–1255, C-62, folder 9, LSU; William Shields Account Book, p. 70, DU; "Memorandum of agreement between James Chaney on the one part and John M. Pintard on the other . . . ," 22 February 1809, John M. Pintard Papers, #887, LSU; H. P. Womack to Pleasant H. Womack, 24 April 1853, Hatchett Family Papers, DU.

6. Benjamin Drew, ed., *The Refugee: A North-Side View of Slavery* (1855; Reading, Mass.: Addison-Wesley, 1969), 58; Receipt, 9 June 1856, Joseph Embree Papers, #692, LSU; Charlotte Lewis to Farish Carter, 16 July 1828, Farish Carter Papers, #2230, folder 4, SHC.

7. Will of James Wallace, 1753/1754, Thom Family Papers, section 19, VHS; *Fulkerson v. Ballard,* 35 Tenn. 261 (1855); Robert E. Corlew, "Some Aspects of Slavery in Dickson County," in Elinor Miller and Eugene D. Genovese, eds., *Plantation, Town, and County: Essays on the Local History of American Slave*

Society (Urbana: University of Illinois Press, 1974), 123; *Jimison v. Smith*, 37 Ala. 185 (1861); *Bailey v. Poindexter*, 55 Va. 133 (1858); *Mercer v. Kelso*, 45 Va. 106 (1847).

8. Briscoe G. Baldwin to William Shumate, 1 January 1839, Byers Family Papers, Box 4, Folder 3, WM; Hiring Contract, W. L. Lyon to Henry Watson, Henry Watson, Jr. Papers, DU; Robert Baylor Lyne to Edward Ware, 12 December 1859, Ware Family Papers, Section 2, VHS; Selina Powell to Rebecca Powell, 3 January 1849, Powell Family Papers, Box 1, Folder 3, WM; Richard Blow to Samuel Proctor, 21 January 1806, Blow Family Papers, VHS.

9. Allan Kulikoff, *Tobacco and Slaves: The Development of Southern Cultures in the Chesapeake* (Chapel Hill: University of North Carolina Press, 1986), 406; Charles L. Perdue, Jr., Thomas E. Barden, and Robert K. Phillips, eds., *Weevils in the Wheat: Interviews with Virginia Ex-Slaves* (Charlottesville: University Press of Virginia, 1976), 190; Levi Coffin, *Reminiscences of Levi Coffin, The Reputed President of the Underground Railroad* (1898; New York: Arno Press, 1968), 407–08.

10. William Spotswood Fontaine to Messrs. Hill and Dabney, 1 May 1840, Robert Hill Papers, Brock Collection, HL; Socrates Maupin to Addison Maupin, 23 September 1843, Socrates Maupin Papers, #2769-a, UVA; I. L. Twyman to Thomas Austin, 2 April 1852, Austin-Twyman Papers, WM. Emphasis in originals.

11. Frederick Douglass, *My Bondage and My Freedom*, William L. Andrews, ed., (Urbana: University of Illinois Press, 1987), 126; *Deloach v. Turner*, 6 S.C. (Richardson) 117 (1853); Shearer Davis Bowman, *Masters and Lords: Mid-19th-Century U.S. Planters and Prussian Junkers* (New York: Oxford University Press, 1993), 61; Charles W. Montague to Francis Thruston Hughes, 22 November 1845, Montague Family Papers, section 5, VHS; James Lindsay Smith, *Autobiography of James L. Smith* (New York: Negro Universities Press, 1969), 25; Edward J. Thomas, *Memoirs of a Southerner: 1840–1923* (Savannah, Ga., 1923), 20.

12. Hannibal Harris to Frederick A. Harris, 28 May 1826, and 29 July 1826, Frederick A. Harris Papers, DU; Account Book, 1842–1852, pp. 40, 42, Henry D. Mandeville and Family Papers, #491, LSU; Dew Gilpin Faust, *James Henry Hammond and the Old South: A Design for Mastery* (Baton Rouge: Louisiana State University, 1982), 107.

13. F. Nims to Horace Nims, 31 January 1853, Nims and Rankin Family Papers, #4255, folder 6, SHC.

14. John Austin to Iverson L. Twyman, 29 December 1851, Austin-Twyman Papers, WM; Charles W. Montague to Francis Thruston Hughes, 22 November 1845, Montague Family Papers, section 5, VHS; P. M. Tabb & Son to Robert W. Carter, 18 November 1846, Beverley Randolph Wellford Papers, VHS; John Taylor, Jr., to Lewis Hill, 1 January 1842, Lewis Hill Papers, HL. For the effects of railroad construction on local markets, see Iverson L. Twyman to John Austin, 25 December 1851, Austin-Twyman Papers, WM. For the effects of a failed corn crop, see Paulina Read to William Cabell, 22 November 1806, Cabell Family Papers, box 4, folder 9, WM.

15. Wilson J. Cary to Virginia Cary, 2 January 1823, Carr-Cary Papers, #1231, Box 2, UVA; Patrick Catlett to Elizabeth Catlett, 4 January 1847, John Catlett Family Papers, #9398-j, UVA; Rebecca B. Yongue to William H. Gilliland, 10 January 1858, William H. Gilliland Papers, DU.

16. Jonathan W. McCalley to William J. McCalley, 7 January 1849, Jonathan W. McCalley Letter, VHS; Iverson L. Twyman to John Austin, 25 December 1851, Austin-Twyman Papers, WM; *Burke, F.W.C. v. Clarke*, 11 La. 206 (1837); *Robert G. Beverley v. Captain and Owners of Steamer Empire*, 15 La. 432 (1860).

17. Iverson Twyman to John Austin, 25 December 1851, Austin-Twyman Papers, WM; L. M. Walton to John T. Hargrave, 10 February 1837, Shepherdstown, Virginia Papers, #11104, box 1, UVA; Ann Elliott to Ann R. Smith, 12 October 1829, Elliott and Gonzales Family Papers, #1009, folder 16, SHC; B. Tucker to William N. Berkley, 14 March 1847, Berkley Family Papers, UVA; James Redpath, *The Roving Editor, or Talks with Slaves in the Southern States,* John R. McKivigan, ed. (University Park: Pennsylvania State University Press, 1996), 164.

18. Lucy Battle to William Battle, 6 January [1852], Battle Family Papers, #3223, folder 26, SHC; Lucy Battle to William Battle, 2 January 1854, Battle Family Papers, #3223, folder 30, SHC. Emphasis in originals.

19. Margaret L. Brooke to Robert S. Brooke, 26 December 1842, Brooke Family Papers, #38–137, UVA. Emphasis in original.

20. Edgar B. Montague to Elizabeth B. Chowning, 1 March 1862, Harrison Family Papers, section 10, VHS; Octavia O. Bullitt to R. H. Smith, n.d., Richard H. Smith and Family Papers, LSU; Sarah Brockenbrough to LH, 26 April 1842, Port Royal, Lewis Hill Papers, HL. Emphasis in originals.

21. Frances Austin to Martha E. Twyman, 29 October 1849, Austin-Twyman Papers, WM; Notebook, 1848, 1858–1860, Henry Alderson Ellison Papers, #1432-Z, SHC; Frederick Kimball, "Dear Nephew and Niece," 7 November 1806, Frederick Kimball Letters, LSU; "Hires & cost of negroes belonging to Emma, Susan, St. George, & Simon B. Mason, minor children of J. Y. Mason, deceased," 1860, Mason Family Papers, VHS; "List of Dower Negroes Belonging to the Estate of Dabney Minor," unidentified compiler, inventory, 1860, VHS.

22. Bell v. Cummings, 35 Tenn. 275 (1855).

23. Angus v. Dickerson, 19 Tenn. 459, 469 (1838).

24. L. M. Young to Joseph S. Copes, 14 November 1861, Joseph S. Copes Papers, TU; unidentified writer to I. L. Twyman, 23 March 1861, Austin-Twyman Papers, WM; A. J. Holliday to A. K. Farrar, 28 January 1841, Alexander K. Farrar Papers, #782, 850, 1348, LSU; *DeBow's Review* 3 (May 1847): 419.

25. Robert A. Jones Account Book, 1817–1829, #389-Z, p. 350, SHC.

26. *Ricks v. Battle,* 29 N.C. 6 (1852).

27. George H. Young to James McDowell, 7 December 1844; George H. Young to James McDowell, 22 May 1844; George H. Young to James McDowell, 20 September 1843, James McDowell Papers, DU. Emphasis in originals.

28. George H. Young to James McDowell, 17 July 1843, James McDowell Papers,

DU; Thomas Clement Read to Henry Carrington, 22 October 1847, Carring-
ton Family Papers, pt. G, section 1, VHS; Iverson L. Twyman to Thomas
Austin, 2 January 1851, Austin-Twyman Papers, WM; William H. Terrill to
George Morton, 26 December 1839, Morton Family Papers, #9755, UVA.;
J. S. Grasty to W. C. Grasty, 2 July 1860; J. S. Grasty to W. C. Grasty, 10 May
1860, William C. Grasty and J. F. Rison Papers, DU. Emphasis in originals.

29. William Brent to David Rees, 21 January 1815, David Rees Papers, TU; "The
Condition of the Nigers. Mr. Bryan Bennett & Isaac Wright as spetial admin-
sitrators . . . ," 12 February 1852, John L. Clifton Papers, DU. On the "social
economy" of hiring, see Eugene D. Genovese, "Yeoman Farmers in a Slaveholding Democracy," *Agricultural History* 49 (1975): 338, and Harry L. Watson, "Conflict and Collaboration: Yeomen, Slaveholders, and Politics in the
Antebellum South," *Social History* 10 (1985): 280.

30. "Conditions of the hiring of the negroes belonging to the minor heirs of Titus
Carr, deceased," 1 February 1841, Carr, Barnes, and Branch Family Papers,
#1392-Z, folder 1, SHC; Andrew Leslie to Lewis Hill, 18 January 1843; James
Govan to Lewis Hill, 23 December 1843; Edmund Taylor to Lewis Hill, 4 Jan-
uary 1852, Lewis Hill Papers, HL. Emphasis in originals.

31. Edward W. Phifer, "Slavery in Microcosm: Burke County, North Carolina," in
Miller and Genovese, *Plantation, Town, and Country*, 93; Elkanah Talley to
Benjamin Brand, 10 September 1809, Benjamin Brand Papers, VHS; "The
conditions of hiring the negroes belonging to the minor heirs of Francis
Harper, deceased," 3 January 1848, Francis Harper Papers, DU; Charles W.
Montague to Francis Thruston Hughes, 22 November 1845, Montague Family Papers, section 5, VHS. See also *Heirs of Capal v. McMillan*, 8 Porter (Ala.)
197 (1840), which involved a dispute between an estate administrator and the
estate's heirs over whether "the negroes would be exposed to injury in health
and morals, by removing them to Mobile."

32. *Rasco and Brantley v. Willis*, 5 Ala. 38 (1843).

33. Frank Hawkins to William Hawkins, 4 January 1849, Mary Ann S. M. Buie
Papers, DU; Ebenezer Cooley to Thomas Jefferson Cooley, 21 December
1829, John G. Devereux Papers, #2149, folder 1, SHC; George Taylor to William A. Burwell, 5 May 1833, Burwell Family Papers, #112, folder 12, SHC;
Edward Garlick to Messrs. Hill and Dabney, 4 January 1838, Robert Hill Papers, HL; John Taylor, Jr., to Lewis Hill, 1 January 1842, Lewis Hill Papers,
HL; William Starke to Lewis Hill, 5 January 1844, Lewis Hill Papers, HL.

34. Mark V. Tushnet, *The American Law of Slavery, 1810–1860: Considerations
of Humanity and Interest* (Princeton: Princeton University Press, 1981);
Thomas D. Morris, *Southern Slavery and the Law, 1619–1860* (Chapel Hill:
University of North Carolina Press, 1996), 132–158.; *Forsyth v. Perry*, 5 Florida 337 (1853); A. Leon Higginbotham, Jr., and Barbara K. Kopytoff, "Property First, Humanity Second: The Recognition of the Slave's Human Nature
in Virginia Civil Law," *Ohio State Law Journal* 50 (1989), 520.

35. *Horsely v. Branch*, 20 Tenn. 199 (1839).

36. William H. Terrill to George Morton, 29 January 1837, Morton Family Pa-

pers, #9755, UVA; Iverson L. Twyman to Thomas Austin, 2 January 1852, Austin-Twyman Papers, WM.

37. Northup, *Twelve Years a Slave,* 163; Iverson Twyman to John Austin, 25 December 1851, Austin-Twyman Papers, WM; Joseph S. Watkins to Thomas Walker Gilmer, 26 December 1835, John Tyler Scrapbook, p. 75, WM; Emphasis in originals.

38. Hiring Contract, John B. Dey and William R. Stubbs to Thomas B. Montague, 1 January 1862, Montague Family Papers, section 12, VHS; Hiring Contract, Angus McDonald and John McDonald to Nathaniel Burwell, 2 January 1805, Angus McDonald Indenture, VHS; Hiring Contract, Edward Sydnor Saunders to Jeremiah Webb, 20 January 1836, Edward Sydnor Saunders Bonds, VHS; Hiring Contract, Isaac Fletcher and John E. Fletcher to Henry Dulans, 1859, John E. Fletcher Papers, section 8, VHS; Barbara Jeanne Fields, *Slavery and Freedom on the Middle Ground: Maryland during the Nineteenth Century* (New Haven, Conn.: Yale University Press, 1985), 84; William Danieley to John L. Clifton, 15 March 1858, John L. Clifton Papers, DU; George G. Lyon to Alfred D. Kerr, 17 January 1850, Rufus Reid Papers, #2712, folder 13, SHC. On the price of slave clothing, see Eugene D. Genovese, *Roll, Jordan, Roll: The World the Slaves Made* (New York: Vintage Books, 1974), 551.

39. Hiring Contract, E. W. Wall to Joseph S. Hicks (for Samuel Smith Downey), 21 January 1836, Samuel Smith Downey Papers, DU; Hiring Contract, Muse & Greenleaf to William H. Wyche, Sr., and William Wyche, February 1829, Wyche and Otey Family Papers, #1608, folder 30, SHC.

40. Hiring Contract, E. W. Wall to Joseph S. Hicks (for Samuel Smith Downey), 21 January 1836, Samuel Smith Downey Papers, DU; Hiring Contract, A. J. M. Rust to Sanford J. Raney, 10 January 1854, Rust Family Papers, #9706, UVA; Hiring Contract, S. Marmion to Elizabeth Allstadt, 1 January 1851, Marmion Family Papers, section 4, VHS; Hiring Contract, D. S. Wooldridge to Catherine McKenney, 1 January 1860, McKenney Family Papers, VHS.

41. Hiring Contract, [?] to Rhoda Stephenson, 2 January 1855, Britton and Moore Family Papers, #4136, folder 6, SHC; Hiring Contract, William L. Coughlin and James G. Maynard to Mary H. Claiborne, 1 January 1859, Jones Family Papers, VHS; Hiring Contract, John Fitzgerald and Samuel Scott to Patrick H. Foster, 31 December 1855, John Fitzgerald Papers, VHS.

42. "Agreement of Dr. Sextus Barbour with Edmund Pendleton Barbour," n.d., Barbour Family Papers, VHS; David Outlaw to Emily Outlaw, 20 December 1847, David Outlaw Papers, #1534, folder 1, SHC; "Conditions of the hiring of the negroes belonging to A. K. Simonton by his Guardian J. F. Alexander," 1 January 1851, Account Book, vol. 2, McElwee Papers, #2692-Z, folder 4, series 2, SHC. For slaves who got smallpox while hired out, see *Latimer v. Alexander,* 14 Georgia 267 (1853) and *Wallace v. Searles and Wife,* 36 Mississippi 53 (1858).

43. Hiring Contract, Muse & Greenleaf to William H. Wyche, Sr., and William Wyche, February 1829, Wyche and Otey Family Papers, #1608, folder 30,

SHC; "The condition of the hire of the negroes belonging to the estate of
Thomas Bennett, deceased," 3 January 1853, John L. Clifton Papers, DU;
"Agreement of Dr. Sextus Barbour with Edmund Pendleton Barbour," n.d.,
Barbour Family Papers, VHS; Hiring Contract, A. J. M. Rust to Sanford J.
Raney, 10 January 1854, Rust Family Papers, #9706, UVA.

44. *Mims v. Mitchell,* 1 Texas Reports 443.

45. Hez Ford to James E. Cooke, 29 November 1849, Barker-Cooke Papers, WM;
J. F. North[?] to James R. Grist, 18 August 1853, James Redding Grist Papers,
DU.

46. Alexander McDowell to Charles Mallett, 16 January 1838, Thomas David
Smith McDowell Papers, SHC; Farish Carter to Thomas Grimes, 20 March
1824, Thomas W. Grimes Papers, DU; Iverson L. Twyman to Frances Austin,
31 December 1852, Austin-Twyman Papers, WM; John Austin to Iverson
L. Twyman, 29 December 1851, Austin-Twyman Papers, WM; Iverson L.
Twyman to John Austin, 31 December 1849, Austin-Twyman Papers, WM.
Emphasis in originals.

47. Samuel Drewry to John Buford, 20 January 1854, and Samuel Drewry to Pas-
chal Buford, 13 December 1853, John Buford Papers, DU. On slave life insurance, see Todd L. Savitt, "Slave Life Insurance in Virginia and North Carolina," *Journal of Southern History* 43 (November 1977): 583–600.

48. Genovese, *Roll, Jordan, Roll,* 5; Henry Bibb, *Narrative of the Life and Adven-
tures of Henry Bibb, an American Slave,* in Gilbert Osofsky, ed., *Puttin' On
Ole Massa* (New York: Harper & Row, 1969), 65; William Wells Brown, *Nar-
rative of William Wells Brown, a Fugitive Slave,* in ibid., 173–223; Etta
Kosnegary to "My Dear Mother and Sisters," 12 November 1862, Etta
Kosnegary Letter, #2897, LSU; T. Lindsay Baker and Julie P. Bakers, eds., *The
WPA Oklahoma Slave Narratives* (Norman: University of Oklahoma Press,
1996), 80; Drew, *The Refugee,* 54.

4. Compromised Mastery

1. George Frederick Holmes quoted in Kenneth S. Greenberg, *Masters and
Statesmen: The Political Culture of American Slavery* (Baltimore: Johns Hopkins University Press, 1985), 96; Frances Anne Kemble, *Journal of a Residence
on a Georgian Plantation in 1838–1839,* John A. Scott, ed. (New York: Knopf,
1961), 105, 122–123; John C. Calhoun quoted in Charles B. Dew, "Disciplining Slave Iron Workers in the Antebellum South: Coercion, Conciliation,
and Accommodation," *American Historical Review* 79 (1974): 393.

2. *Redding v. Hall,* 1 Kentucky 536 (1809).

3. T. G. Mitchell to Iveson L. Brookes, 27 November 1838, Iveson Lewis
Brookes Papers, #3249, Folder 4, SHC; E. D. Williams to Farish Carter, 8 January 1840, Farish Carter Papers, #2230, folder 18, SHC; Hiring Contract,
names illegible, 28 December 1844, Orange Grove Plantation Records,
Nathaniel Evans and Family Papers, LSU.

4. John G. Gamble to J. H. Cocke, 5 January 1825, Cocke Family Papers, #640,
box 42, UVA; W. H. Oram to Joseph S. Copes, 5 December 1841, Joseph S.

Copes Papers, #733, TU; Emily Jordan to Daniel W. Jordan, 6 November 1845, Daniel W. Jordan Papers, DU.

5. James Redpath, *The Roving Editor, or Talks with Slaves in the Southern States,* John R. McKivigan, ed. (University Park: Pennsylvania State University Press, 1996), 196; John Wilkes to "My Dear Father," 26 August 1856, Wilkes Family Papers, DU. Emphasis in originals.

6. Sarah S. Hughes, "Slaves for Hire: The Allocation of Black Labor in Elizabeth County, Virginia, 1782 to 1810," *William and Mary Quarterly* 35 (April 1978): 268; Randolph B. Campbell, "Slave Hiring in Texas," *American Historical Review* 93 (February 1988): 111.

7. George P. Rawick, ed., *The American Slave: A Composite Autobiography* (Westport, Conn.: Greenwood Press, 1972-), supplement, series 2, Texas Narratives, vol. 4, pt. 3, 1282; ibid., vol. 8, pt. 7, 3295; Charles L. Perdue, Jr., Thomas E. Barden, and Robert K. Phillips, eds., *Weevils in the Wheat: Interviews with Ex-Slaves* (Charlottesville: University Press of Virginia, 1976), 318; Frederick Douglass, *My Bondage and My Freedom,* William L. Andrews, ed. (Urbana: University of Illinois Press, 1987), 135.

8. John G. Gamble to J. H. Cocke, 22 September 1823, Cocke Family Papers, #640, box 39, UVA; E. F. Ricker to Farish Carter, 21 November 1853, Farish Carter Papers, #2230, folder 54, SHC; E. D. Williams to Farish Carter, 8 January 1840, Farish Carter Papers, #2230, folder 18, SHC.

9. John B. Baird to Farish Carter, 28 December 1845, Farish Carter Papers, #2230, folder 28, SHC; George W. Johnson to William Johnson, 14 November 1837, William Johnson Papers, #380, folder 6, SHC; George W. Johnson to William Johnson, 19 July 1839, William Johnson Papers, #380, folder 7, SHC.

10. Henry Langhorne to J. H. Cocke, 27 January 1830, Cocke Family Papers, #640, box 62, UVA; George Foster to Joseph S. Copes, 2 September 1855, Joseph S. Copes Papers, TU; G. W. Mussfield to Bowker Preston, 23 December 1835, John Hook Papers, #247, UVA; *The Black Worker: A Documentary History from Colonial Times to the Present,* vol. 1: *The Black Worker to 1869,* Philip S. Foner and Ronald L. Lewis, eds. (Philadelphia: Temple University Press, 1978), 15. Emphasis in originals.

11. *Womack v. Nicholson,* 3 La. Robinson's 248 (1842).

12. James E. Horner to Iverson L. Twyman, 13 January 1854, Austin-Twyman Papers, WM; Samuel Griswold to Farish Carter, 7 March 1850, Farish Carter Papers; Beverly Hutchison to George Millam, 28 March 1858, Beverly Hutchison Papers, #3272, folder 1, SHC; William Campbell to Caroline Foscue, 23 October 1860, Foscue Family Papers, #4643, folder 19, SHC.

13. C. G. Fulks to William Massie, 8 December 1857, William Massie Papers, in Kenneth Stampp, ed., *Records of Ante-bellum Southern Plantations from the Revolution through the Civil War* (Frederick, Md.: University Publications of America, 1985-), series G, pt. 2, reel 26. Emphasis in original.

14. James Oakes, *Slavery and Freedom: An Interpretation of the Old* South (New York: Vintage Books, 1990), 93, 109. See also, Victoria E. Bynum, *Unruly Women: The Politics of Social and Sexual Control in the Old South* (Chapel Hill: University of North Carolina Press, 1992), 7–8.

15. *DeBow's Review,* vol. 30, issue 1 (1861): 74.

16. E. B. Weed to Farish Carter, 19 December 1851, Farish Carter Papers, #2230, folder 45, SHC; E. B. Weed to Farish Carter, 25 December 1852, Farish Carter Papers, #2230, folder 49, SHC; John L. Clifton to William Darden, 2 January 1852, John L. Clifton Papers, DU; R. W. Shaw to Iverson L. Twyman, 29 August 1853, Austin-Twyman Papers, WM.

17. Emily Jordan to Daniel W. Jordan, 6 November 1845, Daniel W. Jordan Papers, DU; Mrs. Shoburn to Archibald Henderson, 28 December 1856, John Steele Henderson Papers, #327, folder 22, SHC.

18. Mrs. M. S. Wolfe to Joseph S. Copes, 15 August 1844, Joseph S. Copes Papers, TU; Mrs. Harris to Joseph S. Copes, April 1853, Joseph S. Copes Papers, TU; Emma L. C. Beard to Joseph S. Copes, 23 June 1855, Joseph S. Copes Papers, TU.

19. Perdue, Barden, and Phillips, *Weevils in the Wheat,* 186; Henry Bibb, *Narrative of the Life and Adventures of Henry Bibb, an American Slave,* in Gilbert Osofsky, ed., *Puttin' On Ole Massa* (New York: Harper & Row, 1969), 65; Sarah H. Bradford, *Harriet: The Moses of Her People* (New York: Lockwood, 1886), 19; Redpath, *The Roving Editor,* 196. Emphasis in originals.

20. Hinton R. Helper, *The Impending Crisis: How to Meet It* (New York: Burdick, 1860), 148–149; John C. Inscoe, "The Civil War's Empowerment of an Appalachian Woman: The 1864 Slave Purchases of Mary Bell," in Patricia Morton, ed., *Discovering the Women in Slavery: Emancipating Perspectives on the American Past* (Athens: University of Georgia Press, 1996), 70; Thomas W. Grimes to Farish Carter, 11 April 1824, Thomas W. Grimes Papers, DU; Alexander Campbell to Joseph S. Copes, 5 December 1841, Joseph S. Copes Papers, #733, TU.

21. Plantation Journal, 4 January 1859, George Scarborough Barnesley Papers, #1521, folder 20, SHC; Henry A. McCormick to William Weaver, 29 December 1855, Weaver-Brady Papers, #38–98, UVA; J. H. Gibbon to "My Dear Sir," 14 January 1850, Wilkes Family Papers, DU; William H. Carrick to William S. Royston, 14 December 1853, William S. Royston Papers, DU.

22. John Faggart to A. Henderson, 5 December 1853, John Steele Henderson Papers, #327, folder 19, SHC; John F. Glenn to "Sir," 8 November 1858, Leonidas Chalmers Glenn Papers, #3052, folder 17, SHC.

23. Harriet Beecher Stowe, *The Key to Uncle Tom's Cabin* (Boston: Jewett, 1854), 147–48; Eugene D. Genovese, *Roll, Jordan, Roll: The World the Slaves Made* (New York: Vintage Books, 1974), 35.

24. *State v. Mann,* 13 N.C. 263 (1829).

25. *James v. Carper,* 4 Sneed (Tenn.) 397 (1857).

26. *Mullen v. Ensley,* 27 Tenn. 429 (1847); *Seay v. Marks,* 23 Ala. 532 (1853); *Jones v. Fort,* 36 Ala. 457 (1860).

27. *Kelly, Timanus & Co. v. Wallace,* 6 Fla. 690 (1856).

28. *Alston v. Balls and Adams,* 12 Ark. 669, 670 (1852); *Wilder v. Richardson,* 1 Dudley (S.C.) 324 (1838).

29. *George v. Elliott,* 12 Va. 5 (1806). Emphasis in originals.

30. *Harmon v. Fleming,* 25 Mississippi 139 (1852).

31. *Lennard v. Boynton,* 11 Georgia 109 (1852).

32. *Federal Union* (Milledgeville, Ga.), 12 December 1854, quoted in Ulrich Bonnell Phillips, *American Negro Slavery: A Survey of the Supply, Employment, and Control of Negro Labor As Determined by the Plantation Regime* (Baton Rouge: Louisiana State University Press, 1918), 407; *Brooks v. Smith,* 21 Georgia 261 (1857). On the Georgia legislature's changes in the law, see David J. Langum, "The Role of Intellect and Fortuity in Legal Change: An Incident from the Law of Slavery," *American Journal of Legal History* 28 (January 1984): 1–16.

33. *Nelson v. Bondurant,* 26 Ala. 341 (1855).

34. [?] Countz to William B. Randolph, 12 July 1845, Papers of William B. Randolph, LC.

35. Frederick Douglass, *My Bondage and My Freedom,* 120; Anonymous, "A Slave's Story," *Putnam's Monthly Magazine* 9 (New York, June 1857): 619.

36. Perdue, Barden, and Phillips, *Weevils in the Wheat,* 135; Alma Hibbard Journal, p. 55, 1854, DU.

37. H. C. Bruce, *The New Man: Twenty-Nine Years a Slave, Twenty-Nine Years a Free Man* (1895; Lincoln: University of Nebraska Press, 1996), 70.

38. D. B. McLaurin to William H. B. Richardson, 27 January 1855, James B. Richardson Papers, DU; Thomas J. Hawkins to Joseph S. Copes, 17 January 1845, Joseph S. Copes Papers, TU.

39. Douglass, *My Bondage and My Freedom,* 150; F. B. Deane to J. H. Cocke, 4 April 1835, Cocke Family Papers, #640, box 81, UVA. Emphasis in originals.

40. F. B. Deane to J. H. Cocke, 4 April 1835, Cocke Family Papers, #640, box 81, UVA; Samuel Dixon to JM, 5 February 1844, James McDowell Papers, DU; Samuel Griswold to Farish Carter, 7 March 1850, Farish Carter Papers, #2230, folder 39, SHC; Oakes, *Slavery and Freedom,* 144.

41. Memorandum Book, 1851–1863, Lewis Stirling and Family Papers, #1866, LSU; Inscoe, "The Civil War's Empowerment of an Appalachian Woman," 64–65; Drew Gilpin Faust, *Mothers of Invention: Women of the Slaveholding South in the American Civil War* (Chapel Hill: University of North Carolina Press, 1996), 71–72.

42. Bruce, *The New Man,* 68; Perdue, Barden, and Phillips, *Weevils in the Wheat,* 27; Douglass, *My Bondage and My Freedom,* 161.

43. Walter G. Baylor to Joseph S. Copes, 30 November 1851, Joseph S. Copes Papers, TU; Robert S. Starobin, *Industrial Slavery in the Old South* (New York: Oxford University Press, 1970), 111.

44. Mrs. Harris to Joseph S. Copes, April 1853, Joseph S. Copes Papers, TU; D. B. McLaurin to William H. B. Richardson, 27 January 1855, James B. Richardson Papers, DU; William Anderson to Farish Carter, 5 August 1853, Farish Carter Papers, #2230, folder 53, SHC; Farish Carter to William Anderson (copy), 1 October 1853, Farish Carter Papers, #2230, folder 54, SHC.

45. William D. Cabell to Iverson L. Twyman, 25 December 1858, Austin-Twyman Papers, WM.

46. William Anderson to Farish Carter, 5 August 1853, Farish Carter Papers, #2230, folder 53, SHC; Bruce, *The New Man,* 66–67.

47. John E. Jones to John Buxton Williams, 8 January 1855, John Buxton Williams Papers, DU; W. Gill to Iverson L. Twyman, 1 January 1859, Austin-Twyman Papers, WM; John Rutherfoord to William B. Randolph, 6 December 1855, William B. Randolph Papers, LC; Petition of J. S. Reid to the Senate and House of Representatives of the State of South Carolina, Abbeville District, November 1856, South Carolina Department of Archives and History, in Loren Schweninger, ed., *Race, Slavery, and Free Blacks: Petitions to Southern Legislatures, 1777–1867* (Bethesda, Md.: University Publications of America, 1998), accession #11385601.

48. Kate E. R. Pickard, *The Kidnapped and the Ransomed* (1856; Lincoln: University of Nebraska Press, 1995), 50. Emphasis in originals.

49. Sarah H. Bradford, *Harriet: The Moses of Her People* (New York: Geo. R. Lockwood, 1886), 40–41. Emphasis in originals.

5. Resistance and Abuse

1. William F. G. Garrett to William Gouldin and Lewis Hill, 22 May 1844, Lewis Hill Papers, HL; Plantation Record Books, vol. 3, 28 August 1848, Nicholas Bryor Massenburg Papers, SHC; *Thornton v. Towns,* 34 Georgia 125 (1865). Emphasis in original.

2. *State v. Mann,* 13 N.C. 267 (1829).

3. Charles L. Perdue, Jr., Thomas E. Barden, and Robert K. Phillips, eds., *Weevils in the Wheat: Interviews with Virginia Ex-Slaves* (Charlottesville: University Press of Virginia, 1976), 318.

4. *Moran v. Davis,* 18 Georgia 722 (1855); William Wells Brown, *Narrative of William Wells Brown, A Fugitive Slave, Written by Himself* (Boston, 1847), reprinted in Gilbert Osofsky, ed., *Puttin' On Ole Massa* (New York: Harper & Row, 1969), 184; H. C. Bruce, *The New Man: Twenty-Nine Years a Slave, Twenty-Nine Years a Free Man* (1895; reprinted Lincoln: University of Nebraska Press, 1996), 69; *State v. Mann,* 13 N.C. 229 (1829).

5. Frederick Douglass, *My Bondage and My Freedom,* William L. Andrews, ed. (Urbana: University of Illinois Press, 1987), 140.

6. Ibid., 140–142.

7. Ibid., 142–143, 192.

8. Martin Webb to John Buford, 12 June 1857, John Buford Papers, UVA; Brown, *Narrative,* in Osofsky, *Puttin' On Ole Massa,* 183 (Brown), 184–185 (Aaron); Dick Coleman to Benjamin Palmore, 2 May 1860, Palmore Family Papers, #38–149, UVA.

9. *Judge v. Moore,* 9 Florida 269 (1860); *Wooddy v. Flournoy,* 20 Virginia Reports 506 (1820); *Berry v. Diamond,* 19 Arkansas 262 (1857).

10. Kate E. R. Pickard, *The Kidnapped and the Ransomed: Being the Personal Recollections of Peter and Vina Still after Forty Years of Slavery* (1856; Lincoln: University of Nebraska Press, 1995), 54–55; D. Cogden to J. C. McRae, 6 November 1852, quoted in Robert S. Starobin, *Industrial Slavery in the Old South* (New York: Oxford University Press, 1970), 111.

11. John Thompson, *The Life of John Thompson, a Fugitive Slave; Containing His*

History of 25 Years in Bondage, and His Providential Escape (1856; New York: Negro Universities Press, 1968), 55–56.

12. Ibid., 72–74.

13. George P. Rawick, ed., *The American Slave: A Composite Autobiography* (Westport, Conn.: Greenwood Press, 1972-), supplement, series 2, vol. 1, pt. 3 (Arkansas), 116; ibid., supplement, series 1, vol. 3, pt. 1 (Georgia), 142; *Harris v. Maury*, 30 Alabama 679 (1857).

14. M. A. Franklin to Farish Carter, 13 January 1852, Farish Carter Papers, SHC; John Jerdone to William Jerdone, 5 March 1839 and 12 April 1839, Jerdone Family Papers, box 9, folder 1, WM; *Hall v. Goodson*, 32 Ala. 277 (1858); George H. Young to James McDowell, 17 February 1846, James McDowell Papers, DU.

15. Horace Cowles Atwater, *Incidents of a Southern Tour* (Boston: J. P. Magee, 1857), 51.

16. *Caldwell v. Dickson*, 17 Missouri 575 (1853); *Helton v. Caston*, 2 Bailey (S.C.) 95 (1831).

17. *Tennent v. Dendy*, 1 Dudley (S.C.) 83 (1837).

18. *DeBow's Review*, vol. 18, number 6 (1855), 717; Eugene D. Genovese, *From Rebellion to Revolution: Afro-American Slave Revolts in the Making of the Modern World* (Baton Rouge: Louisiana State University, 1979), 5; Eugene D. Genovese, *Roll, Jordan, Roll: The World the Slaves Made* (New York: Vintage Books, 1974), 5–7.

19. On slaves complaining to owners about abusive overseers, Philip D. Morgan writes: "This major channel of communication between master and slave was therefore double-edged: it represented a way for field hands to assert their rights but at the same time easily drew them into a more complete dependence on their masters for the amendment of their complaints." *Slave Counterpoint: Black Culture in the Eighteenth-Century Chesapeake and Lowcountry* (Chapel Hill: University of North Carolina Press, 1998), 333.

20. Douglass, *My Bondage and My Freedom*, 140; Pickard, *The Kidnapped and the Ransomed*, 54–55.

21. Howard McGary and Bill E. Lawson, *Between Slavery and Freedom: Philosophy and American Slavery* (Bloomington: Indiana University Press, 1992), 1–15; James W. C. Pennington, *The Fugitive Blacksmith: or, Events in the History of James W. C. Pennington* (1850; Westport, CT: Negro Universities Press, 1971), iv–v; *DeBow's Review*, vol. 18, number 6 (1855), 714–715.

22. See James C. Scott, *Domination and the Arts of Resistance: Hidden Transcripts* (New Haven, Conn.: Yale University Press, 1990), and Robin D. G. Kelley, "'We Are Not What We Seem': Rethinking Black Working-Class Resistance in the Jim Crow South," *Journal of American History* 80 (June 1993): 75–112.

23. Robert Allen to R. D. Buford, 1 July 1857, John Buford Papers, UVA; William H. Fitzhugh to Lewis Hill, 26 May 1853, Lewis Hill Papers, HL.

24. *Wier v. Buford*, 8 Ala. 134 (1845); *McNeill and Forniss v. Easley*, 24 Ala. 455 (1854); *Maury v. Coleman*, 24 Ala. 455 (1854).

25. Genovese, *Roll, Jordan, Roll*, 609–610; Alex Lichtenstein, "'That Disposition

to Theft, with Which They Have Been Branded': Moral Economy, Slave Management, and the Law," *Journal of Social History* 21 (Spring 1988): 421–422.

26. Peter Randolph, *Sketches of Slave Life; or, Illustrations of the "Peculiar Institution"* (Boston, 1855), 47.

27. Kenneth S. Greenberg, "The Nose, the Lie, and the Duel in the Antebellum South," *American Historical Review* 95 (February 1990): 65.

28. *Commonwealth v. Hart,* 29 Kentucky 119 (1831).

29. Similarly, Ariela Gross argues that the introduction of slave testimony, however indirect, in Southern courtrooms "impugned a white man's honor in the deepest way." Ariela Gross, "Pandora's Box: Slave Character on Trial in the Antebellum South," in Paul Finkelman, ed., *Slavery and the Law* (Madison, Wis.: Madison House, 1997), 318.

30. *West v. Forrest,* 22 Missouri 344 (1856).

31. *M'Gowen v. Chapen,* 6 N.C. 61 (1811); *Hall v. Goodson,* 32 Ala. 277 (1858).

32. Andrew Fede, "Legitimized Violent Slave Abuse in the American South, 1619–1865: A Case Study of Law and Social Change in Six Southern States," *American Journal of Legal History* 29 (1985): 117–126, 138–146.

33. *Mims v. Mitchell,* 1 Texas 443 (1846). For similar rulings in other states see *Tallahassee Rail-Road Company v. Arthur Macon,* 8 Florida 299 (1859); *Latimer v. Alexander,* 14 Georgia 266 (1853); *Jones v. Glass,* 13 Iredell (N.C.) 305 (1852).

34. *Craig's Adm'r v. Lee,* 53 Kentucky 96 (1853).

35. *White v. Arnold,* 6 Richardson (S.C.) 138 (1853).

36. See, for example, *Young v. Thompson,* 3 Smedes and Marshall's (Mississippi) 129 (1844), and *Thornton v. Towns,* 34 Georgia 125 (1865).

37. *Tillman v. Chadwick,* 37 Ala. 317 (1861); *Robinson v. Varnell,* 16 Texas 384 (1856). See also *Young v. Thompson,* 3 Smedes and Marshall's (Mississippi) 129 (1844). On the implicit presence of slave "testimony" in Southern courtrooms, see Gross, "Pandora's Box," and Walter Johnson, "Inconsistency, Contradiction, and Complete Confusion: The Everyday Life of the Law of Slavery," *Law and Social Inquiry* 22 (Spring 1997): 419–430.

38. *Peters v. Clause,* 37 Missouri 337 (1866); *Trotter v. McCall,* 26 Mississippi 411 (1853).

39. Greenlee Diary, vol. 1, 128–129, SHC, quoted in Edward W. Phifer, "Slavery in Microcosm: Burke County, North Carolina," in Elinor Miller and Eugene D. Genovese, eds., *Plantation, Town, and Country: Essays on the Local History of American Slave Society* (Urbana: University of Illinois Press, 1974), 93.

40. John T. Day to Shanks, Anderson & Anderson, 9 November 1849, quoted in Charles B. Dew, "Disciplining Slave Ironworkers in the Antebellum South: Coercion, Conciliation, and Accommodation," *American Historical Review* 79 (April 1974): 399; T. H. Burns to John T. Day, 18 December 1849, Anderson Family Papers (UVA), quoted in ibid., 400.

41. Joseph S. Watkins to Thomas Walker Gilmer, 26 December 1835, John Tyler Scrapbook, p. 75, WM.

42. "List of Servants to be Hired," n.d., Cocke Family Papers, #640, box 65, UVA.

43. Samuel Drewry to John Buford, 30 December 1854 and 16 January 1855, John Buford Papers, DU.

44. Frederick Law Olmsted, *A Journey Through Texas; or, A Saddle Trip on the Southwestern Frontier* (1860; New York: B. Franklin, 1969), 119–120.

6. Working Alone

1. James Redpath, *The Roving Editor, or Talks with Slaves in the Southern States*, John R. McKivigan, ed. (University Park: Pennsylvania State University Press, 1996), 157.
2. Frederick Douglass, *My Bondage and My Freedom*, William L. Andrews, ed. (Urbana: University of Illinois Press, 1987), 199.
3. Frederic Bancroft, *Slave Trading in the Old South* (1931; New York: Frederick Ungar, 1959), 162–163; Robert S. Starobin, *Industrial Slavery in the Old South* (New York: Oxford University Press, 1970), 135. For use of the term "quasi freedom" (along with such variations as "quasi-independent" or "quasi-free") to describe self-hired slaves, see Richard B. Morris, "Labor Controls in Maryland in the Nineteenth Century," *Journal of Southern History* 14 (August 1948): 386; Richard B. Morris, "The Measure of Bondage in the Slave States," *Mississippi Valley Historical Review* 41 (1954): 220; Marianne Buroff Sheldon, "Black-White Relations in Richmond, Virginia, 1782–1820," *Journal of Southern History* 45 (February 1979): 27; Douglas R. Egerton, "Gabriel's Conspiracy and the Election of 1800," *Journal of Southern History* 56 (May 1990): 195; Loren Schweninger, "The Underside of Slavery: The Internal Economy, Self-Hire, and Quasi-Freedom in Virginia, 1780–1865," *Slavery and Abolition* 12 (September 1991): 10; Joseph P. Reidy, *From Slavery to Agrarian Capitalism in the Cotton Plantation South: Central Georgia, 1800–1880* (Chapel Hill: University of North Carolina Press, 1992), 105. Eugene D. Genovese argues that self-hired slaves were in a position of "enormous advantage" and that "they could live approximately as did the free Negroes." See *Roll, Jordan, Roll: The World the Slaves Made* (New York: Vintage Books, 1972), 392.
4. Douglass, *My Bondage and My Freedom*, 197.
5. Ibid., 188.
6. Schweninger, "The Underside of Slavery," 12–13. As Schweninger notes, "I have, judging from a variety of sources, made what I believe to be a conservative estimate." See ibid., 21, n.30.
7. Quoted in Ulrich Bonnell Phillips, "The Slave Labor Problem in the Charleston District," in *Plantation, Town, and County: Essays in the Local History of American Slave Society*, Elinor Miller and Eugene D. Genovese, eds. (Urbana: University of Illinois Press, 1974), 13.
8. Henry W. Farnam, *Chapters in the History of Social Legislation in the United States to 1860* (Washington, D.C.: Carnegie Institute of Washington, 1938), 191–192; William Goodell, *The American Slave Code in Theory and Practice: Its Distinctive Features Shown by Its Statutes, Judicial Decisions, Illustrative Facts* (New York: American and Foreign Anti-Slavery Society, 1853), 97–104.
9. Petition of McCulley Righton, William Moir, James Mitchell, et al., to the House of Representatives of the State of South Carolina, Charleston District, December 1793, in Loren Schweninger, *Race, Slavery, and Free Blacks: Peti-*

tions to Southern Legislatures, 1777–1867 (Bethesda, Md.: University Publications of America, 1998), accession #11379309 (hereafter, Petition #11379309); Petition of John Allan, William Keddie, Normand MacLeod, et al., to the General Assembly of the State of North Carolina, New Hanover County, November 1802, in Schweninger, *Race, Slavery, and Free Blacks,* accession #11280206 (hereafter, Petition #11280206); Petition of James Long, A. Russell, Jacob N. Land, and James Jeffrey to the Senate of the State of South Carolina, Charleston District, 8 October 1858, in Schweninger, *Race, Slavery, and Free Blacks,* accession #11385805 (hereafter, Petition #11385805); Columbia *Bulletin* quoted in Ulrich Bonnell Phillips, *American Negro Slavery: A Survey of the Supply, Employment and Control of Negro Labor As Determined by the Plantation Regime* (1918; Baton Rouge: Louisiana State University Press, 1966), 412.

10. Petition #11280206; Petition of William McKewn, Aaron Barton, Henry S. Egan, et al., to the Senate of South Carolina, Charleston District, 1828, in Schweninger, *Race, Slavery, and Free Blacks,* accession #11382813 (hereafter, Petition #11382813); Petition of Elly Godbold, A. McDuffie, C. D. Evans, et al., to the Senate and House of Representatives of South Carolina, Marion District, 1858, in Schweninger, *Race, Slavery, and Free Blacks,* accession #11385803 (hereafter, Petition #11385803).

11. Douglass, *My Bondage and My Freedom,* 199; William L. Gwyn to Hamilton Brown, 1 March 1836, #1090, folder 5, SHC; Petition #11382813.

12. Charles White to Hamilton Brown, 20 December 1832, Hamilton Brown Papers, #1090, folder 4, SHC; Alfred Steel to Mary Steele, 15 November 1835, John Steele Papers, #689, folder 71, SHC; Thomas Clement Read to Henry Carrington, 22 October 1847 and April 1852, Carrington Family Papers, pt. G, section 1, VHS.

13. John Blassingame, ed., *Slave Testimony: Two Centuries of Letters, Speeches, Interviews, and Autobiographies* (Baton Rouge: Louisiana State University Press, 1977), 186; [J. C. Lovejoy,] *Narratives of the Sufferings of Lewis and Milton Clarke, Sons of a Soldier of the Revolution, during a Captivity of More than Twenty Years among the Slaveholders of Kentucky, One of the So Called Christian States of North America* (Boston: Bela Marsh, 1854), 30; Blassingame, *Slave Testimony,* 274, 455; William L. Gwyn to Hamilton Brown, 2 March 1835, Hamilton Brown Papers, #1090, folder 5, SHC.

14. *South Carolina Gazette,* 24 September 1772, quoted in Robert Olwell, *Masters, Slaves, and Subjects: The Culture of Power in the South Carolina Low Country, 1740–1790* (Ithaca, N.Y.: Cornell University Press, 1998), 161. For a complaint about the nonenforcement of laws against living out, see Petition of S. T. Robinson, Samuel Stoney, William H. Peronneau, et al., to the Senate and House of Representatives of the State of South Carolina, Charleston District, 1843, in Schweninger, *Race, Slavery, and Free Blacks,* accession #11384301.

15. James D. Watts to Iverson L. Twyman, 20 February 1852, Austin-Twyman Papers, WM; William L. Gwyn to Hamilton Brown, 1 March 1836, Hamilton Brown Papers, #1090, folder 5, SHC. For an example of a slave hired out by a sheriff to pay for jail fees, see Petition of Henry Winfree to the General Assem-

bly of Virginia, December 1802, Chesterfield County, in Schweninger, *Race, Slavery, and Free Blacks,* accession #11680205.

16. Charles White to Hamilton Brown, 20 December 1832, Hamilton Brown Papers, #1090, folder 4, SHC; Jack Lewis to Christopher Tompkins, 22 July 1832, Tompkins Family Papers, VHS.

17. Anderson F. Henderson to Archibald and Mary Henderson, 26 January 1849, John Steele Henderson Papers, #327, Folder 17, SHC.

18. Anderson F. Henderson to Archibald and Mary Henderson, 14 June 1857, John Steele Henderson Papers, #327, Folder 23, SHC.

19. Bethany Veney, *The Narrative of Bethany Veney, a Slave Woman* (Worcester, Mass., 1889), 32; Blassingame, *Slave Testimony,* 455; Testimony of Charlotte, American Freedman's Inquiry Commission (AFIC), Letters Received by the Adjutant General's Office, M-619, RG 94, reel 201, file #7, 84, NA; Testimony of Lavina Bell, AFIC, reel 201, file #7, 89, NA.

20. Hez Ford to James E. Cooke, 18 March 1851 and 20 January 1852, Barker-Cooke Papers, WM.

21. Henry Laurens to James Laurens, 2 July 1775, in *The Papers of Henry Laurens,* Philip M. Hamer, ed. (Columbia: University of South Carolina Press, 1968–), vol. 10, 203; Elijah Fuller to Alexander McDowell, 29 March 1845, Thomas David Smith McDowell Papers, #460, folder 60, SHC; D. R. Carroll to George Lewis Collins Davis, 5 November 1845, George Lewis Collins Davis Papers, #644, TU.

22. Douglass, *My Bondage and My Freedom,* 199; Blassingame, *Slave Testimony,* 420; George P. Rawick, ed., *The American Slave: A Composite Autobiography* (Westport, Conn.: Greenwood Press, 1972-), supplement, series 2, Texas Narratives, vol. 8, pt. 7, 3203; Blassingame, *Slave Testimony,* 490–491.

23. Blassingame, *Slave Testimony,* 216 (Garrison), 469 (Crissman), 440 (Jackson); Moses Grandy, *Narrative of the Life of Moses Grandy; Late a Slave in the United States of America* (London: C. Gilpin, 1843), 47.

24. Grandy, *Narrative of the Life of Moses Grandy,* 17; Blassingame, *Slave Testimony,* 330 (Charlton), 437 (Williams).

25. Richard C. Wade, *Slavery in the Cities: The South, 1820–1860* (New York: Oxford University Press, 1964), 48–49; *DeBow's Review,* vol. 11, issue 2 (August 1851): 196.

26. Morris, "Measure of Bondage in the Slave States," 220, 234; Eaton, "Slave-Hiring in the Upper South," 663; Wade, *Slavery in the Cities,* 48; Schweninger, "The Underside of Slavery," 10.

27. Douglass, *My Bondage and My Freedom,* 199.

28. Blassingame, *Slave Testimony,* 364 (Smith), 27 (Watts).

29. John B. Murison to G. L. C. Davis, 27 August 1842, George Lewis Collins Davis Papers, #644, TU.

30. George Renkins to William B. Randolph, 21 February 1852, William B. Randolph Papers, LC; Isaac Ballandine to William B. Randolph, 2 December 1857, William B. Randolph Papers, LC; Testimony of Charlotte, AFIC, reel 201, file #7, 84, NA.

31. Thomas H. Jones, *The Experience of Thomas H. Jones, Who Was a Slave for*

Forty-Three Years. Written by a Friend, as Related to Him by Brother Jones (Boston: Bazin & Chandler, 1862), 32.

32. Peter Randolph, *Sketches of Slave Life; or, Illustrations of the "Peculiar Institution"* (Boston: Published for the Author, 1855), 58.

33. Michael Mullin, *Africa in America: Slave Acculturation and Resistance in the American South and the British Caribbean, 1736–1831* (Urbana: University of Illinois Press, 1992), 227–228; Douglas R. Egerton, *Gabriel's Rebellion: The Virginia Slave Conspiracies of 1800 and 1802* (Chapel Hill: University of North Carolina Press, 1993), 24–26; Douglass, *My Bondage and My Freedom*, 102.

34. Blassingame, *Slave Testimony*, 395.

35. Blassingame, *Slave Testimony*, 364 (Smith), 490 (Johnston); Governor Wickliffe quoted in John Ashworth, *Slavery, Capitalism, and Politics in the Antebellum Republic*, vol. 1: *Commerce and Compromise, 1820–1850* (New York: Cambridge University Press, 1995), 103.

36. Petition of James Goodwyn, John Bynum, John Creyon, et al., to the Legislature of the State of South Carolina, Richland District, November 1819, in Schweninger, *Race, Slavery, and Free Blacks*, accession #11381905 (hereafter, Petition #11381905); Petition #11379309; Petition #11382813; Petition #11385803.

37. "Memorial of the Citizens of Charleston to the Senate and House of Representatives of the State of South Carolina (Charleston, 1822), reprinted in Philip S. Foner and Ronald L. Lewis, eds., *The Black Worker: A Documentary History from Colonial Times to the Present*, vol. 1: *The Black Worker to 1869* (Philadelphia: Temple University Press, 1978), 84.

38. "The Humble Remonstrance of Your Majesty's Governor, Council, and Assembly of South Carolina," 9 April 1734, in *Documents Illustrative of the History of the Slave Trade to America*, Elizabeth Donnan, ed., Carnegie Institution of Washington Publication no. 409, vol. 4 (Washington, D.C., 1935), 288; Petition of Daniel Cameron, Stephen Shrewsbury, John Clement, et al., to the House of Representatives of the State of South Carolina, Charleston District, February 1783, in Schweninger, *Race, Slavery, and Free Blacks*, accession #11378304 (hereafter "Petition #11378304"); *Augusta Chronicle*, 9 July 1828, quoted in Michele Gillespie, *Free Labor in an Unfree World: White Artisans in Slaveholding Georgia, 1789–1860* (Athens: University of Georgia Press, 2000), 157; J. S. Grasty to W. C. Grasty, 19 November 1862, William C. Grasty and J. F. Rison Papers, DU.

39. Petition #11381905; Petition #11378304; Petition #11382813.

40. Brenda L. Stevenson, *Life in Black and White: Family and Community in the Slave South* (New York: Oxford University Press, 1996), 258–319; Michael P. Johnson and James L. Roark, "Strategies of Survival: Free Negro Families and the Problem of Slavery," in *In Joy and In Sorrow: Women, Family, and Marriage in the Victorian South*, Carol Bleser, ed. (New York: Oxford University Press, 1991), 88–102; Larry Koger, *Black Slaveowners: Free Black Slave Masters in South Carolina, 1790–1860* (Jefferson, N.C.: McFarland & Company, Inc., 1985), 201–234.

41. "Negro Mechanics," typescript copy from *The Woodville Republican*, 18 September 1847, "Slavery" Subject File, MDAH.

42. Petition #11280206; Douglass, *My Bondage and My Freedom*, 189–190; Arkansas petition quoted in Ashworth, *Slavery, Capitalism, and Politics*, 104; *Southern Cultivator* quoted in Reidy, *From Slavery to Agrarian Capitalism*, 118; Douglass, *My Bondage and My Freedom*, 188.

43. Petition #11379309; Petition #11382813; Petition #11385805.

44. *Richmond Enquirer* quoted in Claudia Dale Goldin, *Urban Slavery in the American South, 1820–1860* (Chicago: University of Chicago Press, 1976), 30; *DeBow's Review*, vol. 27, issue 1 (1859): 102; *DeBow's Review*, vol. 25, issue 4 (1858): 412.

45. Petition of John Mayo, Jr., William Gathright, Hebron Owen, et al., to the Virginia House of Delegates, Henrico County, 8 June 1782, in Schweninger, ed, *Race, Slavery, and Free Blacks*, accession #11678201; Petition of John Utsey, Daniel Utsey, William Harrison, et al., to the Senate of the State of South Carolina, Colleton District, 1820, in Schweninger, *Race, Slavery, and Free Blacks*, accession #11382017; Petition of William Galtin, Calvin Burch, Nathan Whitford, et al., to the General Assembly of the State of North Carolina, Craven County, December 1831, in Schweninger, *Race, Slavery, and Free Blacks*, accession #11283107; Petition of Isaac Croom, Matthew M. Carr, John B. Kennedy, et al., to the General Assembly of North Carolina, Lenoir County, November 1831, in Schweninger, *Race, Slavery, and Free Blacks*, accession #11283105.

46. *DeBow's Review*, vol. 26, issue 5 (1859): 600.

Epilogue

1. Frederick Douglass, *My Bondage and My Freedom*, William L. Andrews, ed. (Urbana: University of Illinois Press, 1987), 29.

2. Ibid., 95.

3. *Bell v. Cummings*, 35 Tenn. 275, 281–282 (1855).

4. Douglass, *My Bondage and My Freedom*, 78.

5. Thomas Jefferson to Nicholas Lewis, 19 December 1786, *The Papers of Thomas Jefferson*, Julian P. Boyd, ed. (Princeton, N.J.: Princeton University Press, 1950–), vol. 11, p. 615.

6. Isaac Mason, *Life of Isaac Mason As a Slave* (Worcester, Mass., 1893), 14.

7. Douglass, *My Bondage and My Freedom*, 192.

8. Edmund Ruffin, "The Effects of High Prices of Slaves," *DeBow's Review* 26 (1859): 656.

Acknowledgments

This book was a long time in the making, and I owe more debts than I can hope to acknowledge appropriately. First of all, for tremendous assistance in tracking down sources on a topic only haphazardly indexed, if at all, I would like to thank the generous archivists who guided me through manuscript collections at the following repositories: the Library of Congress, the Huntington Library, the Southern Historical Collection at the University of North Carolina, the William Perkins Library at Duke University, the Earl Gregg Swem Library at the College of William and Mary, the Alderman Library at the University of Virginia, the Virginia Historical Society, the Mississippi Department of Archives and History, the Howard-Tilton Memorial Library at Tulane University, and the Louisiana and Lower Mississippi Valley Collections at Louisiana State University.

The book began under the guidance of Danny Walkowitz, a Zen master of the historical profession. An inimitable scholar and an even better mentor, Danny provided the unfailing encouragement and intelligent insights that I needed to make each version of the manuscript better. He has taught me more than anyone else about how to be a historian. The book is also the product of many discussions with Martha Hodes, discussions that coaxed from me whatever nuance and clarity the book might display. For a long time she has nurtured my love for nineteenth-century social history and offered countless examples of how to practice the craft of history with precision and grace. Finally, I have learned more about slavery from Walter Johnson than from anyone else. On numerous occasions he pushed me to ask better questions, posed a few of his own that I still can't answer, and demonstrated how to write history that breathes with everyday experience. Tom Bender and Karen Kupperman also read the entire manuscript in an early incarnation and offered smart and constructive feedback. In later stages of the project I profited from close readings of the manuscript by anonymous readers for Harvard University Press. Joyce Seltzer, my editor at Harvard University Press, provided the cheering guidance and sharp editorial comments that helped me steer my way through difficult stages. I wrote and rewrote every sentence with her voice ringing in my ears. Susan Abel copyedited the manuscript and saved me from many imprecisions, though not nearly so many as she would have liked. Needless to say, none of the above are responsible for any errors that might still persist as a result of my failure to heed their advice.

A cadre of excellent friends supported me throughout the project. Greg and Rebecca Guest have been the truest of friends and have significantly underwritten my quest to avoid the working world. Chris Scala, Amy Ho Tai, and Laura Mills offered necessary support and even more necessary diversions, making the writing of this book a much less solitary endeavor than it could have been. Others deserve my gratitude as well, but lest I prove forgetful, I'll leave it at this: you know who you are, and I thank you. As for friends of an even higher sort, Allison, Francisco, and Tim have done their best to keep their brother from becoming too nerdy. I am not an adequate testimonial to their efforts.

My greatest debt will always be to my parents, and this book is for them. My father taught me the joys of intellectual curiosity. He also taught me, by example and precept, how to write. Though I cursed it at the time, I learned the patience and care that writing requires through the seemingly endless revisions he demanded of my grade-school book reports. One of the highlights of this project early on was a midsummer trip to New Orleans with my mother. She went as a tourist, but when I could see time getting short I handed her a spare laptop and enlisted her as an unpaid research assistant. She gladly gave up walking tours for the stillness of the archive, and even got attached to a hired slave named Mabin, who unfortunately never made his way into the book. Then she drank beer with me on Bourbon Street. Everyone should have parents this cool; the dedication is just a small acknowledgment that mine truly are.

Index